BRITISH ESTABLISHMENT PERSPECTIVES ON FRANCE, 1936–40

STUDIES IN MILITARY AND STRATEGIC HISTORY
General Editor: Michael Dockrill, Professor of Diplomatic History, King's College, London

Published titles include:

Nigel John Ashton
EISENHOWER, MACMILLAN AND THE PROBLEM OF NASSER: Anglo-American Relations and Arab Nationalism, 1955–59

G. H. Bennett
BRITISH FOREIGN POLICY DURING THE CURZON PERIOD, 1919–24

David A. Charters
THE BRITISH ARMY AND JEWISH INSURGENCY IN PALESTINE, 1945–47

Paul Cornish
BRITISH MILITARY PLANNING FOR THE DEFENCE OF GERMANY, 1945–50

Robert Frazier
ANGLO-AMERICAN RELATIONS WITH GREECE: The Coming of the Cold War, 1942–47

Brian Holden Reid
J. F. C. FULLER: Military Thinker

Stewart Lone
JAPAN'S FIRST MODERN WAR: Army and Society in the Conflict with China, 1894–95

Thomas R. Mockaitis
BRITISH COUNTERINSURGENCY, 1919–60

Roger Woodhouse
BRITISH FOREIGN POLICY TOWARDS FRANCE, 1945–51

Studies in Military and Strategic History
Series Standing Order ISBN 0–333–71046–0
(*outside North America only*)

You can receive future titles in this series as they are published by placing a standing order. Please contact your bookseller or, in case of difficulty, write to us at the address below with your name and address, the title of the series and the ISBN quoted above.

Customer Services Department, Macmillan Distribution Ltd
Houndmills, Basingstoke, Hampshire RG21 6XS, England

British Establishment Perspectives on France, 1936–40

Michael Dockrill
Professor of Diplomatic History
King's College, London

First published in Great Britain 1999 by
MACMILLAN PRESS LTD
Houndmills, Basingstoke, Hampshire RG21 6XS and London
Companies and representatives throughout the world

A catalogue record for this book is available from the British Library.

ISBN 0–333–63439–X

First published in the United States of America 1999 by
ST. MARTIN'S PRESS, INC.,
Scholarly and Reference Division,
175 Fifth Avenue, New York, N.Y. 10010

ISBN 0–312–21544–4

Library of Congress Cataloging-in-Publication Data
Dockrill, M. L. (Michael L.)
British establishment perspectives on France, 1936–40 / Michael Dockrill.
p. cm. — (Studies in military and strategic history)
Includes bibliographical references and index.
ISBN 0–312–21544–4
1. Great Britain—Foreign relations—France. 2. Public opinion–
–Great Britain—History—20th century. 3. Great Britain—Foreign relations—1936–1945. 4. France—Foreign public opinion, British. 5. France—Foreign relations—Great Britain. 6. World War, 1939–1945—Great Britain. 7. World War, 1939–1945—France.
I. Title. II. Series.
DA47.1.D63 1998
327.41044—dc21 98–3710
CIP

---

10 9 8 7 6 5 4 3 2 1
08 07 06 05 04 03 02 01 00 99

Printed and bound in Great Britain by
Antony Rowe Ltd, Chippenham, Wiltshire

This book is dedicated with all my love to Saki

Contents

Preface

In the late 1930s the British 'establishment' was still a relatively small and tight-knit group, mostly products of the leading British public schools and of Oxford or Cambridge university. Politicians, senior officials and other members of the elite were *habitués* of the small world of the London clubs, while they often met at dinners and house parties hosted by grandees such as the Londonderrys or rich Americans such as the Astors. For example, Neville Chamberlain joined shooting parties at country estates with Lord Halifax, who was also a friend and Yorkshire neighbour of Geoffrey Dawson, the influential editor of *The Times*.

Government ministers, officials and high-ranking military, air and naval officers also discussed foreign, strategic and defence issues at the Committee of Imperial Defence, its many sub-committees and at the inter-departmental meetings which proliferated throughout Whitehall. These men were responsible for the formulation of British defence and foreign policies during the increasingly threatening international environment of the late 1930s. Most were cautious and conservative in outlook, only too aware of the Britain's vulnerability in a world in which the British Empire faced three potential enemies, Germany, Italy and Japan, with financial, military, naval and air resources which were less than adequate for the task. The bulk of these men agreed with Chamberlain that Britain's security dilemma could only be resolved by agreement with Germany, the closest and most dangerous of its likely foes. The belief that, if handled carefully, Hitler could be won over to an Anglo-German rapprochement was, of course, completely fallacious: the German dictator was not interested in Britain's idea of a European settlement, which in return for removing Germany's outstanding Versailles grievances would require Germany to return to the League of Nations and agree to arms limitation measures. Agreements of this kind were never on Hitler's agenda. He sought an Anglo-German agreement which would give Germany a free hand in Eastern and Central Europe. Such an abdication of Britain's great power status was never a realistic proposition, even for Chamberlain, although, in the name of 'self-determination', the British prime minister and French prime minister, Edouard Daladier, assisted Hitler's efforts to destabilise Central Europe at Munich in 1938 by conniving at the dissolution of Czechoslovakia as a viable state.

The existence of the Anglo-French entente imposed some restraint on Chamberlain's efforts to appease Germany. Although the entente was, for a variety of reasons, an object of suspicion in Britain in the inter-war period, most British policy-makers were reluctantly compelled to recognise the crucial importance of France as Britain's only potential great power ally in a hostile world. Whatever the shortcomings of France, Britain could never afford to let the entente collapse completely. As it was, Britain's dismissive attitude towards France's genuine security concerns did nothing to sustain French morale or encourage a more vigorous French stance towards Germany's violations of international treaties. The more thoughtful British policy-makers realised that if France became too demoralised it might seek such terms as it could get from Germany and leave Britain isolated. An isolated and militarily ill-prepared Britain would have been in no position to counter a German-dominated continent, as events after 1940 demonstrated. Hence the British government was forced to offer France an occasional gesture of solidarity to shore up France's waning self-confidence. Such gestures were scarcely impressive – a grudging acceptance of extremely limited military conversations in 1936, and their renewal in 1938, a few tepid assurances by Chamberlain of Britain's loyalty to France and a Royal visit to Paris in 1938. It was little enough. The British government would not promise to send an expeditionary force to France in the event of war and did little to prepare the British army for operations on the continent: the only measure that would convince both France and Germany that Britain was genuinely prepared to resist aggression. In 1939 Chamberlain was forced to change course in the face of mounting evidence of Hitler's increasingly bellicosity, which convinced most of his cabinet colleagues that Britain must now draw closer to France and do more to prepare for war than the leisurely efforts which had marked Britain's defence preparations hitherto.

This book examines British 'establishment' policy towards, and perceptions of, France from 1936, when, as Anthony Adamthwaite points out, Hitler began to wage an 'undeclared war' against Britain and France.

I would like to thank Tim Farmiloe and Annabelle Buckley of the Macmillan Press at Basingstoke for their support and cooperation not only while I was writing this book but also during the many years in which I have been general editor of this series. I am also grateful to the copy editor, Ruth Willats, for her painstaking work in editing the typescript. I thank the School of Humanities at King's College, London, for a grant which enabled me to finance the research. Finally I owe a huge debt to Saki Dockrill, for her encouragement and devotion, a source of great strength to me while I was writing this book.

Acknowledgements

Crown Copyright material in the Public Record Office is reproduced by permission of the Director of the Public Record Office. The Syndics of the Cambridge University Library have granted me permission to quote from the private papers of Sir Samuel Hoare, Lord Templewood. The Trustees of the Liddell Hart Centre for Military Archives, King's College, London, have given me permission to examine and reproduce extracts from the papers of Sir Basil Liddell Hart, General Sir John Dill, Field Marshal Lord Alanbrooke, Major General Francis Davidson and Field Marshal Sir Archibald Montgomery Massingberd. Lady Avon has kindly given me her permission to quote extracts from the papers of Anthony Eden, Lord Avon, at the University of Birmingham. Quotations from the papers of Philip Kerr, Lord Lothian, at the National Library of Scotland are reproduced with the permission of the Keeper of the Records of Scotland. Copyright permission to quote extracts from the private papers of David Lloyd George and J.C.C. Davidson in the custody of the Record Office, House of Lords, has been granted by the Clerk of the Records acting on behalf of the Beaverbrook Trustees. I am grateful to Professor Ann K.S. Lambton for permission to quote extracts from the papers of Lord Robert Cecil in the Department of Manuscripts at the British Library. I am indebted to the University of Birmingham for permission to publish material from the private papers of Neville Chamberlain. The Masters and Fellows of Balliol College, Oxford, have given me permission to quote from the private papers of Walter Monckton at the Bodleian Library, Oxford. The Bodleian Library, Oxford, and the Viscountess Simon have kindly granted me permission to quote from the private papers of Sir John Simon in the Bodleian Library, Oxford. Mr and Mrs William Bell have kindly granted me permission to quote from the private papers of Geoffrey Dawson in the Bodleian Library, Oxford. The present Lord Ponsonby has kindly allowed me to quote material from the private papers of Lord Ponsonby in the Bodleian Library, Oxford. Extracts from the papers of Hugh Dalton and Sir Warren Fisher are reproduced with the permission of the Librarian, the British Library of Economics and Political Science. Quotations from the papers of Leslie Hore-Belisha, Sir Maurice Hankey and Sir Eric Phipps in the Churchill Archives Centre, Cambridge, are reproduced with the permission of the Master, Fellows and Scholars of Churchill College, Cambridge. Extracts from the papers of Sir Alexander

Cadogan in the Churchill College Archives Centre, Cambridge, are reproduced by permission of Mr A.M. Farrer of Farrer and Co., London. Extracts from the private papers of Lord Halifax (the Hickleton Papers) in the Borthwick Institute of Historical Research, the University of York, are reproduced with the permission of the present Lord Halifax. The present Lord Caldecote has kindly given me permission to quote from the private papers of Sir Thomas Inskip, Lord Caldecote, at the Churchill College Archives Centre, Cambridge. Colonel J.A. Aylmer has given me permission to quote from the private papers of Major General Sir Edward Spears in the Churchill College Archives Centre, Cambridge. Sir Colville Barclay has kindly given me permission to quote 'The Ode to France' in the private papers of Lord Vansittart in the Churchill Archives Centre, Cambridge, although neither of us is convinced that Lord Vansittart actually composed the 'Ode'.

I wish to thank the archival staff at all the institutions listed above for their generous assistance and unfailing courtesy while I was undertaking the research for this volume in their archives. I am also grateful to Mr Correlli Barnett for allowing me to quote a passage from his book *The Collapse of British Power* and Sir Martin Gilbert and Richard Gott have kindly given me permission to quote an extract from *The Appeasers*.

I have attempted to trace all the copyright holders of the private papers from which I have quoted in this book but in a very few cases I was not successful. I apologise if I have unwittingly infringed other copyrights.

Michael Dockrill

Ode to France at 'Entertainment' at the Foreign and India Office Arranged by Sir Robert Vansittart on the Occasion of the State Visit of the President of France and Madame Lebrun to London in March 1939

France, whom we welcome to our Kingdom,
France, who bore the lilies in her banner.
Then the Bees, and now the Triple Colour
For the threefold virtues you are vowed to
Know that to the English you are ever
France the Beautiful, to whom our people
Utter thanks for centuries of Glory …
France, be welcome in our midst,
and take
These our revels, wrought for France's sake.
Epilogue
Farewell most lovely France, we will remember
The saying of the Sage, that 'Everyman
Owes service to the lords, his own and France …'

(in Lord Clarendon to Halifax, 24 March 1939, Vansittart Mss., I, 3/8)

1 Introduction

> ... while I admit that the French between 1870 and 1914 had their tails well down and therefore assumed a veneer of moderation, during the rest of their centuries-old existence, they had played the part of bullies ... and they are doing so now.
>
> (Warren Fisher, 19 July 1923)[1]

THE POLITICAL BACKGROUND: ANGLO-FRENCH RELATIONS BEFORE 1936

Anglo-French relations have, over the centuries, been characterised by mutual suspicion and antagonism, punctuated by brief periods of détente.[2] As Nicholas Rostow has put it,

> Language, history, even differences in government structure, emphasised that the British and French were distinct peoples of definite character. They looked at the world differently. To different habits of mind and government, the past added strands of rivalry and cooperation which were revealed in contradictory feelings and attitudes in both countries.[3]

Brigadier T.G.G. Heywood, the British military attaché to France, attempted to emphasise the positive aspects of the French character in a lecture on 'The French and French Policy' at Rhodes House, Oxford, on 28 November 1936, although in doing so he also suggested the innate differences between the two peoples:

> There are many types of Frenchmen just as there are many types of Englishmen ... The traditional representation of a Frenchman as a short, rotund little man, with black hair and with a painted black beard is as wrong as the extremely cadaverous looking individual with red hair and flowing red whiskers by which the Englishman is traditionally regarded in France ... The nation as a whole presents a mass of complex, often contradictory, qualities, which render it, especially to the Anglo-Saxon, extraordinarily difficult to understand. The French possess great intellectual qualities, method, continuity, logic and an inordinate craving to

> plan everything beforehand, to define and limit areas of thought and action, to lay down rules and provide for all possible contingencies.[4]

Having reached their nadir during the revolutionary and Napoleonic Wars, relations between the two countries improved during the three decades after 1830, but soured again after 1860 as a result of increasingly frenzied naval and colonial rivalry. The intense competition between the two countries culminated in the Fashoda incident of 1898 when they came close to war. However the growing threat to the interests of the two countries of the economically expanding and ambitious German Empire, itself formed after the defeat of France by Prussia in 1871, brought the two countries together in 1904 in an agreement which settled their outstanding colonial disputes, but which gradually developed into an informal military and naval alignment against Germany. This was not an alliance, as the British refused to tie their hands irrevocably by entering into a commitment to send troops to France in the event of a Franco-German war.

The two countries fought together against the common enemy, Germany, between 1914 and 1918, although it was never an easy partnership. Even at the outset of the European war, there were bitter debates within the British cabinet about whether Britain should become involved at all.[5] The defeat of Germany in 1918 removed the cement which had held the entente together since 1904. Shortly before the Paris peace conference opened, Lord Curzon, the lord president of the council, told the eastern committee,

> We have been brought, for reasons of national safety, into an alliance with the French, which I hope will last, but their national character is different from ours in many cases. I am afraid that the Great Power from whom we most have to fear in the future is France ...[6]

General J.C. Smuts, the South African politician and member of the imperial war cabinet, shared Curzon's prejudices, writing in December 1918 that France 'has always been ambitious, is militant and imperialist in temperament ... I fear we shall find her a difficult and intolerable neighbour. She will do her best to remain mistress of the Continent.'[7]

At the Paris peace conference in 1919 the two countries were in broad agreement that Germany's aggression should be punished, and that the clauses of the Versailles Treaty should contain territorial, financial and other measures designed to prevent Germany from threatening the peace of Europe in the future. Where they disagreed, however, was over the severity of the measures to contain Germany. France, with a smaller population than Germany's, and only too aware of Germany's superior industrial and military potential, sought to redress the balance by removing the Rhineland from Germany's sovereignty and by entering into treaties with the new Rhenish states providing for the garrisoning of French troops on their soil. The prospect of creating more 'Alsace-Lorraines' in Europe, and thus a source of permanent German grievance against the allies, alarmed the British, who refused to accept this solution. Instead, France was persuaded to settle for an allied occupation of the Rhineland for 15 years, severe restrictions on the size of Germany's armed services and on the quality and quantity of its armaments, accompanied by an Anglo-American guarantee that the two countries would come to the assistance of France if it was invaded by Germany again.

At the same time France fostered the territorial ambitions of the Central and Eastern European states which had emerged from the collapse of the Habsburg Empire – Poland, Czechoslovakia, Romania and Yugoslavia – as barriers to any future German expansion. After 1920 France signed alliances with Poland and Czechoslovakia, and, in the West, with Belgium, all directed at Germany. These efforts to weaken and encircle Germany alarmed the British delegation at Paris, since, as Lord Hardinge, the permanent under-secretary at the Foreign Office, put it, 'the French are opening their mouths very wide and would like to reduce Germany to servitude for the next 50 years.'[8] In March, and again in June 1919, David Lloyd George, the British prime minister, attempted to secure some modifications in Germany's favour in the draft treaty, but only managed to persuade the French and Americans to accept some relatively insignificant changes. In French eyes the genesis of what became British 'appeasement' was apparent even before Germany signed the peace treaty.[9]

Britain wanted a close alignment with the United States, not France, to help Britain preserve postwar peace and stability. President Woodrow Wilson's idealism, as publicly expressed during the latter stages of the war in his 14 points and other public statements, sought to create a postwar world order based on national self-determination, democracy and the promotion of peace and peaceful change through a League of Nations. Wilson appealed to large swathes of Liberal, Labour and even moderate Conservative opinion in Britain, although the British government and its officials were extremely doubtful about the practicability of Wilson's programme. However the widespread popularity of Wilson's ideals suggested to the British government that it would be politic at least to pay lip-service to them, especially as ambiguities could be, and were, exploited to serve British interests. The illusion of shared Anglo-American traditions and common purposes encouraged British ministers to believe that the two countries could collaborate successfully across the world. The 'greedy'

French, as they were described by Arthur Balfour, the British foreign secretary in 1919, would have to adjust their policies to the new Anglo-American hegemony.[10] Those senior Foreign Office officials who were committed to the Anglo-French connection, such as Sir Eyre Crowe, cautioned the foreign secretary in vain about the perils of ignoring French concerns, since 'we must remember that our friend America lives a long way off. France sits at our door.'[11]

Over the following two decades the deep psychological wounds inflicted on the country by the blood-letting on the western front made British politicians and officials, who, on this subject at least, reflected British public opinion, determined to avoid involvement in a renewed conflict in the killing grounds of Western Europe. The myth also became widely accepted in Britain that the country had sacrificed the cream of its young manhood for the sake of France and of French interests. French policies after 1920 seemed to demonstrate the truth of this perception of French selfishness. Hence the mistaken assumption that the Anglo-French military and naval conversations before the war had saddled Britain with a commitment to assist France against German attack in 1914 was stressed repeatedly by politicians and officials, and in the British press after 1919. In 1925, Winston Churchill, then chancellor of the exchequer, expressed his strong opposition to any new military commitment to France, denying that 'our fate was involved in that of France'.[12] In these years, the chorus of vituperation against the French mounted steadily, with Lloyd George and Winston Churchill leading the way in 'cursing the French for their avarice and intransigence'.[13]

At the end of 1919 and again in early 1920 the US Congress rejected the Treaty of Versailles, and Britain's hopes for future Anglo-American cooperation lay in tatters as the United States retreated into isolationism. French security also suffered a severe blow, as the American guarantee to France lapsed, along with the Versailles Treaty. The British took the opportunity to denounce their guarantee as well, which provided the French with further evidence of British perfidity.

Thus, after 1920, the two remaining great powers, Britain and France, were left to uphold the treaty they had so recently negotiated. As it turned out, their increasing divergence about how Germany should be treated made it impossible for them to cooperate in this task. British Germanophobia, so intense in the immediate aftermath of the war, soon subsided, while British politicians wanted to encourage Germany's economic recovery, which, they believed, would provide Britain with the trading opportunities necessary to overcome the difficulties Britain was facing during the postwar recession: prior to 1914 the two countries had been close trading partners. Given the destruction inflicted on France's northern provinces by Germany during the Great War and France's abiding fear that Germany's economic and hence military revival would in the future threaten it with a repetition of that savage conflict, French politicians insisted that the punitive clauses of the treaty should be rigorously imposed on Germany.

Between 1920 and 1925 Anglo-French quarrels centred largely on Germany's reparations liabilities to the allies. The British were prepared to yield to frequent German requests for temporary moratoria on its reparations payments on the grounds of the postwar dislocation of its economy. France suspected that Germany was wilfully defaulting on its payments, and insisted on repayment in full as a means of impeding Germany's revival. Anglo-French-German disputes over this issue culminated in the French and Belgian occupation of the Ruhr on 11 January 1923 in an attempt to force Germany to resume reparation payments and deliveries of timber and coal to France, which Germany had suspended in December. Britain condemned the occupation as of doubtful legality but otherwise remained aloof. To make matters worse, after 1920 the two countries quarrelled bitterly over the future of Turkey and their respective claims to former Ottoman territory in the Middle East. The entente was now badly fractured.

France's aggressive policy in the Ruhr convinced many British politicians and officials that France was seeking hegemony in Europe, and this was reinforced by a scare – largely manufactured by the chief of the air staff, Marshal of the Royal Air Force Sir Hugh Trenchard, in his battle for increased Royal Air Force funding – that the superior French Air Force might be used to blackmail Britain into supporting its anti-German policies. In 1923, Lord Curzon, the foreign secretary, feared that given 'a [French] preponderance of air power and increased strength in submarines ... it would be possible for her to dictate her policy to the whole world'; while Arthur Balfour doubted 'if we possessed sufficient confidence in the French nation, who were at present in a somewhat hysterical condition'.[14]

In fact, as more moderate politicians such as Austen Chamberlain, who became foreign secretary in 1925, appreciated, French policy was dictated, not by an impulse to dominate the continent, but by its deep sense of insecurity vis-à-vis Germany.[15] Before 1925 British refusal to give France a guarantee of its security forced the French to provide for their own security by insisting on the imposition of the Versailles Treaty clauses on Germany, and by entering into alliances and agreements with Poland, Czechoslovakia and the little entente, which further increased Britain's fears of its involvement in a European war as a result of French commitments to these Eastern

European countries. The issue of French security also destroyed any chance of progress on disarmament in the League of Nations during these years: France would not consider arms limitation without cast-iron guarantees against renewed German aggression.

However these problems seemed to be partially resolved when the French accepted the Dawes Plan in 1924, which temporarily settled the vexed issue of reparations. They evacuated the Ruhr and joined Britain, Germany, Belgium and Italy in signing the treaty of Locarno in December 1925, the main feature of which was a treaty of mutual guarantee of the Franco-German and Belgian-German frontiers between Germany, Belgium, France, Britain and Italy. At the same time Chamberlain rejected any British association with France's eastern alliances.

Austen Chamberlain hoped that, as a result of Locarno, a new balance of power could be established in Western Europe in which Germany would be able to recover economically, while a more secure France would join Britain in seeking ways of ameliorating the more draconian clauses of the Versailles Treaty in Germany's favour. The British were confident that in the new atmosphere of goodwill thus created in Europe, they would never have to fulfil their guarantee. In any case the despatch of a British expeditionary force to the continent was hardly a realistic proposition given the steady reduction in the size and quality of the British army since 1920, a trend which was to continue after 1925. The British army had returned to its traditional role as an imperial police force.

Until 1930 Britain, France and Germany managed to coexist peacefully, but it was not an easy relationship. Germany paid the reparations due to France and Belgium under the timetable laid down by Dawes Plan, while the French agreed to the relaxation of some of the Versailles clauses, for instance, agreeing to a partial evacuation of their troops from the Rhineland in 1926 and the withdrawal of the inter-allied control commission which had been set up under the Versailles Treaty to supervise the restrictions imposed on Germany's arms production. However, these concessions never went far enough, nor were they fast enough, to satisfy German aspirations.

The onset of the depression in Europe in 1930 wrecked whatever chance there may have been for the establishment of a peaceful and stable Europe. The effects of the depression on the Weimar Republic were devastating. Undermined by left-wing and right-wing extremism, partly a product of mass unemployment, the virtual collapse of law and order and the steady descent of successive governments into authoritarian rule, its leaders began to clamour for the immediate relaxation of the Versailles clauses if the Republic was to survive at all. France now resisted making further concessions in the disordered state of Europe, and as a result, relations between France and Germany became increasingly strained, while this renewed French intransigence alienated Britain. During the early 1930s the main, but not the only, area of Franco-British-German controversy was over disarmament (the depression led to the abandonment of reparations in April 1932).

During the long and tedious debates over disarmament during the world disarmament conference between 1932 and 1934, Britain repeatedly pressed France to accept proposals the French believed would increase Germany's military strength at the expense of France, while Britain, for its part, refused to ease French apprehensions by giving a security guarantee to France. In October 1933, Germany, now under National Socialist control, withdrew from the disarmament conference and from the League of Nations. On 17 April 1934, the French announced that in future they would look after their own security rather than participate in further fruitless debates over disarmament. The conference finally collapsed in June, with Britain blaming France for its demise.[16] British bitterness was reflected in accusations by the foreign secretary, Sir John Simon, in June 1934:

> The French in present circumstances do not want a Disarmament Agreement or indeed, any agreement about arms at all. They ... may hope to surround Germany on the East ... and no doubt they calculate that, whether we like it or not, we must stand with them in the end against Germany.[17]

Anti-French feelings in Britain did not diminish during the Locarno years, despite the improvement in the international atmosphere.[18] The Labour chancellor of the exchequer, Philip Snowden, for example, remained 'virulently anti-French' throughout.[19] After 1930 Francophobia rose to new heights in British political circles. In 1934 the prime minister, James Ramsay MacDonald, described France as 'selfish' and possessed of a 'true war mentality'.[20] French intransigence towards the Weimar Republic was blamed for Hitler's rise to power, while French rejection of a 'reasonable' German offer of a disarmament agreement in 1933 was regarded in London as an opportunity missed to clinch a deal with Hitler while Germany was still militarily weak. France was accused of using its financial strength, based on the gold reserves it had accumulated in the late 1920s, to impose its will upon Europe, for instance, when it prevented the formation of an economic *Anschluss* between Germany and Austria in 1931.

As Germany grew stronger and Japan more menacing, Britain began to consider some modest improvements in its military, air and naval strength, but progress in achieving these was slow, mired in a labyrinth of chiefs of staff and cabinet committees, in which supporters of Royal Air Force expansion, like Neville Chamberlain, clashed with the War Office and the chief of the imperial general staff over the latter's proposals for the expansion of the expeditionary force. Against this background of ministerial and inter-service rivalry, Britain's relations with France deteriorated further during 1935. There were bitter wrangles between the two countries over the criteria for a new approach to Hitler for a disarmament agreement and a general settlement of outstanding European problems.[21] In the wake of Hitler's repudiation of the military clauses of the Versailles Treaty in February 1935, Britain, France and Italy met at Stresa between 11 and 14 April 1935 and issued a declaration in which they promised to uphold international treaties. Britain's contribution to this conference was, to say the least, half-hearted, making it clear from the outset that the declaration would not be accompanied by any British military commitment to support it. Britain did reaffirm its Locarno obligations, but French demands for the League to impose sanctions on countries that violated treaties exasperated MacDonald, who commented: 'one cannot trust the French further than they can be seen.'[22] Pierre Laval, the French foreign minister (who became prime minister as well on 7 June), and General Maurice Gamelin, the chief of staff of the French army, entered into staff talks with Italy, whereby France was to send an army corps to Italy in the event of German aggression against Austria.[23]

For its part, Britain signed a naval agreement with Germany in June 1935, which restricted the German surface fleet to 35 per cent of the size of the British navy. The French were not consulted in advance about this agreement, and condemned it as a betrayal of the Stresa Declaration, as well as active British connivance in a serious breach of the Versailles Treaty.[24] Cabinet ministers accepted the proposed ratio unanimously as a measure which removed the threat of a recurrence of the pre-1912 Anglo-German naval race. At the same time they hoped that it would enable the Admiralty to concentrate on the Japanese menace in the Far East.

On 7 June 1935, Stanley Baldwin replaced Ramsay MacDonald as prime minister. Sir Samuel Hoare took Simon's place as foreign secretary. Baldwin was not interested in foreign policy issues and his foreign secretaries were left to formulate foreign policy with relatively little prime ministerial interference. In October Anglo-French relations were further envenomed when Italy invaded Ethiopia. While the motives for Britain's denunciation of the invasion were partly based on the forthcoming general election in November and the anxiety of the Baldwin government to identify itself with British public opinion's fervent support for international law and the League of Nations, it was determined not to become involved in a war with Italy. The government calculated that once the election was over, Anglo-French negotiations with Mussolini would result in an agreement whereby Mussolini obtained the bulk of his territorial demands in Ethiopia, but with a gesture to British public opinion in allowing the emperor of Ethiopia to reign over what little was left of his country. In public the government trumpeted its support for the League – although Hoare's speech to the League assembly on 11 September was widely misinterpreted as threatening League military action to stop an Italian takeover of Ethiopia. Britain reluctantly promoted League economic sanctions against Italy, but their actual application was limited and unconvincing.

Hoare hoped that the failure of sanctions to dislodge Italy from Ethiopia could be blamed on French refusal to cooperate, since Laval insisted that he would take no action which would disrupt the close Franco-Italian relations which he had forged after Stresa. Indeed, Laval laboured behind the scenes to weaken sanctions even further. The French naval staff was unenthusiastic about naval cooperation and staff talks with Britain. French intransigence over Ethiopia provoked the permanent under-secretary at the Foreign Office, Sir Robert Vansittart, to exclaim that the French 'were a race that has never known the meaning of loyalty' and of 'disloyalty and treachery in its dirtiest and blackest form'. In January 1936, Sir George Clerk, the British ambassador to France, told Anthony Eden that 'two main tendencies inform M. Laval's character: a genuine horror of war and a natural inclination to double dealing.'[25] At a cabinet meeting on 16 October 1935, where ministers expressed doubts about French reliability, 'the French withdrawal from Chanak was recalled'.[26] Finally, after much British pressure, Laval gave way later in October and promised full cooperation with Britain in the Mediterranean and in imposing sanctions on Italy. Anglo-French naval, air and military staff talks followed.

In the general election in November, Baldwin's national government secured a majority of 247. Freed from electoral pressures, Hoare visited Paris on 8 December. There he reached an agreement with Laval which would have given Mussolini the bulk of his territorial demands in Ethiopia. The Hoare–Laval pact was stillborn after its contents were leaked to the French and British press. This caused an explosion of indignation in Britain, and Hoare was compelled to resign. Anthony Eden, the minister for League of Nations affairs, who had gained a public reputation as an advocate of collective security, replaced him as foreign secretary. The Foreign Office blamed the French for the disastrous press leak. The Ethiopian crisis was the lowest point in Anglo-French relations during the

1930s. French right-wingers blamed Britain for the loss of Italian friendship, while British officials complained that French support throughout the crisis had been at best half-hearted.[27]

British confidence in the French was also undermined by the relentless decline of the French economy after 1934 and by its continuing governmental instability. Frequent changes of government in France, which usually entailed the same politicians transferring to different portfolios, politicians who seemed to be either corrupt or immoral, the violent riots in Paris in February 1934 which came close to destroying the Republic altogether, and the growing fissure between left and right, did not suggest to the British that France was either a stable power or a reliable partner. Unemployment in France rose to two million in 1935 as industrial production fell, overseas trade collapsed, the balance of payments showed increasing deficits, bank failures multiplied, capital fled the country and internal investment collapsed. Laval attempted to deflate the economy, but his measures merely worsened the situation; while in order to avoid devaluation, which was regarded as likely to fracture an already deeply divided society, the government imposed quotas and tariffs on a wide range of agricultural and manufactured imports, whose adverse effects on British trade with France increased British impatience with France. France did not begin to climb out of the depression until the end of 1938.[28]

Nor was the French army in these years as strong and as confident as Winston Churchill was apt to proclaim or as French propaganda asserted. The original strategic justification for the building of the Maginot line was that it would enable the French army to destroy initial enemy attacks, which would then be followed by a major French offensive into Germany. By the 1930s, however, the line had come to symbolise French defensive-mindedness. British military observers noted the many imperfections in the construction of the line, and that it terminated just before the Ardennes. Moreover by the early 1930s the French army had lost the capability to embark on a rapid advance into Germany. Successive cuts in military expenditure after 1933 resulted in the dismissal of many professional regular and non-commissioned officers, shortages of essential armaments, armour and equipment, inadequate troop training and plummeting morale. Despite the reductions in the size of the officer corps, many elderly senior officers managed cling to the top posts in the army.[29] Matters did not improve until after September 1936, when Léon Blum's popular front government inaugurated a rearmament programme, which procured new equipment and weapons for the French army.

However sketchy British knowledge was about the state of the French army, the strength of pacifist and anti-war feeling in France could not be overlooked. This was, of course, mirrored by similar pacifist sentiments in the United Kingdom, but the bulk of the British population would have accepted phlegmatically a call to arms in an emergency, as they did in 1939, but in 1935 and 1936 there was less confidence that the French people would do so. During the latter stages of the Ethiopian crisis, the press attaché in Paris, Sir Charles Mendl, reported that, in the event of war with Italy, 'there would, in my considered opinion, be riots and almost certain civil war ... and that there would be hostile demonstrations in every town against mobilisation in that event.'[30]

THE BRITISH DOMESTIC BACKGROUND: WHITEHALL AND WESTMINSTER

The only British government department which sought to maintain friendly relations with France in these years was the Foreign Office, although it was by no means united or consistent in this policy. The affinity of many of its senior officials with France was criticised by Neville Chamberlain, the chancellor of the exchequer until 1937 and then prime minister, who wanted to reach an agreement with Germany, and who saw the Foreign Office's allegedly pro-French and anti-German bias as an impediment to the fulfilment of this task. R.A. Butler,[31] who became under-secretary of state for foreign affairs in 1938, blamed the Francophilia of many of the Foreign Office's top officials on the years they had spent in France learning the French language in their youth, when French had been the language of diplomacy. They had, as a result, he was convinced, absorbed French ideas and perspectives uncritically.[32] Geoffrey Dawson, the editor of *The Times*, a fervent advocate of the need 'to explore every avenue' for an Anglo-German settlement, regarded Foreign Office collaboration with the French 'architects of disorder in Europe' as being largely responsible for Britain's alienation from Germany.[33] Similarly, a newspaper correspondent, Peter Borneau, blamed the 'whole pro-French nest in the Foreign Office' for 'pursuing exactly the same policy as in 1905–1914, and it will probably have the same results.'[34] Henry Channon, the anti-French American-born Conservative Member of Parliament for Southend, who became Butler's parliamentary private secretary in March 1938, described Foreign Office officials as 'the Mandarins in the Forbidden City', thought France 'decadent' and argued that 'we should let gallant little Germany glut her fill of the Reds in the East.'[35]

Contrary to many of these assumptions, however, the Foreign Office was by no means united behind a pro-French policy, particularly at the more junior levels. Sir Samuel Hoare recalled his experiences as foreign secretary during the Ethiopian crisis, when each official seemed to have his own opinion as to a solution: 'There appeared to be no generally accepted body of opinion [in the Foreign Office] on the main issues. Diametrically opposed views were pressed upon me, and sometimes with the intolerance of an *odium theologicum*.'[36] Those officials whom Brian McKercher has described as the 'Edwardians' in the Office, who supported the traditional policy of the 'balance of power' and the maintenance of the entente, lost much of their influence after 1937, when Neville Chamberlain began to impose his own, rather different, ideas on British foreign policy. As late as July 1939 an observer thought that, with Chamberlain's ascendancy over foreign policy, 'as in the worst days of Lloyd George there is now a second F.O. at number 10.'[37]

Sir Robert Vansittart,[38] who had been permanent under-secretary at the Foreign Office since January 1930, was the leading exponent of the 'Edwardian' school of thought. He became intensely suspicious of Nazi Germany's ambitions after Hitler's rise, and called for the acceleration of Britain's rearmament as a counterweight to Germany's increasing military and air might. In keeping with his balance of power convictions, however, Vansittart had not hesitated to condemn France in the early 1930s for the 'blind ... selfish ... and vindictive' use of its hegemony in Europe in the previous decade.[39] Neither he nor the bulk of his officials initially opposed Anglo-German negotiations which might lead to the satisfaction of German grievances within an overall European settlement. However, by 1937, he had despaired of reaching any acceptable agreement with the Nazi regime.[40]

Vansittart's role in the negotiations for the abortive Hoare–Laval Pact in December 1935 discredited him in the eyes of many of his associates,[41] while Eden was irritated (as were many other politicians) by Vansittart's long-winded and florid 'Old Adam'[42] memoranda on the German danger and by the cabinet's assumption that the youthful Eden was merely the mouthpiece for Vansittart's views.[43] Eden was also concerned about Vansittart's mental stability, commenting in November 1936, after being addressed 'rather hysterically' by Vansittart about the formation of the anti-Comintern Pact, that 'he is not balanced and is in such a continual state of nerves that he will end by making would-be aggressors think the more of us as a possible victim!'[44] Baldwin and Eden tried to persuade Vansittart to move to the Paris embassy in 1936, but the permanent under-secretary refused to go, arguing that his transfer 'would be taken in many countries as a sign of a change in Britain's policy' and 'the effect on our own position, with France in her present condition, would be harmful.'[45]

Vansittart was not finally dislodged from his post until January 1938, when Chamberlain 'promoted' him to a new position as chief diplomatic adviser, an ornamental post which allowed Vansittart, as was intended, little influence on policy-making. It was described as 'a convenient, and polite means of dispensing with V[ansittart]'s services'.[46] Prophetically, Vansittart warned Eden at this time, 'I have long been identified with you in the eyes of the world as the greatest supporter in your policy' and 'my removal [will be] the first step towards undermining or sidetracking *you*.'[47]

Vansittart was replaced as permanent under-secretary by a more conventional official, Sir Alexander Cadogan, the deputy under-secretary, regarded by Chamberlain and Eden as a safer pair of hands, who would not attempt to direct Britain's foreign policy in the trenchant manner Vansittart had adopted. Bitter at being replaced, Vansittart described Cadogan as 'a tame and colourless civil servant, with less character, less knowledge and less persistence in arguing with politicians'.[48] Slightly more charitably, A.J. Sylvester, David Lloyd George's secretary, described Cadogan as 'a public servant who carries out instructions to the best of his ability – which is considerable. But unlike Vanisttart he has not a strong personality. Neither has he any strong convictions as Vansittart has, some of which are good and some are bad.'[49] Until September 1938, Cadogan supported Chamberlain's appeasement policy, writing in 1936 that 'cunctation' had left the initiative to Germany in foreign affairs and that 'our so-called "policy" has been a complete disaster since 1933.'[50] However, in September 1938, he was appalled by Chamberlain's willingness to accept Hitler's Godesberg *dictat* and persuaded Halifax to reject it. In 1939 he advocated a firm British policy towards Hitler, and admitted that Vansittart had been right all along in his assessment of German ambitions. Cadogan confessed to Halifax in February 1939 that he now had 'the profoundest suspicion of Hitler's ambitions. I believe they are strictly dishonourable and I believe what he would like best, if he could do it, would be to smash the British Empire.'[51] In July 1939, an informant told Sir Archibald Clark-Kerr, the British ambassador to China, that he had 'heard' that Chamberlain was 'disappointed with Cadogan and does not trust him any more.'[52] As a result of Cadogan's conversion to a hard line towards Germany, Vansittart recovered some of the influence in the Foreign Office which he had lost in the previous year.[53]

Clive Wigram was head of the Central Department until his death at the end of December 1936. He was intensely suspicious of Nazi Germany, and kept Winston Churchill informed about the progress of Germany's rearmament and the latest developments in British foreign policy. However, he too could be privately critical of the French. He complained in April 1935 that 'the French are so untrustworthy and broken reeds, whenever there is a crisis they crack and their government is turned out.'[54] He was succeeded as head of the Central Department by William Strang, a counsellor in the Department, who did not share Wigram's hostility towards Germany. In late 1937, however, he too began to doubt the possibility of reaching any worthwhile agreement with Hitler. Nevertheless he supported Chamberlain's policy towards Czechoslovakia in September 1938.[55]

Orme Sargent, the superintending under-secretary of the Central Department, supported the maintenance of the entente and wanted Britain to back France and Czechoslovakia against Germany in 1938.[56] In 1934, Sargent complained that the British habit of '"hating" France ... as the experience of the last fifteen years shows, can be indulged in with complete impunity and has no disagreeable after effects.'[57] One of Lloyd George's informants told the former prime minister that Sargent was 'the most convinced of our Francophiles'.[58] However, Sargent could also be waspish about the French; for instance, he complained in December 1936, that 'a Frenchman is always more frightened for his pocket than he is for his own skin.'[59] He also opposed the Franco-Soviet pact, which he described in January 1936 as 'the first step in the direction of the fatal policy which can, to my mind, only lead to one ultimate result, namely a European war in which the Soviet Government, in their capacity of agents of the Third International, would probably be the only beneficiaries.'[60] After Munich, Sargent was disgusted by France's betrayal of Czechoslovakia, although this did provide him with the opportunity to press for the abandonment of France's remaining East European commitments.

Disunity amongst Foreign Office officials and diplomats assisted Chamberlain's efforts to come to terms with the dictators. One of his most enthusiastic supporters in the diplomatic service was Sir Nevile Henderson,[61] who was appointed ambassador to Germany in April 1937. He became an extreme exponent of a pro-German line, inveighing against what he described as the 'Crowe tradition' in the Foreign Office which, he believed, regarded war with Germany as 'inevitable'.[62] Henderson wanted the entente with France to take second place to a rapprochement with Germany, telling the Labour Member of Parliament, Hugh Dalton, in October 1937, 'I would not trust the French'[63] and Halifax in February 1938 that 'most of our ills during the past twenty years must be ascribed to excessive deference to French policy'.[64] He thought that 'if France herself would be quiet, Germany would be quiet vis-à-vis France. French policy however is not only based on fear for herself, which is legitimate, but on opposition to German unity and consequent German greatness.'[65] He was not the only British diplomatic representative who was antagonistic towards the French. Sir Percy Loraine, appointed British ambassador to Rome in 1939, supported Chamberlain's appeasement policy, while Miles Lampson in Cairo, who was briefly considered for the Berlin embassy in 1937, wrote to Henderson in 1938 complaining that Britain was 'tied to France's chariot'.[66]

Sir Eric Phipps,[67] Vansittart's brother-in-law, was transferred from Berlin to Paris as British ambassador to France in April 1938 after much lobbying of friends in high places in Whitehall. He was a Francophile, having served on three previous occasions as a junior secretary at the Paris embassy. He had been educated in Paris and in the *Dictionary of National Biography* Sargent wrote:

> This education gave a foreign and especially a French tinge to his character and tastes, which showed itself in the profound knowledge which he acquired of French politics and culture, and in the sympathy which he felt for France throughout his life.[68]

Nevertheless this did not prevent him from identifying with French defeatists like Georges Bonnet, foreign minister during the September crisis in 1938, and urging Neville Chamberlain to accept any settlement with Germany over Czechoslovakia which would avoid war. Phipps had become depressed about the weakness of France and was convinced that, if the Sudeten crisis led to war between Germany and France, France would be defeated. His support for Chamberlain's appeasement policy discredited him within the Foreign Office, and particularly with Vansittart, who accused Phipps of undermining Foreign Office attempts to stiffen British and French policy towards Germany.

Inside the Foreign Office Sir George Mounsey, an assistant under-secretary responsible for the League of Nations and Western Departments, supported Chamberlain's appeasement policy and strongly criticised Vansittart's pro-French attitude during the Munich crisis.[69] On the other hand, the head of the Northern Department, Laurence Collier, was an 'arch anti-appeaser', opposed to any compromise with the Axis Powers, and a firm believer in the virtues of the balance of power and the need for an Anglo-French alliance. As early as January 1936 he was writing that 'we can only have a rapprochement with Germany on German terms and … it is not worth that.'[70] Reginald Leeper, the head of the Foreign Office News Department since 1935, shared Vansittart's view of German malevolence. He tried to influence the British press to disseminate the Foreign Office version of foreign policy as an antidote to the Chamberlain line propagated by George Steward, the pro-German press relations officer at 10

Downing Street, and by Sir Joseph Ball, director of the Conservative Research Department, and one of Chamberlain's closest aides.[71]

Many junior officials did not share the pro-French and anti-German feelings of their superiors. A junior member of Collier's Department, Robert Henry Hadow, complained to Nevile Henderson in May 1938:

> here the clique who would not allow of any right on the German side are still doing what they can to bring on the day of reckoning … . But, as usual, there is a disinclination, or inability, to DO anything, or to say directly and plainly to the French 'for fear of upsetting our Allies' (the very words of a Cabinet Minister) which … has left France to play her traditional game in Europe and may mean our being dragged in.

He hoped that Henderson would succeed in his efforts to improve relations with Germany, 'and wish I could help but in the Northern Department one is side-tracked & anyhow a 1st Secretary is easily smothered.'[72] Owen St Clair O'Malley, the head of the Southern Department until he was appointed minister to Mexico in 1937, believed that his opposition to the prevailing pro-French line in the Foreign Office had led to his being transferred to Mexico, a country he disliked. He had not endeared himself to Vansittart by his strident support for the satisfaction of Germany's 'legitimate grievances and a loosening of Britain's ties to France to enable Britain to adopt the role of mediator between Germany and France.'[73]

The foreign secretary who presided over this discordant department from 1935 until 1938, Anthony Eden, was widely regarded in government circles as a supporter of close relations with France. Since 1931 he had served in the national government successively as parliamentary under-secretary for foreign affairs, lord privy seal and minister without portfolio for League of Nations affairs with a seat in the cabinet from June 1935, and then foreign secretary after Hoare's resignation in December 1935. Eden had gained a reputation as a supporter of the League of Nations, chiefly as a result of his relatively high profile at the world disarmament conference and subsequently at the League assembly at Geneva. His performance at the League contrasted favourably with Sir John Simon's disdain for the organisation, which was clearly evident on the rare occasions when he addressed it. In fact Eden was never a pro-League zealot like Lord Robert Cecil, had not supported League sanctions against Japanese aggression in Manchuria after 1931, and by 1934 had come to the conclusion that the best hope of preserving peace was for a close association between Britain, France and Italy to uphold collective security.[74] His pro-League credentials made him the natural replacement for Hoare when the latter was forced to resign on 22 December 1935. Nevertheless Eden's anxiety to maintain the entente did not prevent him from supporting efforts to secure a general settlement with Germany, which was later to divide him further from Vansittart, who had concluded that Hitler would only accept an agreement which would give Germany hegemony in Central and Eastern Europe.[75] In 1938 Eden's differences with Neville Chamberlain over negotiations with Italy led to his resignation.

Eden's difficulties in formulating foreign policy were increased by the presence in the cabinet of two former foreign secretaries, Simon and Hoare, and also of Neville Chamberlain, who took a close interest in foreign affairs. However, until the end of 1937, Eden's relations with Chamberlain were relatively cordial.

Sir John Simon has seldom received a good press.[76] A distinguished lawyer with a considerable forensic intellect, Simon was a private person, shy and socially inept. He set up the National Liberal Party after defecting from the Liberal Party in 1931 over the tariff issue and joined Ramsay MacDonald's National Government as foreign secretary after the 1931 elections. He was generally regarded as a failure as a foreign secretary and was removed from the post by Baldwin in June 1935. In fact the intractability of many of the foreign problems with which Britain was faced during his period in office would have taxed the ingenuity of any other holder of the post – Japan's invasion of Manchuria, the rise of Hitler and the long drawn out and ultimately futile world disarmament conference. Moreover Britain's weakened economic, naval and military situation placed severe limitations on what Britain could achieve in its foreign policy. However it was Simon's indecisiveness and lack of drive which exasperated his officials and cabinet colleagues alike. But as a representative of a small, breakaway party in a government dominated by Conservatives, his position was scarcely a strong one, especially after the departure of the Samuelite Liberals from the government in September 1932. It was weakened still further by the dislike felt towards him by the prime minister, James Ramsay MacDonald, who in any case believed that he had much greater expertise in foreign policy than Simon.

Like his predecessors, Simon was opposed to any commitment to France which might saddle Britain with an obligation to go to war. However in January 1935 he did suggest offering France and Belgium staff conversations in return for French agreement to Germany's return to the League, but he was overruled by the cabinet. In June 1935 Simon was appointed home secretary. When Neville Chamberlain became prime minister in 1937, Simon replaced him as chancellor of the exchequer. He was preoccupied at the Treasury with the rising costs of rearmament. He worked closely with Chamberlain in late 1937 to impose a ceiling of

£1500 million on defence expenditure for four years, tightened Treasury control over the service departments, and fully supported the Inskip Report's recommendation that the defence of allies should be relegated to the fourth position in Britain's defence priorities – thus further reducing the role of the British army, on which further economies could now be implemented. This led him into conflict with Eden, who challenged the Treasury's pessimistic assumptions about Britain's financial and strategic difficulties.

After Eden resigned there remained no serious obstacle in the cabinet to Chamberlain's search for appeasement with Italy and Germany and in this he was fully supported by Simon – indeed, with Hoare and Halifax, Simon became one of Chamberlain's inner cabinet which determined policy during the crisis over Czechoslovakia in September 1938. After some hesitation Simon supported British acceptance of Hitler's Godesberg demands, and attempted to browbeat the French into accepting them as well. After Munich Simon agreed to a limited relaxation of Treasury controls on defence expenditure, but continued to resist pressure from Halifax and others to expand the field force on the grounds that the Maginot line was probably 'the strongest system of fortification that had ever been constructed', and that therefore the French did not need British reinforcements.[77] However by February 1939, intense pressure by Halifax, Lord Chatfield, the new minister for coordination of defence, and the chiefs of staff forced Simon to agree to 12 territorial army divisions being provided with full training equipment, and later in the same month to the creation of a field force of four regular and four territorial army divisions and two mobile divisions. While increasingly concerned by the escalating expenditure on armaments after March 1939, which was draining the country of its scarce gold reserves, Simon's grip on the finances slipped even further as conscription was introduced and further naval and air force expansion authorised. His close association with the failed Munich policy had in any case completely discredited him with the growing band of Conservative anti-appeasers in the House of Commons. His activities since 1937 had marked him out as one of the leading Francophobes in the cabinet, opposed to the despatch of an expeditionary force to France and always thinking up fresh pretexts for opposing staff talks with the French. Oliver Harvey, private secretary to Eden and then Halifax, described Simon as 'slippery and evasive, a moral coward'.[78]

The other pro-Chamberlain former foreign secretary in the Cabinet after 1936 was Samuel Hoare.[79] He had been an intelligence officer during the Great War in Russia and in Italy, and had served as secretary of state for air and secretary of state for India in successive Conservative administrations and in the National Government before taking Simon's place as foreign secretary on 7 June 1935. Given his wide experience of public affairs, his colleagues confidently expected a more determined foreign policy after the indecisiveness of the Simon years. As it turned out, Hoare lasted only for a few months in office, forced into resignation after the débâcle of his deal with Laval over Ethiopia in December. Oliver Harvey claimed that Hoare had 'never forgiven A[nthony] E[den] for succeeding him'.[80]

In June 1936 Baldwin recalled Hoare from the backbenches to be first lord of the Admiralty, and when Chamberlain became prime minister he appointed Hoare to be home secretary in place of Simon. As one of Chamberlain's few close friends and a member of the inner cabinet, Hoare fully supported the prime minister's appeasement policy, but after Munich he gradually became dissatisfied with what he now regarded as Chamberlain's passivity in the face of the German threat, and began to press for faster progress in rearmament. He was instrumental in persuading a reluctant Halifax and Chamberlain to agree to open the Anglo-French negotiations in the spring and summer of 1939 with the Soviet Union for an alliance and a military convention. Hoare's attitude towards France was at best ambivalent: his bruising experience after his experiences over the pact with Laval in 1935, which had temporarily destroyed his career, and the widespread belief that the leak to the press about the pact had emanated from the Quai d'Orsay, led him to distrust the French, as was evident from the many disparaging remarks he made about them down to 1938.

Lord Halifax,[81] who replaced Anthony Eden as foreign secretary in February 1938, was a wealthy aristocrat, a former viceroy of India, who was appointed lord president of the council by Chamberlain in May 1937, where he acted mainly as Eden's understudy. A compromiser in foreign affairs, Halifax fully supported Chamberlain's appeasement policy until Hitler's Godesberg *dictat* in September 1938; he then revolted against Hitler's aggressive tactics, which angered Chamberlain, who was never comfortable with opposition to his chosen policies. Their relations never fully recovered. Thereafter Halifax adopted a more pro-French line, urging the cabinet to strengthen Britain's military support for France, since otherwise, demoralised by Munich, France might sign a separate agreement with Germany. Channon, who turned against Halifax after the latter distanced himself from Chamberlain, 'reflected' in 1940 'on Halifax's extraordinary character; his high principles, his engaging charm and grand manner ... his sublime treachery which is never deliberate, and, always to him, a necessity dictated by a situation. Means are nothing to him, only ends. He is insinuating but not unloveable.'[82] After lunching with Halifax in April 1938 Sir Robert Bruce Lockhart, a journalist and former diplomat, described Halifax more kindly as 'gentle and not awe-inspiring, yet has considerable dignity and gives one an impression of great intellectual honesty. He would make a very fine judge.'[83]

As for the rest of the Chamberlain cabinet, Oliver Harvey, who had little regard for any politician except Eden, described Kingsley Wood[84] as 'a severe critic of A.[nthony] E.[den] and ... a pushy professional politician', and Earl de La Warr,[85] Malcolm MacDonald,[86] W. Ormsby-Gore[87] and Oliver Stanley[88] as 'all lightweights ... who haven't got the courage of their convictions'.[89]

The personality and policies of Neville Chamberlain have been thoroughly dissected by historians.[90] He was undoubtedly sincere in his search for agreement with Germany, which, he believed, would solve many of Britain's financial and strategic problems. His genuine hatred of war placed him at a severe disadvantage, to say the least, when dealing with Hitler in September 1938. The German dictator was more than willing to use force against Czechoslovakia, while Chamberlain sought to avoid war at almost any cost. For Chamberlain, the weakness of France was an additional motive for his appeasement policies; to an American correspondent he wrote in January 1938 that 'France's weakness is a public danger just when she ought to be a source of strength and confidence.'[91]

Of the civil servants outside the Foreign Office, Sir Maurice Hankey,[92] the long-standing secretary to the cabinet and the committee of imperial defence, was an influential figure. He was more concerned with the security of the British Empire and with British naval strength than he was with European issues, but recognised that the safety of the Empire depended on the defence of France and Belgium against German expansionism. While doubtful of France's staying power in war, he advocated the maintenance of close ties with France as an insurance against potential German aggression, although he was not consistent in this view. He told Phipps in January 1936 that, while France 'was not very reliable except when her own safety was at stake' and that 'most people' in Britain believed that France would 'throw a Chanak' in the event of hostilities, 'I do not think that anyone inside has any doubt that we must stick to her – with all her trickiness, unreliability and instability. Our interests are too closely intertwined.'[93] Later in the summer, however, Hankey concluded that, 'in the present state of Europe, with Spain and France menaced by Bolshevism, it is not inconceivable that it might pay us to throw in our lot with Germany,' so echoing the fears of many Conservatives that communism was a greater danger to European stability than national socialism.[94] He opposed any prior commitment to the despatch of the British expeditionary force to France in the event of war, and even then, if the government decided that it should be sent, the French should be told firmly that four divisions would be the maximum of Britain's land effort on the continent. The chief secretary to the Treasury until 1939, Warren Fisher, shared Hankey's views on foreign and defence policies, although he thought the British army should be increased to a maximum of 600,000 men.[95]

The chiefs of staff were not, for different reasons, enthusiastic about sending an expeditionary force to the continent. One can sympathise with their predicament since, by 1935, all three services were suffering from the underfunding of the previous ten years, with the army particularly affected by the cutbacks. Despite their efforts to present a united front to the politicians, chiefs of staff meetings were usually riven by bitter infighting as each service chief sought to secure as much money as possible for his own service from the limited budget allocated to defence. When the cabinet was unable to make up its collective mind about service priorities, it usually referred the issue back to the chiefs for consideration, thus allowing further opportunities for delay and procrastination. Of course, each service had its own strategic agenda: the Royal Navy concentrated its attention on the Far East and the Japanese naval threat, the Royal Air Force was wedded to the doctrine of the strategic offensive, while the army, 'the Cinderella Service' as Lord Hailsham, a former secretary of state for war, described it, was absorbed in policing the Empire. These differences became glaringly apparent during the meetings of the defence requirements sub-committee of the committee of imperial defence (DRC), set up by the government in November 1933 in the wake of the Manchurian crisis to recommend measures to remedy the worst deficiencies in Britain's defences. Hankey was chairman of this sub-committee, with Vansittart, Warren Fisher and the chiefs of staff as members. Vansittart and Warren Fisher overcame the objections of Admiral Sir Ernle Chatfield, the first sea lord, and Hankey, who were more concerned about the danger of an expansionist Japan to Britain's interests in the Far East than about the potential German threat in Europe, and secured the insertion of a passage in the final report that Germany was 'the ultimate potential enemy against whom our "long range" defence policy has to be directed'.

The chiefs of staff, who had long and bitter experiences of the parsimony of successive governments where the nation's defences were concerned, contested what they regarded as the civilian members' unrealistic expectation that the National Government would accept the relatively large sums of money which Vansittart, Hankey and Warren Fisher were prepared to recommend for what would turn out to be a programme of military, naval and air rearmament rather than merely remedying the worst deficiencies in the armed services. It was a bizarre spectacle to witness civil servants arguing for greater expenditure on the armed services while the military, naval and air members proposed more modest amounts based on political and financial restraints.[96]

The first report was completed on 28 January 1934. It was then examined by the ministerial committee on disarmament, whose conclusions fully justified the chiefs of staff's forebodings. The ministerial committee focused its attention on the DRC's recommendations for the creation of an expeditionary force of one cavalry division, four infantry divisions and a tank brigade to take the field one month after mobilisation. Neville Chamberlain led the opposition to this proposal and, after lengthy debates with Lord Hailsham, the secretary of state for war, who strenuously supported army expansion, persuaded the committee to reduce the DRC's recommended expenditure on the expeditionary force, and to expand the size of the Royal Air Force instead.

Chamberlain was convinced that the Royal Air Force would be a more credible deterrent to potential aggressors than the army. The sensitivity of politicians to what they rightly believed was the hostility of public opinion to a continental commitment was reflected in a committee of imperial defence decision in November 1934 to ban the use of the term 'Expeditionary Force' in speeches by politicians and in official papers since, as the dominions secretary, J.H. Thomas put it, 'the expression "Expeditionary Force" had unpleasant inferences in the public mind.' It was to be replaced by the euphemism, 'the Field Force'. No war planning followed the DRC report, since, while the despatch of the expeditionary force to the continent had been accepted in principle, it was not certain that the politicians would agree to its going to France or the Low Countries in the event of war with Germany. Even the then chief of the imperial general staff, Field Marshal Sir Archibald Montgomery-Massingberd, was unenthusiastic about such a commitment.[97]

A second DRC report was completed on 24 July 1935. In the light of the worsening international climate, it recommended a new two-power naval standard for the navy, an expeditionary force of five regular divisions (one of which was to be mechanised) and 12 territorial army divisions, and further expansion of the Royal Air Force. This programme was to be completed by 1939, based on Vansittart's belief that Germany would be ready to go to war in that year. A third DRC report, in November 1935, repeated the recommendations of the second about the future size of the expeditionary force. It was examined by a new cabinet committee, the defence policy requirements committee. Chamberlain again led the way in opposing army expansion, particularly the recommendation that 12 territorial army divisions should be equipped with war reserves. He succeeded in postponing further consideration of this proposal for three years.[98] The controversy over the size and role of the expeditionary force, and the related question of staff talks with the French, was not resolved until 1939. Until then the chiefs of staff continued to oppose a firm commitment to the despatch of the expeditionary force to France and to Anglo-French staff talks, in the belief that to support closer military ties with the French would redound to their discredit with politicians and with public opinion if it was leaked to the press. The French did not know that the British service chiefs opposed staff talks and blamed British ministers for Britain's reluctance to authorise them.[99]

Of those outside the charmed circle of government, civil servants and chiefs of staff, Winston Churchill's pro-French and anti-German sentiments in this period are well known. Discredited by his opposition to the introduction of constitutional reforms in India and by his quixotic support for King Edward VIII during the abdication crisis, he was nevertheless a thorn in the side of the government with his constant pressure for faster rearmament and his calls for closer Anglo-French relations in the face of the menace from Germany. Churchill's belief in the strength of the French army was contested by the pro-German and pro-Chamberlain proprietor of the *Daily Mail*, Lord Rothermere, who wrote to Churchill in October 1937 that 'the French Army is slowly but surely sinking into a condition of chaos and confusion such as is beginning to distinguish the life of France.' This was not information likely to appeal to Churchill.[100]

Churchill was supported in his views by a small group of Conservative rebels, who included General Sir Edward Spears, Robert Boothby and Brendan Bracken. Spears, who had been born in France and had served as a liaison officer to the French general staff during the Great War, was close to Churchill during these years. He was accused by his critics of misleading Churchill by exaggerating the strength of the French army. Spears, whose encouragement of Georges Mandel, the French minister of the colonies, and a friend from the war years, to resist the partition of Czechoslovakia in September 1938, upset Edouard Daladier, the French prime minister. Spears was active during these years in trying to foster closer Anglo-French relations in the upper-class milieu in which he moved. He was a member of the committee of an Anglo-French luncheon club, for which he secured speakers from France, who included the journalist 'Pertinax' (André Géraud), General Alphonse Georges, deputy to General Gamelin, and the politician Joseph Paul-Boncour. Spears considered that the 'club does admirable work in keeping together English people who love France and in entertaining distinguished Frenchmen who visit London.'[101] He was also joint chairman, with the former French foreign minister Pierre-Etienne Flandin, of the Anglo-French parliamentary group, until Flandin was removed after he had publicly congratulated Hitler on the Munich settlement.[102] During the 'phoney war', Spears wrote: 'I have always felt that unless the British and French stand together there was no hope for the future of Europe and I have preached this view in season and out if season ever since the last war.'[103]

However, there were British residents in France who did not think that the average French person was capable of fulfilling the role which Francophiles like Spears believed to be essential if the entente was to become a central feature of the future European order. A Mr H.E. Drew, who worked in the Gironde, complained to R.A. Butler in January 1939:

> We British subjects who are working in France are really not welcomed, but are merely tolerated. On several occasions I have been asked by French citizens 'And what are YOU doing in France?' The only type of foreigner who is wanted here is the tourist (particularly English and American) who arrives with his purse full and leaves soon afterwards with his purse empty ...
>
> It does seem to me – and I believe that this opinion is shared by all the British subjects of my acquaintance – the attitude of Frenchmen towards the representatives of her Allies in France should be less rigorous. If such rigour is at all necessary it should rather be confined to her enemies and perhaps neutrals.[104]

The bulk of elite opinion-formers in Britain supported appeasement and belittled the importance of the French connection for British security. Geoffrey Dawson, the editor of *The Times* until 1941, was probably one of the most fervent pro-Germans down to 1939. His assistant editor, Robert Barrington-Ward, shared Dawson's opinions. Dawson regarded the Versailles Treaty as unjust in its treatment of Germany and argued that it should be substantially modified in Germany's favour. He was friendly with Stanley Baldwin, Neville Chamberlain and Halifax, his neighbour in Yorkshire. He summed up his attitude to France in a leading article in *The Times* on 6 July 1936:

> British opinion accepts as an axiom the existing friendship with France ... There is nothing anti-French or pro-German about it ... What British opinion is not prepared to accept is the leadership of France over the

> whole field of foreign policies, or to admit responsibility for all the liabilities which she has been accumulating in the shape of alliances on the farther side of Germany.

While he did not write the famous editorial in *The Times* of 7 September 1938, advocating the outright transfer of the Sudetenland to Germany, which embarrassed Halifax, he did make alterations to it and authorised its publication.[105] Sargent warned Phipps in June 1936 that Barrington-Ward 'has strong pro-German prejudices, which are all the more dangerous in view of the influence which he exercises on "The Times" and elsewhere'.

The attacks by Dawson and Barrington-Ward on the pro-French and anti-German bias of the Foreign Office were supported by Lord Lothian, who, as Philip Kerr, had been Lloyd George's private secretary before and during the Paris peace conference in 1919, and had played an important role in the negotiations leading to the Versailles Treaty. He had been a member of Lord Milner's Round Table group, dedicated to the closer union of the British Empire. Like Lloyd George, Lothian had little regard for the French or for the Foreign Office. He wanted an Anglo-German agreement based on the removal of Germany's Versailles grievances. His meetings with Hitler in January 1935 and May 1937 had impressed him with the evident sincerity of the German dictator's desire for peace and Anglo-German friendship. His opinions were, of course, anathema to Vansittart, who, like many other Foreign Office officials, had encountered Lothian at the Paris peace conference and had resented his interference in foreign policy-making there.[106]

David Lloyd George had been equally impressed with Hitler when he met him at Berchtesgaden in September 1936. Lloyd George was accompanied by Dr Thomas Jones, the former deputy secretary of the committee of imperial defence, a confidant of Lloyd George and Baldwin, who shared Lloyd George's Francophobia, and who also campaigned for an accommodation with Germany. His activities scarcely endeared him to Eden and Vansittart, while he was equally hostile to Eden, whom he accused of preferring 'to cling to France and the Treaty of Versailles' rather than seek friendship with Germany and Italy. However, Jones turned against appeasement after Munich.[107]

Another pro-German who influenced Lloyd George was Professor M.S. Gerothwohl, who described himself as a Belgian journalist, resident in the United Kingdom, and 'associated' with the American Hearst press. He was in contact with French politicians and claimed that he gleaned information, which, as it turned out, was not always very reliable, from informants within the Foreign Office about British foreign policy. Gerothwohl fed Lloyd George a diet of anti-French and anti-Foreign Office gossip during these years, and from Lloyd George's marginalia and underlinings on Gerothwohl's reports, the former prime minister appeared to read them avidly. Gerothwohl's criticisms of the role of the Foreign Office were meat and drink to Lloyd George, who harboured a long-standing animus towards the Foreign Office.

These were the figures who either shaped policy towards, or influenced public opinion about, France in this period. Most of them, apart from a few Foreign Office officials and Churchill and his small band of supporters, were antagonistic towards France and they believed that in this they reflected the perceptions of the broad mass of British public opinion. There were, of course, other members of the British establishment who shared their prejudices. While the notion of the 'Clivedon Set', based on house parties at the home of Lord and Lady Astor, supposedly influencing government policy in an anti-French and pro-German direction has been exposed as the myth that it was, there is no doubt that many of those who clustered around the Astors shared Lady Astor's 'vivid personal dislike of the French'. As Gilbert and Gott have suggested in their book *The Appeasers*, to people of this ilk:

> While Germany gained a new master and a new discipline in 1933, France remained slovenly, excitable, under the influence of left-wing politicians ... German excesses there indeed were, but French weakness was as great a crime. It was a weakness the communists could exploit; a weakness which offered a chance of power to the agents of Moscow. A deal with France would be a deal with danger.[108]

2 Britain, France and the Rhineland Crisis, March to December 1936

The ways of French politics are incalculable.

(Orme Sargent)[1]

A great deal of consideration was given to the question from the military point of view but the military situation developed out of the diplomatic situation. Were our relations with the France so tightly bound, it was asked, that we should have trouble if the Cabinet were first to survey the situation for themselves and then consider a policy towards Germany?

(Cabinet minutes, 9 January 1936)[2]

Pierre Laval resigned as French prime minister on 22 January 1936, after a vote of no confidence in his administration in the Chamber of Deputies. With a general election due in May, Albert Saurraut formed a caretaker government, with Pierre-Etienne Flandin as foreign minister. Laval's fall from power was welcomed in British official circles, where he had become widely disliked and distrusted. Sir Horace Rumbold, a former British ambassador to Germany, told Geoffrey Dawson in December 1935 that 'the only white thing about Laval was his tie and even that was only washed occasionnlly (*sic*).'[3] Sir George Clerk, the British ambassador to France, wrote that 'unhappily his character is such that it is almost impossible for him to believe that anyone can run straight and he cannot distinguish between legitimate and friendly criticism and intrigues such as he would indulge in similar circumstances.'[4]

It was not only the poor quality of its politicians which discredited France in the eyes of British politicians. Its economy, after Laval's deflationary measures in 1935, was failing, its gold reserves were flowing out of the country at an alarming rate, and its armaments production falling at a time when German rearmament was expanding rapidly. Laval's disastrous foreign policy had resulted in estrangement from Italy and the loss of British confidence in French reliability. Given his experiences of France's opportunist diplomacy during the previous six months, Anthony Eden's complaint that, if France had followed 'a strong policy towards Italy, the Abyssinian War could have been prevented or curtailed, and France would be in a strong position in Europe today, instead of in a very weak one', did not seem unreasonable.[5]

Under these circumstances Saurraut's government was in no position to respond effectively to Germany's re-militarisation of the Rhineland on 7 March 1936.[6] The feeble Anglo-French handling of the Ethiopian crisis had prompted Hitler to act in the belief that the two countries would not challenge him in Western Europe.[7] Germany justified the re-militarisation on the grounds that the ratification of the Franco-Soviet alliance by the French Chamber of Deputies on 27 February had undermined the Locarno Treaty.[8] The ensuing clamour by Flandin for a determined Anglo-French response to force German troops out of the Rhineland carried little conviction with his French cabinet colleagues,[9] while the British cabinet had already decided on 5 March 1936 that:

> the reality of the situation was that neither France nor England was really in a position to take effective military action against Germany in the event of a violation of the Treaty of Locarno. M. Flandin ought to be put up against [*sic*] this reality.[10]

Colonel H.R. Pownall, the military assistant secretary to the committee of imperial defence, echoed the opinion of most British officials in concluding that Hitler 'will get away with it ... We are certainly in no position (even if we wanted to) to use force – nor are the French though they will squeal and sulk and ask for help.'[11] On 11 March the chiefs of staff warned the cabinet that the bulk of British naval, air and ground forces were concentrated in the Mediterranean against Italy, and that 'if there was the smallest danger of war with Germany', they would have to be brought back to England, a process which would take some time to complete. The chiefs added that they were aware 'that the main object of the Government's policy is to avoid any risk of war with Germany.' On 16 March the joint planning sub-committee pointed out that the only British land forces which could be spared for France in the event of war with Germany were two infantry divisions, and that even these would not be ready for despatch to the continent until three weeks after the beginning of hostilities. Furthermore the two divisions would be dependent on horses for their transport, and they possessed no tanks, anti-tank guns or infantry mortars.[12]

British Francophobes were quick to blame Germany's decision to re-militarise the Rhineland on France's past refusal to approach Germany's legitimate grievances in a conciliatory spirit. Gerothwohl, writing to Lloyd George on the day of the re-militarisation, attributed Germany's action to its frustration after France's rejection of previous German offers of direct talks to settle the Rhineland issue. At the same time France had also offended Germany by trying to revive 'the old Poincaré policy of encirclement', since Gerothwohl accepted the German argument that the Franco-Soviet Pact was 'a moral violation and a political violation' of Locarno.[13] Lord Lothian, writing to Lloyd George on 8 March, also excused Hitler's action 'because of the folly of the Franco-Russian Treaty and the still greater folly of the British Foreign Office having approved of the idea'. While reluctantly accepting that Britain was right to 'side with France, because it is very important in the present uncertainties that we should not alienate her needlessly until Hitler's proposals have been put to the test', Lothian nevertheless hoped that Britain should not 'stand on the letter of the Locarno Treaties'.[14]

Lord Robert Cecil, a former Conservative disarmament minister and, after 1923, president of the League of Nations Union, warned Winston Churchill in April 'not [to] underrate the very strong anti-French feeling that is raging in this country', which was, as Harold Nicolson, National Labour Member of Parliament and a former diplomat, noted, also reflected in the 'terribly pro-German' and Francophobic mood which was infecting the broad mass of Conservative MPs in the House of Commons.[15] When Austen Chamberlain attended a meeting of Conservative MPs in the House on 17 March, he also encountered intense hostility towards the French for 'their continual coercion [of Germany] and everlasting complaining',[16] while Roger Lumley, Eden's parliamentary private secretary, warned the foreign secretary in September that 'any commitment to France which would bring us in on the side of the Bolshevists would never be passed by the Country.'[17]

While Eden thought that Germany's coup had 'now exploded ... the myth ... that Herr Hitler only repudiates treaties imposed on Germany by force', he seized on Hitler's offers, which accompanied Berlin's announcement of the re-militarisation, to negotiate new security and air pacts to replace the Locarno Treaty, to sign non-aggression pacts with Germany's eastern neighbours and to rejoin the League of Nations,[18] as a means of circumventing Flandin's pressure for Anglo-French-Belgian action against Germany under the Locarno Treaty. Eden accepted that 'in the face of this fresh and gross insult to the sanctity of treaties, it will be difficult to persuade the French to sign any fresh agreement with Germany in present circumstances', but this was not going to discourage him from exploring Hitler's proposals. While Eden thought that 'France is not in the mood for a military adventure', like Pownall he feared that

> between military action on the one hand and friendly action on the other, there lies a policy of sulking and passive obstruction, and it is this policy to which the French Government in their weakness, will be inclined to have recourse, and out of which we shall have to persuade them.[19]

This was not to prove an easy task, and nor was it made any easier by a wave of anti-British revulsion in France over Britain's passivity in the face of this latest German breach of international treaties. Hugh Lloyd-Thomas, the British minister in Paris, reported to the Foreign Office at the end of March that:

> opinion in all circles is converging towards the same point – indignation at the alleged failure of His Majesty's Government to carry out their obligations to support France in this critical hour ... Laval and Co. say: 'we told you so ... We always knew that British enthusiasm for collective security and the sanctity of treaties was a ramp.'[20]

After reading this, Ralph Wigram hoped that Britain would try to prevent Franco-British relations from deteriorating further, since, 'unless we take care, we shall see France actually coming to some arrangement with Italy against us [over sanctions] ... That may be a very unpleasant and immoral possibility to suggest but it seems to me that foreign policy has to be framed with such possibilities in mind.' In responding to Wigram's minute, Eden expressed his intense irritation with French behaviour since October 1935:

> Franco-British relations do not depend upon this country alone. I have done my utmost to meet [the] French Govt & can go no further. If they persist in talking about the reconstruction of the 'Stresa' front, we shall have to continue to make it plain that we will have nothing to do [with] it. If France then decides to prefer Italy to ourselves that will only add one more miscalculation to that country's innumerable miscalculations since the war.[21]

While Eden did not believe that France would use force against Germany, he could not entirely rule out the possibility, although he suspected that French Anglophobia was being fermented by the French government in order to demonstrate to its own public opinion that Britain, not France, was responsible for the lack of any effective entente action against Germany.[22]

In fact, Flandin's aim was to secure a firmer British guarantee of French security than that contained in the Locarno Treaty, which all French politicians correctly regarded as worthless. The purpose of the French foreign minister's persistence in pressing Britain to agree to sanctions against Germany was to persuade London to agree to closer Anglo-French military relations as an alternative.[23] Flandin was well aware of British opposition to sanctions, claiming later that the British prime minister, Stanley Baldwin, had told him on 14 March that he (Baldwin) was determined to avoid war over the Rhineland issue at all costs.[24]

At a preliminary meeting at the Quai d'Orsay on Tuesday 10 March 1936, between Eden, Halifax, Flandin and Paul Van Zeeland, the Belgian prime minister, to discuss their response to the Rhineland crisis, Flandin demanded that the remaining Locarno powers should adopt a series of economic, financial and, ultimately, military measures to force the German army to evacuate the Rhineland. Eden's parliamentary under-secretary, Lord Cranborne, on reading these demands, hoped that the foreign secretary would 'be able to deal firmly with the French, who seem to be beginning to behave in a very obstreperous manner.'[25] Eden, given his previous assumption that France would do nothing, was taken aback by the French foreign minister's evident determination to act against Germany, and by the support Van Zeeland gave Flandin's proposals.[26] Eden told Flandin and Van Zeeland that he would have to return to London to consult the cabinet before he could reply. He also persuaded them to agree that future meetings of the remaining Locarno powers should be held in the British capital.

After Eden's return to London, a special cabinet meeting was convened in the evening of 11 March to determine how Britain should react to Flandin's demands. The outcome was predictable. The cabinet unanimously rejected sanctions against Germany since these might lead to a general European war for which Britain was militarily unprepared. It resolved that, instead, negotiations with Germany should be initiated for a general European settlement based on Hitler's 7 March proposals. One minister pointed out that British 'public opinion was strongly opposed to any military action against', Germany while 'the ex-Servicemen were very anti-French'. The prime minister voiced the cabinet's unanimous hostility towards French pressure for sanctions in stating that

> at some stage it would be necessary to point out to the French that the action they proposed would not result only in letting loose another great war in Europe. They might succeed in crushing Germany with the aid of Russia, but it would probably only result in Germany going Bolshevik.

Eden 'pointed out that at bottom the French nation was very pacifist'. The prime minister then complained that British military unpreparedness

> was perfectly well known to the French Government, and it seemed very unfriendly of them to put us in the present dilemma. People would take a long time to forget it ... He felt that the French ought to welcome our coming re-armament rather than expose us to the present embarrassments.

The rejection of forcible measures against Germany, the feeling that there was some justice in Germany's case over the Rhineland and the tendency to blame past French policy towards Germany for the current crisis was by no means confined to Francophobes like Lothian and Gerothwohl, but was shared by government ministers and, it appeared, by the majority of British public opinion.[27]

This negative British response to Flandin's call for resolute entente action prompted the French ambassador, Charles Corbin, to warn Vansittart on 13 March that if Britain failed to stand by its Locarno obligations, the resulting Franco-British estrangement would lead inevitably to a German-dominated Europe. The permanent under-secretary could only try 'to reassure the French Ambassador that we were people who kept our word. I deprecated any undue anxiety and felt that we should best be served by resolute optimism.'[28] This was not much consolation to the French, but given the refusal of the French army chief of staff, General Maurice Gamelin, to take military action against Germany without general mobilisation, a sensitive issue on the eve of a French general election, Eden's initial assumption that France would not move turned out to be correct.

However, the knowledge that the French army was unable to mount a swift response to Germany's action, and that Saurraut was opposed to military measures, did not deter Flandin from continuing his campaign to persuade Britain to adopt a more determined line. He warned Eden that if Britain did nothing to help France in the current crisis, Laval might combine with Edouard Daladier and return to power with a mandate to negotiate a direct settlement of outstanding issues between France and Germany, and one that might ignore British interests. The French foreign minister reminded Eden that 'M. Laval was always urging that it was useless to rely on England'.[29] As Flandin intended, such threats of a possible Anglo-French estrangement worried Eden, who now began to examine methods of meeting France's security concerns in Western Europe without committing Britain to an alliance with France or becoming entangled with France's treaties with the Soviet Union, Czechoslovakia or Poland.[30]

Evidently Vansittart was already working on a solution of this kind in mid-March, since, according to notes made by Samuel Hoare of a conversation with the permanent under-secretary on the 14th, the latter wanted Britain to give France a military guarantee as a safeguard in case Germany again broke an international treaty. According to Hoare, Vansittart was adamant that 'We can't and won't go to war.'[31] At the same time Vansittart was urging Eden to support a League of Nations resolution condemning Germany for its unilateral repudiation of Locarno, otherwise 'the French will become unmanageable (they have plenty of chapter and verse against us, as well as the smart of the pressure [over Abyssinia] we put on them throughout 1935).' Without some British gesture to uphold the Locarno Treaty, he too feared that Germany would succeed in driving a wedge between Britain and France.[32]

British officials recognised that Germany's military reoccupation of the Rhineland would make it difficult in future for France to come to the assistance of Czechoslovakia and Poland in the event of German aggression against them. However, the Foreign Office did not regret this outcome, as Cranborne made clear in a minute on 17 March:

> It is frequently said that France is becoming a second-rate Power. That is not true. What gives colour to the suggestion is that France is at present biting off more than she can chew. If her sphere of influence was limited to Western Europe and Northern Africa she would remain a great and powerful nation. But, as she cannot effectively spread her influence further, the Great Power of Central Europe must inevitably be Germany.

He suggested that, in return for Germany's re-entry into the League of Nations and its participation in a series of European-wide non-aggression pacts, Germany might be allowed 'a freer hand' economically in Eastern Europe. Orme Sargent thought that Britain should offer France a guarantee against a direct German attack in return for the abandonment of France's commitments in Eastern Europe. This was not a policy which commended itself to Vansittart – 'We could not of course ask France to sever her Eastern connections' he minuted – but it remained an attractive option for many cabinet ministers and Whitehall officials, who were concerned that Britain might become involved in a war with Germany as a result of a dispute in Central Europe which led to French intervention on the side of its eastern allies.[33]

Further meetings of the representatives of the four Locarno powers – Eden, Flandin, Van Zeeland and the Italian ambassador to the United Kingdom, Count Dino Grandi – were held in London between 12 and

19 March to try to overcome the impasse between France and Britain over sanctions. Flandin demanded that the League of Nations should condemn Germany for its violations of the treaties of Versailles and Locarno, and he pressed for Anglo-French-Belgian military staff conversations to concert automatic action in advance if Germany defied Europe again. He told Eden that he would not agree to negotiations with Germany while its troops remained in the Rhineland. The chancellor of the exchequer, Neville Chamberlain, who was asked by Eden and Halifax to assist them in trying to persuade Flandin and Van Zeeland to accept a peaceful resolution of the crisis, warned the French foreign minister over lunch at the French embassy on 12 March that British public opinion would not support sanctions against Germany. Flandin retorted that, if Britain and France took a firm stand, Germany would give way without war. Chamberlain retorted that 'we cannot accept this as a reliable estimate of a mad dictator's reactions.' On Sunday, 15 March, during the course of another conversation with Flandin, the latter warned Chamberlain that a failure to force Germany to evacuate the Rhineland might lead to a Fascist takeover in France. He suggested the conclusion of a mutual assistance pact between Britain, France and Belgium, but the chancellor of the exchequer again replied that it would be impossible for Britain to agree to such a pact 'in view of [the] isolationist school'. However, he hinted that Britain might be agreeable to military staff conversations with France.

Ward Price, the *Daily Mail* correspondent in Berlin, told Chamberlain on the 13th that Hitler had intimated to him (Ward Price) that he would be prepared to accept the stationing of an international force on both sides of the Rhineland frontier while negotiations for a new Locarno settlement continued. Chamberlain confided to his diary that Baldwin, Eden and Halifax had 'expressed great satisfaction' when he informed them that Flandin had hinted that he might agree to negotiations with Germany if an international force was placed on the Rhineland frontier.[34]

Despite Chamberlain's optimism about Flandin's willingness to compromise, the latter, during the 18 March meeting of the four Locarno powers, on learning that Hitler had rejected a British suggestion that he order a token withdrawal of German troops from the Rhineland as a prelude to negotiations, threatened to return to France if Britain did not agree to sanctions against Germany.[35] Eden was now convinced, as he told the cabinet on the same day, that France could only be persuaded to agree to negotiations with Germany if the British government approved Anglo-French-Belgian staff conversations. Inevitably this suggestion was not welcomed by the cabinet. 'Several Ministers' pointed out 'that military conversations on that basis would be very unacceptable to public opinion in this country.' While the cabinet was eventually persuaded by Eden to agree to staff talks, the cabinet majority insisted that it be made clear to France and Belgium that:

> such conversations must be strictly limited to mutual arrangements for defence in the event of German aggression against France and Belgium during the period of negotiation, and this would have to be made unmistakeably clear in any announcement to the British public.[36]

Chamberlain continued to support Eden's efforts to achieve a satisfactory compromise with France and Belgium, based on a British promise of staff conversations, urging Van Zeeland on the 19 March that, if the Locarno powers sought a lasting peace, 'we should not say things that might irritate [Hitler]' as 'we were dealing with a lunatic and it was no use to treat him as though he were a sane man.' He (Chamberlain) wanted 'to concentrate on the constructive side'.

On 19 March, after a meeting of the Locarno powers which lasted until the early hours of the following morning, Chamberlain and Halifax (Eden was attending the League of Nations council meeting in London which condemned Germany for repudiating the Versailles and Locarno treaties) persuaded Van Zeeland and Flandin, who had refused to accept the stationing of an international force on the French as well as on the German side of the Rhineland frontier – a 'monstrous inequity'[37] – to agree to the offer of negotiations with Germany in return for British acceptance of Anglo-Belgian-French staff conversations and a reaffirmation by the three powers of their Locarno obligations. The British insisted, in notes to France and Belgium, that 'it is understood that this contact between the General Staffs cannot give rise, in respect of either Government, to any political understanding nor to any obligations regarding the organisation of national defence.' Also, in a letter from the British to the French and Belgian governments, Britain agreed that if conciliation should fail, it would consult with the other two powers on ways to meet the new situation.[38] Chamberlain congratulated himself on the successful outcome of the conference, writing to Hilda Chamberlain on 21 March: 'I have supplied most of the ideas and taken the lead all through …'; while 'the Cabinet were uneasy at one time … they were delighted and amazed at our success in obtaining an agreement which avoided all sanctions, military or otherwise, and rather limited than extended our commitments under Locarno.'[39]

Cabinet acceptance of these agreements was not as easy to obtain as Chamberlain had suggested. They met with stiff opposition from many ministers, the most vociferous of whom was Sir John Simon, the home secretary. He wrote to Baldwin on 25 March objecting to any staff conversations which might imply the automatic commitment of the field force to France in the event of war. He could not 'believe that if London was being heavily bombed we should be despatching regiments of soldiers to France', and he wanted it made clear to the French 'that the British people do not really contemplate sending their sons to the Continent.' He was also concerned that, as a result of Britain's pledge to consult France and Belgium if the negotiations with Germany collapsed, the French

> now feel pretty sure that they have got us so tied that they can safely wait for the breakdown of discussions with Germany. In such circumstances it will be as selfish and as pigheaded as France has always been and the prospect of agreement with Germany will grow dimmer and dimmer.[40]

When the texts of the Anglo-Belgian-French agreements were presented to a meeting of British ministers on 30 March for approval, 'some Ministers', with Simon in the lead, expressed their anxiety that, if the proposed negotiations with Germany failed, France would use the promise of further consultations to inveigle Britain into a war to force Germany out of the Rhineland. They therefore attempted to restrict further the scope of the staff conversations. Lord Swinton, the secretary of state for air, wanted the French to be told that the conversations were only to cover the contingency of German aggression against France for a limited period of time. The lord president of the council, Ramsay MacDonald, urged that the terms of reference for the talks should be drafted carefully, otherwise 'they [the military staffs] would be roaming all over the place'. As foreshadowed in his letter to Baldwin, Simon asked whether the conversations would commit Britain to send an expeditionary force to the continent in the event of hostilities, while the lord chancellor, Viscount Hailsham, opposed the despatch of British troops to the continent under any circumstances, and wanted the French to be informed that Britain would only mobilise the Royal Navy and send to France what aircraft it could spare in the event of a German attack on France. Alfred Duff Cooper, the secretary of state for war, repeated the chiefs of staff's warning that, if it was decided to send an expeditionary force to France in an emergency, only two ill-equipped divisions could be spared.

Baldwin restated the obvious when he said that 'we could not give any effective help [to France] at the moment', although Chamberlain thought the French might be reassured by the information that, in two years' time the Royal Air Force would be much stronger and 'able to hit her [Germany] fairly hard'. Simon feared that Germany might regard the staff conversations as provocative and, as a result, would refuse to put forward any serious proposals for a comprehensive European settlement. Eden rejected this: after all, he said, Germany had broken the Locarno Treaty, entered the de-militarised zone and weakened French security, and therefore had no right to complain if, as a consequence of its illegal action, staff conversations took place between the remaining Locarno powers. Eventually the cabinet, while giving grudging approval to Eden's proposals in principle, asked the chiefs of staff for their views on the staff talks before coming to a final decision. No doubt Chamberlain's support was crucial to this outcome.[41]

The chiefs of staff, in a memorandum of 1 April, supported Simon's objections by pointing out that knowledge of staff talks might upset the Germans and result in German intransigence over negotiations for a new Locarno. Furthermore, the French 'will assume, with justice' that Britain had made 'a moral commitment' to them, which might in turn encourage them to embark on hostilities with Germany in the event of the breakdown of negotiations with Germany, with Britain 'committed to participate with forces which are not only inadequate to render effective support, but incapable of assuring our own security, with grave consequences for the people of this country'.[42] However, the cabinet, meeting on 1 April, agreed that staff conversations should take place in the near future, subject to the restrictions on their scope already laid down.[43]

Vansittart was alarmed by the cabinet's insistence that Britain should not promise France that a British expeditionary force would be sent to the continent in the event of German aggression. He thought that:

> No Frenchman or Belgian would ever accept the proposition that they could do the land fighting and we would, for our own convenience, limit ourselves to air and sea ... It is wholly unnecessary and anything unnecessary is dangerous.[44]

Eden's hope that the immediate crisis had been overcome was disappointed when, on 8 April, Flandin met him in Geneva and asked the foreign secretary for a joint examination of coercive measures against Germany's fortification of its Rhineland frontier, which Hitler had refused to forgo. Eden rejected this demand, since it would entail the abandonment of any negotiations with Germany.[45] He denied the French assertion that conciliation had broken down, since Germany, in a note to the Locarno powers on 31 March, had produced a new peace plan, based largely on Hitler's 7 March offers, and had, at the same time, promised that it would not increase the existing number of its troops in the Rhineland for four months while negotiations proceeded.[46] This latest disagreement with Flandin prompted Eden to exclaim on the following day that 'Our French friends are really difficult to understand and to tolerate with the patience they no doubt deserve.'[47] Later in the month, Hankey agreed that 'the proper policy, of course, is to bring France and Germany together, as we are trying to do. But neither of them are reasonable (least of all the French) and I doubt if we can pull it off.'[48] At a further meeting at Geneva on 10 April, Eden persuaded Flandin to agree to the despatch of a questionnaire to the German government requesting the elucidation of various ambiguities in its 31 March note.[49] This blunted further French pressure for anti-German measures. When the questionnaire was eventually presented to Hitler by Sir Eric Phipps, the British ambassador to Germany, on 14 May, Hitler refused a reply until a new French government was formed in June.[50]

The Anglo-French-Belgian staff conversations, which were held in London on 15 and 16 April, were, on British insistence, restricted, on the naval side, to exchanges of information about the state of naval forces in commission, communications, future exchanges of liaison officers and signal codes; on the military side to a statement of forces available to each side, and a request to the French for information about French port facilities, transport from the ports to the field force's assembly areas (but no discussion as to where the force might go thereafter); and on the air side, to an exchange of information about the strengths of each side's air forces and the availability of Franco-Belgian aerodromes to the Royal Air Force.

At the army talks, the chief French military delegate, General Victor-Henri Schweisguth, stated that the French army could defend the French frontier from Basle to the Belgian frontier without British assistance, and he suggested that British troops should be sent to help Belgium. Brigadier John Dill, the director of military operations at the War Office, representing the British army, thought that Britain might have two infantry divisions available 14 days after mobilisation, but he could not guarantee that they would be despatched to France or Belgium.[51]

It was pretty meagre fare, but as far as the French were concerned, the British had at least agreed, for the first time since before 1914, to staff conversations based on possible collaboration against Germany in the event of war,[52] although Corbin told Eden that they were hardly convincing as an effective reassurance to French public opinion.[53] The chief of the air staff admitted that 'the policy of the Air Ministry had been to confine discussion ... to generalities',[54] and Hankey agreed that 'the military "Conversations" were merely a make-weight thrown in to ease matters for the French.'[55] Orme Sargent described them as 'merely eyewash',[56] while Pownall dismissed them 'as more of a political gesture to please France than as of any real practical value'. He added, 'It's high time the French were "told where they get off" ... It's time we ceased being tied to their apron-strings, and a rare lot of people in this country think so too.'[57] However, at a meeting of the committee of imperial defence in April, ministers were told by the prime minister that they should not assume that 'the French were regarding these conversations largely as "window-dressing" for their electorate.'[58]

The French elections in May 1936 returned a large majority of radical, socialist and communist deputies to the Chamber of Deputies, and on 1 June a Popular Front government took office (without communist participation) under the socialist leader, Léon Blum, with Yvon Delbos as foreign minister.[59] Vansittart thought that the new French prime minister would be 'rather more prodigal of words than deeds',[60] but Eden was impressed, when he met Blum in Paris on 15 May, with Blum's anxiety for close Anglo-French cooperation. Eden wrote in his memoirs that he 'rejoiced at the improvement he [Blum] would be on his predecessors'.[61] Blum told Eden that he wanted a comprehensive international disarmament agreement, which Eden dismissed as 'unattainable in a world of dictators'.[62] After reading Eden's record of this meeting, Phipps announced that he was unimpressed with Blum's 'schoolboy-like utterances', and asked Sargent: 'Did you ever dream such a string of alternate platitudes and stupidities could be put together by a future President of the Council?'[63]

Blum's subsequent appeals for a disarmament agreement irritated Vansittart, who feared that such an initiative

> will put us back into the world of technical unrealities, in which we fruitlessly laboured for 3 years, before we made any real progress in dragging Hitlerite Germany into a world of political and territorial reality. The world was not ripe for disarmament in 1932. I doubt it will be ripe before 1942 in reality. If we put the clock back while pretending to put it forward – and thereby delaying our own long overdue re-equipment – we shall be playing up to ... Left opinion once too often ... We can no longer afford to be anything but realists ...[64]

Vansittart also derided speeches by other Popular Front ministers calling for universal peace, general disarmament and a strengthened League as 'sadder balderdash ... The Germans, who have still not even responded to our modest questionnaire, must smile.'[65] He complained that 'Blum will be a trial with his disarmament flapdoodle.'[66] When, in June, Blum talked to Clerk about the need for an understanding with Germany, suggesting that 'Hitler might ... be a genuine idealist', Vansittart described the French prime minister as 'naif and weak', and complained:

> M. Blum has evidently not the faintest idea of what he is up against in Hitler. He resembles the larger part of our Labour Party. The whole difficulty is to get an agreement in which we shall not be either dupes or accomplices … And the Lothian school would cheerfully make us either or both![67]

Wigram dismissed Blum's suggestions as 'phantasies … But they are silly enough in Paris for anything.' But Eden thought that 'we must make allowances', as Blum had had no previous ministerial experience.[68]

Phipps reported that the Popular Front victory was being used by Hitler as a pretext to delay further a reply to Britain's questionnaire. After reading Phipps's despatch, Sargent warned Eden that, once it was realised 'that the isolation of France is the one and the only thing he [Hitler] is working for, all his manoeuvres became quite clear … We [are] aiming for a general settlement, including France, and Hitler [is] striving for an Anglo-German agreement to the exclusion of France.' Vansittart agreed that 'Hitler has never meant business in our sense of the word. The sooner the Cabinet realise that the better for this long misguided country.' Eden insisted that the British government had to prove to British public opinion that a general settlement was impossible, and that the responsibility for this failure must be laid at the door of Germany, and not Britain or France.[69]

By the midsummer of 1936, London had still received no reply to its questionnaire to Germany. On 6 July, Eden persuaded the cabinet to agree to a further meeting of the four Locarno powers in Brussels, which had been requested by the Belgian government. On the same day he received an appreciation from the joint planners that 'the backwardness of our own preparations for war and the very unreliable military condition of France at the present time have placed us in a very weak position.'[70] Primed by this report, Eden painted a gloomy picture of the international situation to the assembled ministers. He contrasted the weakness of both the League and Britain and France ('the weakness of France was generally recognised at Geneva') with the ever-increasing military strength of Germany, a country 'governed by unscrupulous people'. Eden could therefore 'give no guarantee of the certainty of peace even during the present year'. He suggested that the questionnaire should be abandoned and replaced by an appeal by the three Locarno powers to Germany to work with the other western powers to devise a new Locarno agreement, with Germany's re-admission to a reformed League based on regional and not universal obligations. He told the cabinet that Germany might enter a new Locarno only if Eastern and Central Europe were excluded from its provisions. The cabinet agreed that Eastern and Central Europe should be excluded from any new Locarno, since Britain was not strong enough to defend the area and in any case British public opinion would reject any British involvement there. Neither Sir Samuel Hoare, who had rejoined Baldwin's cabinet in June, nor Lord Stanhope, the first commissioner of works, presumed that France had any confidence either in her Eastern allies or in the Soviet Union. Stanhope doubted that the Blum government would last very long and that, as a result, 'it was possible that by the autumn the situation in France would be very grave.' Ministers complained about the continued drift and vacillation in British foreign policy which could only benefit Germany, given Eden's warning that France appeared to be going to pieces while Germany was growing stronger.

The cabinet eventually resolved that 'the objects of British policy ... were first to secure peace in the world if possible and second to keep this country out of war.' British foreign policy must be based on the fact that it was too weak to defend Eastern Europe (although the cabinet insisted that this should not be announced publicly), and that Britain would henceforward defend only the British Empire and Flanders against aggression. If Germany refused to attend a five-power conference, Britain would have to form a western Locarno with France and Belgium. The cabinet's dismal conclusion was that 'circumstances compelled us to abandon the complete League policy in order to secure half the policy.' When one minister interjected that the present policy of yielding to Germany on every occasion merely encouraged Hitler to pursue his aggressive policy, and suggested that he should be told that there was a definite limit beyond which Britain would not allow him to go, 'it was pointed out ... that at the moment this country had neither the means nor the heart to stop him.'[71]

Earlier in June, Eden had contemplated that, if the negotiations with Germany failed to materialise, Britain might take up a suggestion by Van Zeeland for Anglo-Belgian staff conversations to arrange for the despatch of the British expeditionary force to Belgium in the event of German aggression. He thought the British public would have no hesitation about defending Belgium, since Belgium could not be accused, like France, of using a British commitment to adopt a forward policy elsewhere in Europe.[72] However, the general staff were as hostile to military conversations with Belgium as they were to those with France. At a chiefs of staff meeting on 16 June, the chief of the imperial general staff stated that Anglo-Belgian staff talks could not be kept secret and leaks to the press would compromise negotiations with Germany, while, if Belgium was attacked by Germany, French military support for Britain and Belgium would be essential. This, together with the knowledge that Anglo-Belgian staff conversations were taking place, might encourage France to embark on a forward policy, leading to a war with Germany in which Britain might become entangled if the Germans invaded Belgium in order to attack France.[73]

When Italy refused to attend the Brussels meeting, France pressed for a meeting of the three remaining Locarno powers as soon as possible. At the cabinet committee on foreign policy on 15 July, Eden supported the French request on the grounds that the attitude of Blum's government towards possible negotiations with Germany had been 'more reasonable' than that of its predecessors.[74] On the following day the cabinet agreed that the meeting should take place in London towards the end of July. This was necessary because 'the [French] Government was weak and wanted to show that they counted for something at any rate with the United Kingdom and Belgium. This was to our own interest.'[75]

The three Locarno powers met at 10 Downing Street on the morning of 23 July, and agreed to issue invitations to Germany and Italy to attend a five-power conference in early September. While the French were irritated when Eden refused to answer directly their question about what the next step would be if the five-power conference did not take place, they had no alternative but to acquiesce in the decision. Eden thought that 'our little 3 power Conference was one of the most successful held for some time past, & its success was in the main due to successful preparation by us.'[76] No five-power meeting was ever held: Italy and Germany, coming closer together in the aftermath of the Abyssinian crisis and the outbreak of the Spanish civil war, refused to attend a conference. As he had intended, Hitler's so-called peace initiative of 7 March 1936 petered out. His repeated objections to France's eastern alliances and to the Franco-Soviet pact ensured that the initiative for a new Locarno got nowhere since France refused to abandon its commitments to these countries. Nonetheless the cabinet committee on foreign policy, meeting on 25 August 1936, rejected a French claim that conciliation had collapsed. Eden argued that negotiations for a new western pact had not yet completely broken down, but if Germany refused to make any concessions, 'we should urge France and Belgium to content themselves with whatever satisfaction they can get out of our renewed guarantee of French and Belgian territory ... We should decline to disinterest ourselves from the East and Centre of Europe.'[77] However, in early September the cabinet wanted France to be told 'that we had no intention of being drawn into any troubles arising out of her Eastern commitments.'[78]

During the summer Lothian urged Lloyd George to take the lead in getting 'a square deal' for Germany in Central Europe by advocating border adjustments in areas where Germans predominated. He told Lionel Curtis, a fellow member of the Round Table, in July that Britain was right to renew its Locarno defence commitment to France in the West, but should remain aloof from France's eastern alliances. 'The essence of French folly is to try to get us to go to war with Germany when Germany is merely asking to be given the rights which are still regarded as the inherent rights of any sovereign state.'[79] But, as one of Lothian's correspondents, Sir Andrew Duncan, the South African minister of mines, pointed out, if a Franco-German war broke out as a result of France's commitments in Central Europe, Britain would be presented with the same dilemma as in 1914 'in the face of the possibility of the defeat of France and its conceivable consequences'.[80] Austen Chamberlain, the architect of Locarno, summed up the British predicament in March: he thought it 'curious that the net result of recent events is to throw us more & more back on the essence of the Locarno policy – a definite guarantee of peace in an area where we are vitally interested & the restriction of our obligations elsewhere; but it is exactly what we propose to do "elsewhere" that the real difficulties arise.'[81] During the spring and summer, Gerothwohl kept Lloyd George informed about the Locarno and League council meetings, complaining that 'the pro-French element in the Foreign Office' and a section of the cabinet were encouraging 'the French warmongers … The bulk of our Government and diplomacy are obsessed with the security of France and … Western Europe, which are grossly exaggerated.'[82]

Gerothwohl's strictures were, of course, totally untrue. The Blum government, far from seeking war, was desperately seeking to avert it. On 18 July 1936, when the Spanish civil war erupted, Blum was concerned that intervention by other powers in Spain might lead to its escalation into an international conflict.[83] The civil war posed a severe dilemma for a left-wing French government, whose supporters clamoured for munitions and aid to be despatched to the Spanish republican government. Delbos and Camille Chautemps (the vice-president of the council of ministers) feared that French deliveries of material assistance to the republicans might result in the spread of the Spanish civil war to France. On 7 August, Blum banned all arms exports to Spain, and tried to avoid entanglement in the civil war by promoting an international non-intervention agreement. This French initiative was not inspired by London, although Clerk unofficially urged the French government to handle the issue cautiously. The advice was unnecessary: Blum had already decided on a low-key approach to the struggle, but British support for non-intervention enabled Blum and Delbos to restrain those ministers in the French cabinet who were pressing for French military equipment to be sent to the Spanish republicans.[84]

Germany and Italy paid only lip-service to the non-intervention agreement, sending military assistance and, in the case of the Italians, troops masquerading as 'volunteers' to help the nationalists. The Soviet Union followed suit by sending munitions, oil, tanks, aircraft and specialist advisers to the republican side.[85] This Soviet intervention upset Conservatives such as Hoare, who feared that it might lead to the emergence of a Bolshevik Spain. The first sea lord, Sir Ernle Chatfield, did not respond to a suggestion by Vice-Admiral François Darlan, the chief of the French naval staff, when he visited the Admiralty in August, that Britain and France might act together to prevent a nationalist victory. On 8 January 1937, Hoare led a majority of cabinet ministers against a proposal by Eden that the Royal Navy should help enforce non-intervention.[86]

Meanwhile Blum continued with his fruitless efforts to achieve a European-wide détente. He suggested to the German economics minister, Dr Hjalmar Schacht, when the latter visited Paris in August, that the restoration of Germany's colonies might be examined as part of a general European settlement.[87] Blum also proposed that the bureau and third committee of the League of Nations should be convened to discuss disarmament. On 6 October Vansittart complained 'personally and unofficially' to Corbin that:

> the French were going too far and fast without adequate reflection or giving us an opportunity for reflection ... I thought it only right to warn him [Corbin] that in my personal opinion if these methods were persisted in or if indeed what has already been done by the French Government in some respects became a matter of public knowledge, considerable feelings of irritation might well be created which would militate against rather than help full and cordial Anglo-French collaboration.[88]

These Foreign Office criticisms notwithstanding, in the unlikely event that the Blum government had been able to negotiate a multilateral agreement which met Germany's outstanding grievances and contributed towards the pacification of Europe, it would have gone some way towards improving its battered image in France. Blum's refusal to help the Spanish republicans had divided its erstwhile supporters in the Popular Front coalition. To make matters worse, the escalating economic crisis further undermined the government's credibility in left-wing circles, as well as provoking bitter attacks from the right-wing parties. The Paris embassy's economic report on France for 1935 noted that 'severe and unbroken depression was the keynote of the general economic situation in France throughout 1935; and very few branches of industry or of commerce proved an exception to this prevailing state.'[89] The economy declined further in 1936, and when Blum came to power he was faced with a wave of country-wide industrial disturbances and factory occupations by striking workers. Clerk bemoaned the fact that the industrial chaos 'has for the time being reduced France to the status of "quantité négligeable" in the councils of the nations.'[90]

As the crisis worsened during the summer, the Central Department complained about the paucity of information it was receiving from the Paris embassy about the situation. On 10 June Vansittart asked Clerk, 'What we want to know is how far the swing to the Left has really gone to the danger of law and order or even of the regime?'[91] In reply Lloyd-Thomas tried to explain that 'it is not easy to describe the situation which changes from hour to hour.' He became increasingly despondent as the industrial and economic situation continued to deteriorate. He had heard extravagant rumours circulating in Paris to the effect that a committee of public safety was to be set up, and that Blum was mentally overwhelmed and physically exhausted 'to such an extent that he might disappear in a week or ten days'. Lloyd-Thomas confessed that:

> I try to resist the influence of alarmist exaggerations ... but I confess I do not like the look of things today. The effect on the international situation must be deplorable. One cannot help thinking that the French Government as a fighting force has ceased to exist ...[92]

Clerk also reported that:

> The Government is so taken up with the internal situation that its foreign policy consists of well-intentioned generalities and that for the time being France is a sleeping partner in international affairs.[93]

On the other hand, Clerk shared the British military attaché's opinion that there had not been any weakening of the allegiance of the army and navy to the Republic and that their morale and discipline were good. However, the attaché, Colonel Frederick Beaumont-Nesbitt, feared that the Army's loyalty might be severely strained if it was called upon to clear factories occupied by striking factory workers or to quell civil disorder.[94] In early September, Beaumont-Nesbitt heard from 'an informant', who claimed to be close to the French general staff, that he feared a communist revolution and hoped that the forces of law and order were making contingency plans to deal with it. The 'informant' added:

> A rallying point must be provided and for this role Marshal Pétain was admirably suited. He was respected by all classes ... My informant took a gloomy view of the future ... But, if it was to be a question of a

> Bolshevised France, he, as a Frenchman, would prefer to see Hitler's 'Panzerdivisionen' in the Place Vendôme rather than the establishment of a Soviet Republic.

The Central Department was sceptical about the reliability of such information, which came mostly from right-wing sources. Wigram did not accept that 'the alarming forecasts as to the future are justified', while Sargent thought that the embassy's reliance on opinion in Paris for its information was 'very misleading when trying to form an estimate of the spirit of the country as a whole'.[95] In June, in response to a report by E. Rowe-Dutton, the financial adviser to the Paris embassy, that the director of the Bank of Indo-China, Paul Baudouin, feared a communist revolution, Sargent commented that 'Mr Rowe-Dutton's informants are, of course, not entirely unprejudiced or disinterested, and their wishes may be father to their thoughts.'[96] In the case of the right-wing Baudouin this was certainly true: he was bitterly opposed to the Popular Front.[97] Nevertheless the Foreign Office could not entirely ignore Lloyd-Thomas's gloomy forebodings about the 'curious atmosphere of uncertainty and menace' which prevailed in Paris,[98] especially when fears about the future were also voiced by patriotic French politicians such as Paul Reynaud, Georges Mandel and Edouard Herriot. However, the Foreign Office was not convinced that, as some reports reaching it suggested, the Soviet Union was behind the industrial unrest in France. Laurence Collier would not accept that it was in the Soviet Union's interest to weaken its ally, although Sargent wondered whether the uncertainty about the role of the communists might be the consequence of the rivalry between the various communist agencies in Moscow. He believed that Maxim Litvinov, the Soviet foreign minister, wanted a strong and stable France as a partner against Germany, but that Litvinov was unable to control the activities of the Communist International inside European countries. Clerk was certainly uneasy about the growing strength and influence of the Communist Party in France, while his successor Phipps was a virulent anti-Communist who saw reds under every French bed.[99]

The Foreign Office was also apprehensive about the consequences for the French economy and on French industrial production of Blum's efforts to satisfy working-class demands by conceding the 40-hour week and by promising to nationalise French armaments industries. It feared that the costs and confusion resulting from these measures would have a deleterious effect on French arms production. A particular Foreign Office *bête noire* in Blum's government was the pro-communist air minister, Pierre Cot, who was an enthusiastic advocate of the nationalisation of the

French aviation industry. Cot argued that nationalisation was essential since the private aircraft firms insisted on keeping their factories in or near Paris in order to be in close touch with the service ministries, but where they were vulnerable to enemy air attack. In his opinion the amalgamation of the large number of small and inefficient aviation firms was the only way to increase French aircraft production. Ralph Wigram accepted that the French aircraft industry 'is in confusion and nothing has been done to organise it. To those who know France well and recall that in 1870 and again in 1914 adequate preparations for war was [*sic*] conspicuous by its absence, these facts are not surprising', but he was not convinced that nationalisation would solve the problem.

Foreign Office and Air Ministry officials were scathing about the inflated projections Cot gave of likely French aircraft production in 1936. The Air Ministry pointed out that 600 of the existing 1000 French front-line planes were obsolete, while the various bomber and fighter aircraft France had produced down to 1936 were inferior in performance capabilities to equivalent British and German machines.[100] The French aircraft industry was nationalised on 11 August, with the result, which the Foreign Office had anticipated, that the already abysmal output of aircraft fell even further. To Gladwyn Jebb, Vansittart's private secretary, all this 'will, I suppose, tend to confirm the belief of those who hold that France will in present circumstances only go to war to protect her own frontiers'.[101] However, these British strictures were not entirely justified, since Cot's plans included the dispersal of the bulk of the aircraft industry to the south of France, where it was hoped it would be less vulnerable to German air attack, and until this dispersal was completed, it was bound to retard aviation production.

Anthony Eden and his officials were equally irritated in mid-August when they learned from Clerk that Cot was purging the French Air Force of officers whose political views did not accord with his own. Furthermore Clerk reported that the French air minister had agreed to provide the Soviet Union with technical information about French aircraft. Clerk noted: 'It is obvious that the policy of "sharing" with the Soviets and the tendency to "purge" must be taken into account in making any future estimate of the military importance of France and the possibility of military collaboration with her.' It also prompted an astonishing outburst from Eden, doubtless a result of his increasing distress at the bad news that was reaching him about France:

> I find it impossible to resist a growing conviction that this Spanish horror is going to have repercussions so wide as perhaps profoundly to modify the present alignment of the European powers. To read this

> [Clerk's] despatch is to feel France growing more 'red'. The importance of this indicates a change in the characteristics of French life. The French, we have comforted ourselves, could never be communist, their whole mode of life will not permit of it. But it is the mode of life that is changing. The standard of life of a large lower middle class that is being reduced until (is it possible?) France represents in her own midst the conditions of Spain, or at least conditions approximating thereto. The 'Cot' type can do much damage none the less grave because it may be inflicted unwittingly.
>
> We may once again take comfort that this process cannot be rapid, yet it is precisely in this respect that the Spanish peril plays its part. If events in this country and the failure of the policy of non-intervention cause the less extreme elements of the French Govt to resign what must the consequences be?[102]

Fortunately for Eden's peace of mind, his anxiety about France did not materialise. In October Clerk was able to reassure him:

> A month ago … I painted the immediate future rather gloomily, though not much more so than would have been done by almost every thinking Frenchman. But since then there has been a change for the better. The Government was now acting against the strikers with increasing firmness, and Blum was determined to control the extremists and to maintain order.[103]

Nevertheless the presence in the French cabinet of radicals of the Cot type continued to agitate the Foreign Office, particularly when its officials heard rumours in September that Cot and his supporters were anxious to sign a military convention with the Soviet Union. Clerk doubted the possibility of this given the opposition of the French general staff to military ties with the Soviet Union and Quai d'Orsay fears that a Franco-Soviet military convention would alienate Britain. Wigram minuted that it would 'clearly be a dangerous move and its effect on public opinion here would be very bad'. Sargent wanted Eden to insist that the French consult Britain before they made any changes in their relations with Russia, since Britain would have to come to the assistance of France if France became involved in a war with Germany. 'So long as we continue, as at present we do, to insist that Great Britain's frontier is on the Rhine … France's policy in Europe must always be of direct concern to H.M. Government.' Cadogan was 'afraid that any claim on our part to have any say in French policy in Europe will provoke the counter-enquiry whether *we* are prepared to find France the security she might hope to find in quarters disapproved by us.' Vansittart agreed: 'That danger … is a clear and very constant one, and since we can never give a clear answer to it, it is not wise on our part to put ourselves in the position of being asked the question.' Eden now took a more relaxed attitude. He did not believe that the French would conclude a military convention with the Soviet Union, and in any case, 'our relations with France are now so much more close and cordial than they were in Barthou's prickly days that I can hardly conceive that they would engage upon any departure without previous consultation.'[104]

In April and May 1937, on hearing further rumours about the imminent conclusion of a Franco-Soviet military convention, Vansittart and Eden warned the French government against such a move, pointing out that it would anger important sections of Anglo-American opinion. Undoubtedly British pressure was an important factor in discouraging Blum from proceeding with negotiations with the Soviet military, and, while Clerk was correct in assuming that French military opposition to a military convention was an even more compelling motive, the sweeping purges in the Red Army high command in the spring of 1937 provided Gamelin with an ideal excuse for abandoning talks with the Soviet military attaché, who was himself executed in April.[105]

The already weakened French security system suffered a further blow when, on 14 October 1936, the King of the Belgians, Leopold III, announced Belgium's return to neutrality. The Belgians had become increasingly lukewarm since the early 1930s about their 1920 pact with France.[106] They feared that they would be dragged into war with Germany for the sake of France's eastern commitments. It would not now be possible for the French army to move automatically into Belgium on the outbreak of war. While Eden was upset by Belgium's decision, the new chief of the imperial general staff, Field Marshal Sir Cyril Deverell, took comfort from the fact that the British army would not have been able to arrive in Belgium before the Germans had overrun the country.[107] Nevertheless France still regarded itself as committed to defend Belgium in the event of a German invasion of the country, and Delbos made this clear to the Chamber of Deputies in December in declaring that France would come to the assistance of Britain and Belgium if they were the victims of unprovoked aggression. Wigram described the declaration as:

> indeed satisfactory. Let us hope that no Chief of Staff will succeed in persuading us lightly to abandon the advantages of an assurance of this kind. It will be remembered that not long ago though they admitted that a French guarantee had military advantages for us, the Chiefs of Staff were prepared to see it abandoned![108]

However, the British government was not prepared to improve its small and poorly equipped expeditionary force. Sir Thomas Inskip (who had been appointed to the new post of minister for co-ordination of defence in May[109]) and Chamberlain discussed the future size of this force in October. Both men agreed that Britain could only afford to provide munitions for an expeditionary force of four infantry divisions and a mobile division. Chamberlain rejected the advice of the then chief of the imperial general staff, Field Marshal Sir Archibald Montgomery-Massingberd, that without substantial British military assistance the French and Belgian armies would retire to their fortifications in the event of war with Germany, thereby enabling the German army to pour through the gap thus created and seize the Channel ports. The chancellor of the exchequer retorted, 'Tell that to the Marines.' He agreed that this might be the outcome if Britain failed to inform the French about the paucity of Britain's land contribution, and 'if we do they can't afford to leave a gap.'[110]

Warren Fisher argued that 'our people are not prepared and will never again consent to be conscripted ... for military service on the European continent (or elsewhere)', and, like Chamberlain, insisted:

> we must inform the French in no uncertain terms ... that we have no intention of military (i.e. army) intervention on the scale of the last war, and that we ourselves must decide how our army can be most usefully be employed.[111]

Thus when, in a cabinet paper on 3 December 1936, Duff Cooper urged that a start should be made with the modernisation of 12 territorial army divisions, a counter-memorandum by Chamberlain rejected what he took to be the idea of sending 17 divisions (that is, four regular divisions, one mobile division and the 12 territorial army divisions) to Western Europe on, or shortly after, the outbreak of war. The chancellor pointed out that Britain's industrial resources were inadequate to provide for the re-equipment of the territorial army, while, in any case, Britain's geographical situation made it unnecessary for the country to maintain a large army ready for war 'at a moment's notice'. Chamberlain was convinced that 'the Air Arm has emerged recently as a factor of first class if not decisive importance,' and that this was where any available funds should be spent. Furthermore,

> we must not lose sight of the fact that the political temper of our people is strongly opposed to continental adventures and they will be strongly suspicious of any such preparations made in peace time which might

likely involve us in entanglements or disputes which do not concern us.[112]

Chamberlain confided to his diary: 'I know this view is shared by many Army officers as well as Air Force men & military experts.'[113]

Chamberlain's arguments angered Vansittart who wrote to Eden:

> This [the Chancellor's] memorandum raises some questions which vitally affect our future. So important are they that I trust you will insist that no decision is taken without the Foreign Office having had some opportunity of expressing their considered opinion … if we really let it be known that in any continental war it [the expeditionary force] was likely to be limited to something so small … we should soon be heading towards an isolation which we are in no position to sustain and which I do not believe we shall ever again be able to sustain without larger efforts than we are contemplating now … If we wish to retain any continental influence it will be impossible to carry on with an army considerably smaller than in pre-war days but with equipment that is practically non-existent.[114]

Duff Cooper responded to Chamberlain's memorandum:

> We should have to re-shape our military policy if it is decided we should in no circumstances take part in continental war. Other nations were building up all three services and their financial circumstances were inferior to ours. We should not regret any money spent preparing our defences.[115]

When the cabinet met on 16 December to consider these conflicting proposals, Chamberlain repeated his opposition to 'equipping the Territorial Force for the trenches', insisting that 'It was not for France to dictate to us the distribution of our Forces.' Finally, after much fruitless discussion, Baldwin 'said that it would be impossible to take a decision that morning' and the cabinet referred the matter to the chiefs of staff, who were asked 'to consider further the role of the British Army in time of war'.[116]

These cabinet minutes prompted Vansittart to repeat his warning to Eden that, if the French knew that Britain would just send five regular divisions to help them in a war, 'their whole confidence in us might be shaken and they would be inclined to make their own terms with Germany.' Eden replied: 'it has to be remembered that the question is how to make the best use of our resources.'[117]

The chiefs of staff supported the secretary of state for war's contention that, in the event of a major European war, the French would insist on the despatch of a British expeditionary force to the continent, and that this should consist of four divisions and a mobile division and 12 territorial divisions. However, the chiefs insisted that the French should be told firmly that this would be the maximum contribution that Britain would make to the land effort. The country could not afford a repetition of the trench warfare of 1914–18.[118]

The cabinet defence requirements committee met three times to consider the chiefs of staff's recommendations. Chamberlain continued his campaign against an enlarged army and claimed that he 'had the support of Sam [Hoare] & Swinton & (really though he won't say so) S[tanley] B[aldwin]' in opposing the re-equipping of the territorial army. He was also supported by Lord Weir, the chief industrial adviser, who wanted to build up a powerful offensive air force and dismissed the army's concentration on an infantry army as a product of outdated thinking. Chamberlain asked Baldwin:

> at end of second mtg for next mtg to be of Ministers only & not CoS or Warren Fisher. At this mtg I, supported by Swinton, said plainly what we were after. Duff Cooper of course had to take the opposite view and we got no further. Weir came to me afterwards plainly in despair. I then told SB that he must take the lead – he had hardly said a word. Send for Duff. I urged him ... that he has to accept a much reduced programme for the army ... What he must accept is that we will only undertake to put a limited number of men into France or on the Continent.

On the morning of 19 January 1937, before the third meeting of the committee, Baldwin had taken advantage of Duff Cooper's absence from the War Office (he 'had gone shooting') to persuade the chief of the imperial general staff, Deverell, to agree to Chamberlain's proposals. Thus at the meeting Chamberlain achieved his goal when Baldwin overruled Duff Cooper and insisted that, while the regular field force would remain intact, the Committee's final report must omit any decision about the territorial army.[119] After hearing Chamberlain's arguments, Pownall condemned as 'the most dangerous heresy' the notion of limited liability:

> If war with Germany was renewed the British *would be fighting for their lives* ... The idea of the 'half-hearted' war is the most dangerous in the world. It will be 100% – and even then we may well lose it ... The Chancellor's cold hard calculating semi-detached attitude was terrible to listen to.[120]

At an ensuing cabinet meeting, Baldwin persuaded the ministers to accept the expenditure of £208 million on re-equipping the regular army and two anti-aircraft divisions of the territorial army by April 1940. It allocated £9,250,000 to the rest of the territorial army. Chamberlain's ideas about the future shape of Britain's armed services had largely but not completely prevailed over those of Duff Cooper and the War Office. When Chamberlain became prime minister in May 1937, he moved Duff Cooper to the Admiralty, and promoted Leslie Hore-Belisha, the transport minister, who was in sympathy with Chamberlain's policy, to the War Office. Chamberlain would then be able to proceed to the final stage of his objective: a further reduction in the role of the army in favour of the expansion of the Royal Air Force.[121]

By the end of 1936, Eden, the Foreign Office and others in the British establishment had become increasingly depressed by the evidence reaching them from Paris about the economic decline of France and its increasing demoralisation in the face of a confident and resurgent Germany.[122] To Hankey, France 'is inoculated with the virus of communism, which is at present rattling the body politic, delaying much needed rearmament and causing acute internal dissension ... In her present state she is not a very desirable ally.'[123] Chatfield informed Vansittart that 'France, our only real support, is ... unreliable politically and militarily, especially the former.'[124] To many in high places, the decline of France reinforced their view that Britain had no alternative but to try to reach a comprehensive agreement with Germany, with Neville Chamberlain a leading exponent of this policy. As prime minister, Chamberlain was to pursue the mirage of an Anglo-German settlement to the bitter end, hoping that the knowledge that Britain was building a powerful air force would both deter Hitler and encourage him to respond favourably to British approaches. Not only did Chamberlain completely misjudge the extent of Hitler's ambitions, but also his defence policies ensured that in May 1940 neither the British army nor, as it turned out, the Royal Air Force were capable of giving more than nominal assistance to the beleaguered French army.

3 Anglo-French Relations in 1937

All our information is that the vast majority of French people feel exactly like the vast majority of British people. They do not wish at all costs to be involved in a war at the present time. They are strictly non-interventionists.

(Lord Cranborne, 25 January 1937)[1]

POLITICAL RELATIONS

In a despatch to the Foreign Office written in January 1937, Clerk noted that 'the end of the year finds Anglo-French relations removed from the atmosphere of suspicion and mutual recrimination in which they were at the beginning, to one of close and cordial collaboration as regards all matters of importance.' Clerk attributed much of the credit for this improvement in Anglo-French relations to Léon Blum's conciliatory policy.[2] However, the Foreign Office continued to fear that Blum, in his anxiety to reduce tensions in Europe, might offer Germany over-generous concessions in order to secure an agreement, thereby undermining Anglo-French insistence that it was for Germany, who had so far failed to respond to the British initiative of 1936, and not the entente, to put forward new proposals for a European settlement. When Delbos, in a speech in Paris on 31 January 1937, expressed the hope that a general disarmament conference could meet in the near future, R.C.S. Stevenson, an assistant adviser on League of Nations affairs, commented:

> this seems to foreshadow a French proposal of wide scope at the forthcoming meeting of the Bureau of the Disarmament Conference on May 6th. I think that we should be well advised to approach the French *as soon as possible* and find out what is in their minds. They cannot really wish to embarrass us in our struggle to carry out our rearmament programme at high speed.[3]

Blum also supported proposals drawn up by the French ambassador to Germany, André François-Poncet, for an arms limitation agreement and a protocol on measures for humanising war as the first steps towards the creation of a new western pact and Germany's return to the league. Vansittart described François-Poncet's proposals as 'another of those half-baked schemes which the French are so busy producing at the present time and against which we should be particularly on our guard'.[4]

Sir Frederick Leith-Ross, the chief economic adviser to the British government, who was anxious to reach an economic agreement with Germany, objected that the Foreign Office's negative line would perpetuate the existing deadlock in Europe, while, at the same time, the impression would be created that Britain was encouraging France to adopt an intransigent policy towards Germany. Leith-Ross argued for a settlement with Germany based on an offer of British financial assistance to ease its balance of payments and foreign exchange problems. He proposed that he should meet Schacht in order to discover from the German economics minister the means by which Germany could be made into 'a good European'.[5] The Foreign Office was well aware that the French government was anxious to pursue the conversations Blum had held with Schacht in Paris in August 1936. The French had not given the Foreign Office a full account of the contents of these talks, and London was apprehensive that Blum, despite his promise to Eden, might be tempted to offer Schacht colonial compensation in return for a wide-ranging settlement of outstanding problems, which Eden believed should be dealt with at the proposed five-power conference on the revision of Locarno.[6] On 18 January 1937, Eden and Chamberlain tried to forestall this by agreeing that Leith-Ross should go to Germany to see Schacht first as 'it would be safer if we [Britain] got control of them [the conversations] from the very beginning, instead of allowing them to be conducted by the French.'[7] Eden told Leith-Ross that future discussions with Germany for a general European settlement must include its willingness to re-enter a new Locarno Treaty, to abandon its drive for economic self-sufficiency and territorial expansion, to accept a treaty of 'non-interference' with Czechoslovakia, to demonstrate its willingness to end the arms race and to agree to return to the League – terms which Eden must have realised would not be acceptable to Hitler. However Leith-Ross was to listen to what Schacht had to say rather than put forward any proposals of his own.[8] From what he had learned about Leith-Ross's proposed visit to Germany led Gerothwohl to conclude that Eden and the Foreign Office were still trying to prevent Blum from seeking an agreement with Germany.[9]

Any lingering British hopes that Germany might be willing to discuss a European settlement based on its offers of 7 and 31 March 1936 were completely extinguished by the negative results of a conversation between Phipps and Hitler on 3 February 1937, when the latter stated that French insistence on including Russia in any negotiations for a new Locarno made it impossible for Germany to attend a five-power conference. Nor did the German chancellor believe that an arms limitation agreement was possible in view of Russia's swollen armaments. C.J.W. Torr of the Central Department minuted that Hitler 'would seem almost to have gone deliberately out of his way to put a spoke in Dr Schacht's wheel'. Leith-Ross met Schacht at Badenweiler on 2 February, where the latter merely repeated Germany's demand for the return of its colonies and talked only vaguely about an economic and political settlement.[10]

Eventually the British decided to abandon any further talks with Schacht after it became clear that the French were not prepared to transfer any of their own colonies to Germany and that Schacht's influence with Hitler was declining. Chamberlain, Warren Fisher and Leith-Ross were convinced that the whole episode had been mishandled by the Foreign Office, which had, they believed, misled Leith-Ross in the autumn of 1936 about the extent of Schacht's proposals and had deliberately sabotaged a genuine effort by Schacht to achieve agreement between Germany, France and Britain, at a time when Schacht was still close to Hitler. In fact, Hitler would never have accepted Britain's demands for a peaceful German policy in Eastern Europe, but the affair fuelled Chamberlain's existing suspicions about alleged Foreign Office intrigues to undermine Anglo-German negotiations.[11] When Schacht met Blum in Paris at the end of May there was no meeting of minds and the conversations lapsed.[12]

All this convinced Strang that Britain should continue rearming, and while maintaining close relations with France, should make it clear to Germany what Britain would fight for, while not making it clear what Britain would not fight for. He concluded that Britain should 'wait and see what time brings ... It might bring war. If so, it will be the end of many things, perhaps of the British Empire. I do not think that we are sufficiently master of our fate to decide for certain, one way or the other.'

Lord Lothian continued to accuse France of being responsible for the current tension in Europe. He wrote to General Smuts in March that France had long attempted 'to humiliate and repress' Germany, and its 'intransigence had been responsible for the rise of National Socialism'. Lothian thought that Hitler should be allowed to develop an 'Ottowa economic *Mittel-Europa*', but feared that France and Russia would not agree to this because they sought 'a rigid encirclement' of Germany. He wanted Britain to make a final effort to induce Paris and Moscow to agree to a settlement with Germany by threatening to revert to its 'old policy of detachment' from Europe if they did not.[13] In June, Lord Arnold, an isolationist Labour peer, wrote to Lothian complaining that 'again and again I have evidence of intense anxiety with regard to France's Eastern commitments and the dangers they may involve for Great Britain'.[14] Lothian agreed: the disturbed state of Europe was, in his view, caused by a combination of 'traditional anti-Germans, [the] whole of [the] Left, & [the] F.O.', which 'is [*sic*] pledged to the French view of European politics'.[15]

Hitler's refusal to enter into negotiations led the Foreign Office to increase its pressure on ministers to expand the rearmament programme. The internal divisions in Whitehall about the future size of the expeditionary force and whether it should be sent to the continent at all in the event of war continued during 1937. Hankey wrote a long memorandum on the subject for the prime minister on 18 January 1937, suggesting the creation of a 17 division expeditionary force which would be available for overseas service in the first year of a war. Hankey considered that even 'Seventeen Divisions does not seem to be a very large contribution from a country of our size and strength.'[16] On 28 January 1937 the chiefs of staff also pressed the government to reach a final decision about the future role of the army, insisting that 'it is impossible to discount the contingency of putting considerable land forces into the field or to limit our role to air forces however expanded'. Vansittart fully agreed with this conclusion and supported the chiefs' recommendation in a memorandum which re-emphasised the importance of a British land contribution to the maintenance of the entire Anglo-French position in Europe:

> The principle of our effective cooperation on land will have to be adequately recognised if our mutual guarantee arrangements with France are to continue to inspire confidence and serve as a sound basis for our European policy ... France is no longer in a position to fight our battles on land for us and there is always the danger that if she, and more particularly Belgium, felt that they could not count on immediate British assistance on land, they might in certain eventualities, prefer to make the best terms they could with Germany beforehand and leave Great Britain to face Germany alone.

Without a commitment from France to defend them, the little entente might succumb to German intimidation or force, enabling Germany to establish its predominance in Central Europe, thus in turn isolating and paralysing France. 'In such an event there will be a European landslide which will render vain every object for which we fought in the last war at such cost', and this would reduce Britain 'to impotent and precarious isolation'.[17]

Inskip refused to alter his decision that Britain could not afford a 17 division army, and he reminded the cabinet in February that there was 'almost universal unwillingness of the country to prepare an army on anything like the 1914–18 scale' – a conclusion from which Strang thought it would be 'difficult to escape'.[18] The cabinet on 3 February 1937, after hearing renewed arguments from Inskip and Chamberlain against a large army, resolved to provide 'the most complete and efficient equipment' for only two divisions of the regular army, while the bulk of the territorial army would only receive training equipment.[19]

Delbos, meeting Eden at Geneva on 21 January, told the foreign secretary that the French army was 'in good heart and high efficiency', but France would welcome the formation of a small but powerful British mechanised force of two divisions for the western front. The French foreign minister argued that, since its economic difficulties made it impossible for Germany to contemplate a long war, it would attempt a knock-out blow against the western powers at the outset, which made concentrated allied striking power, not mass armies, essential to crush the initial German assault. Colonel Clark, the military assistant to General R.H. Haining, the director of military operations and intelligence at the War Office, informed the Foreign Office on 29 January that Haining was also facing considerable French pressure to provide two armoured divisions. Haining had responded that the British army could not afford to raise such a force, which would, in any case, be entirely unsuitable for imperial operations.[20] The creation of a small but all-mechanised British force was supported at this time by the maverick military pundit, Basil Liddell Hart, who became unofficial military consultant to the new secretary of state for war, Leslie Hore-Belisha, in June 1937.[21]

Although Hore-Belisha asked the general staff to investigate the possibility of raising a mechanised force, there was no prospect that it would be accepted. As it was the War Office was facing immense difficulties in obtaining sufficient recruits for the regular army, and its problems were made worse by shortages of funding and hence equipment. When Hore-Belisha requested an additional £43 million in June 1937 to re-equip for war purposes four territorial army divisions, Sir John Simon, who had replaced Chamberlain as chancellor of the exchequer in May, rejected any increased expenditure on the army.[22]

The Foreign Office and most British military experts accepted at its face value Delbos's estimation of the strength and high morale of the French army, although this was encouraged by Gamelin in order to convince the British that France was worthy of British support.[23] However, Chamberlain was not influenced by this French propaganda about the strength of the French army, since he was convinced that 'at the moment' Britain 'could not expect very effective support from France'. It did persuade Vansittart that 'the French Army ... has never been in better shape. It is probably still superior to the German, and certainly superior in heavy artillery. Similarly the French navy is proportionately *much* stronger than before the war.' He added: 'As for the numbers and equipment of our Expeditionary Force, the less said the better for the time being.'[24]

When he met Gamelin on 5 July, Phipps, who had replaced Clerk as British ambassador to France in April, was most impressed with the French general. He described Gamelin as 'a man of quite remarkable "sang froid," and unlikely ever to give way to any kind of panic or undue pessimism.' Clerk had been similarly impressed. Gamelin, he wrote earlier in 1937, was

> a small, thick-set man, active, intelligent, practical, and has lost many typical French habits owing to service in other countries amongst all sorts and conditions of men. Extremely amiable ... [with] a lucid and elastic mind.[25]

No doubt the absence of 'many typical French habits' helped to endear Gamelin to the British. However Field Marshal Deverell, in the course of conversations with Liddell Hart and Hugh Dalton, expressed doubts about the 'reliability and efficiency' of the French army.[26] British admiration for the French army was, of course, the product of much wishful thinking on their part, while its alleged strength provided a useful additional justification for Britain's reluctance to despatch an expeditionary force to the continent in the event of war.

The rebuff which Hitler had given Phipps on 3 February, and the failure of the talks with Schacht, did not deflect Chamberlain from his search for agreement with Germany. When he became prime minister in May he was determined to achieve this goal, and he later complained that his task was hindered by the absence of 'courage ... and imagination' in the Foreign Office.[27] On 17 March, Hoare wrote to Chamberlain blaming the anti-German and anti-Italian bias of the Foreign Office for Britain's failure to secure 'any European reconciliation', and warned Chamberlain that the only basis for a successful agreement with Germany was that of 'full equality' for the latter power. He noted that 'the recent F.O. papers invariably try to undermine this conception [of German equality] by falling back on the idea of Anglo-French agreements.'[28] Halifax, who shared Chamberlain's conviction that permanent European peace could only be achieved by agreement with Germany, became lord president of the council in May, thereby strengthening his role not only as Eden's understudy, but also as an advocate of Chamberlain's 'appeasement' policy in the Foreign Office.[29]

Chamberlain soon discovered another kindred spirit in his quest for what Hoare described as a 'great' change in 'the European atmosphere',[30] in the person of Sir Nevile Henderson, who replaced Phipps at the Berlin embassy on the latter's transfer to Paris in April. This disastrous appointment had been supported by both Eden and Vansittart. Henderson became a committed advocate of an Anglo-German agreement as the only means of preserving European peace. Once installed in Berlin, he lost no time in articulating his opinions. On 10 May he wrote a memorandum setting out his ideas on future British policy towards Germany, although he evidently did not forward it to the Foreign Office until 20 July. In this memorandum, while insisting that Britain would have to defend France and the Low Countries from aggression, he recommended that:

> at the same time, it is equally obvious that, if Great Britain's influence in Europe and on the side of peace is to be effective and justifiable, friendship with France must *never be exclusive*. French security is British security but French policy is far from being in British or international interests. The most obvious example of this is the French system of alliances ostensibly based, it is true, on the League of Nations but employing the latter not for the higher purposes for which it was created but as an instrument to serve French policy. In other words, while Britain cannot disinterest herself in Europe she should never identify herself too closely with any single group of Powers.

He complained that further progress in securing agreement with Germany was impossible while France refused to renounce its alliances and agreements with the Soviet Union and the little entente, and he thought that 'The alternative, however disagreeable, would then be a direct Anglo-German understanding based on French security and integrity but including some guarantee of neutrality in the event of a Russo-German conflict.'[31]

When Central Department officials read this memorandum in July, they were astonished by Henderson's rashness in proposing measures which would weaken France's already tenuous affiliations with Central and Eastern Europe and further undermine France's status as a great power. In a draft despatch to Henderson in October 1937 (but not, in the event, sent) the Foreign Office insisted that Britain's 'position as one of the Great Powers of Europe makes it impossible for His Majesty's Government to subscribe to a policy of detachment as regard to international developments in any part of Europe'.[32] Of course, the Foreign Office's opposition to any agreement with Germany which might adversely affect French interests was not shared by Chamberlain and his supporters in the cabinet, Simon, Hoare, Halifax and Kingsley Wood, the minister of health, who were also pressing for a rapprochement with Italy as well as with Germany.

In an effort to prevent these ministers receiving information which would provide them with further ammunition for their criticisms of France, Sargent told Phipps not to include material about French press and parliamentary criticisms of the Blum Government in his *official* telegrams since these were distributed to cabinet ministers:

> certain of whom are only too glad to quote and exploit any criticism of that terrible pseudo-Communist Government ... to the coat-tails of which our F.O. is as usual tied, when it would be so much nicer and more proper to have it tied to the good Conservative and anti-communistic coat-tails of Hitler and Goring.[33]

According to Sargent, Eden and Vansittart agreed that 'in the present state of Europe, French security was identical with British security & that any disagreement between Gt Britain and France would be fatal.'[34]

As part of his search for a settlement with the dictators, Chamberlain supported Halifax's decision to visit Germany between 17 and 21 November, ostensibly to attend a hunting exhibition in Berlin, but in reality to use the opportunity to talk privately with the German leaders. The lord president of the council failed to adhere to a Foreign Office request that he should give no encouragement to Hitler's ambitions in Central Europe, although he did tell Hitler that any changes there should be accomplished by peaceful means. The French government were naturally irritated that they had not been informed in advance about the visit. In his notes for his conversations in Germany, Halifax intended to tell Hitler that the present French government was 'more ready to come to terms than any other post-war Government'.[35] Eden, absent in Brussels at the nine-power conference on the Far East when news of the visit leaked to the British press, attempted a damage limitation exercise on his return to London on the 14th by issuing a press release which emphasised the unofficial nature of the visit, that it represented no fundamental change in British foreign policy and implied no alteration in the cordiality of Anglo-French relations.[36]

Then, in what Sargent described as 'a timely antidote' to the Halifax mission, Eden arranged an Anglo-French ministerial meeting in London between 29 and 30 November 1937. Chamberlain, Halifax, Eden and their officials, Vansittart, Sargent and Strang, met Camille Chautemps (who had replaced Blum as French prime minister on 22 June), Yvon Delbos and their advisers, Charles Corbin, Alexis Léger, the secretary-general of the Quai d'Orsay, René Massigli, the director of the Political Affairs Department, and Roland de Margerie, counsellor at the French embassy in London. At the first meeting at 10 Downing Street on the 29th, Halifax gave the French a version of his discussions with Hitler and Goering. He stated that, in response to Hitler's catalogue of grievances about Czechoslovakia and Central Europe, he had rejoined that, while Britain did not 'stand rigidly in all circumstances on the status quo', Britain was concerned that, if any adjustments were made, 'the form and means of these adjustments should not be such as to involve ugly consequences for Europe and the world.' Chamberlain assured the French that, while he sought a general European settlement, he would never yield to German pressure for a bilateral Anglo-German agreement on the transfer of British colonies to Germany, which Hitler had mentioned to Halifax as 'the only direct issue between Germany and Great Britain'.

The main item on the agenda was Czechoslovakia and the Sudeten question, but there was no meeting of minds. Chamberlain told his French visitors that Britain would not go to war over Czechoslovakia. While Delbos made a half-hearted defence of France's commitment to Czechoslovakia, Chautemps evaded the issue, but he managed to convey to the British his reluctance to go to war over the Sudeten issue. At a subsequent cabinet meeting, on 1 December 1937, the prime minister mentioned that:

> at one time it looked as though they [the French] were going to press the British Ministers to adopt some more forthcoming attitude in Central Europe. No encouragement had been given to them, however, and finally they had agreed that appropriate concessions might be made by Czechoslovakia and ... to reach a general settlement with Germany.[37]

No agreement was reached about Anglo-French relations with Italy. Chautemps and Delbos denounced Mussolini's anti-French policies in Spain and the Mediterranean, while Chamberlain insisted that he intended to approach Italy for an agreement, although he promised to keep France informed of the progress of the negotiations.[38]

The British believed that the meeting had soothed French resentment about Halifax's visit to Germany. Afterwards Chamberlain wrote:

> the meeting with the French Ministers really was, for once, as successful as the papers reported it ... I won their confidence & respect by my handling of the conference. I myself liked the little man [Chautemps]

> very much. He is quick and witty and as it seemed to me quite candid and straightforward.[39]

Sargent believed that the French ministers had returned to Paris 'enlightened and reassured as regard to the P.M.'. Chautemps had 'made a good impression unlike Delbos who appeared somewhat doctrinaire and short-sighted'. He concluded that there had not been 'a moment's disagreement ... It all went happily as a marriage bell.'[40] Sir Alexander Hardinge, the King's secretary, thought 'this ... was mainly due to the fact that they were expecting some unpleasant surprises which did not materialize!'[41]

British satisfaction with the conference was scarcely justified, however, given the paucity of its achievements. Neither the prime minister, Eden nor Halifax mentioned to the French that the cabinet was on the verge of abandoning the continental commitment altogether. On 22 December 1937 the cabinet accepted a report by Inskip recommending that Britain's defence expenditure over the next five years (from 1937 to 1941) should be limited to £1500 million, while assistance to allies would in future occupy the lowest rung in British defence planning. The expeditionary force would in future be equipped only for 'a colonial theatre'. Inskip based this decision on the repeated assurances by France's political and military leaders that the French army could defend the Maginot line without external assistance, and indeed, as has been described, during the 1936 military conversations the French had suggested that the British army should go to Belgium not France.[42] Inskip argued:

> France no longer looks to us in the event of war to supply an expeditionary force on the scale hitherto proposed in addition to our all-important co-operation on the sea and in the air. He did agree, however, that if France was in danger of being overrun by land armies, Britain would have to improvise an army to assist France. Should this happen, the Government of the day would most certainly be criticised for having neglected so obvious a continency.[43]

Hore-Belisha hoped that Britain's decision about the future role of the expeditionary force would encourage the French to extend the Maginot line to the sea, which would, in turn, provide a further justification for not sending the expeditionary force to the continent. In October, Hore-Belisha had drawn up, at Chamberlain's request, a list of proposed army reforms, at the top of which he had put 'the elimination of the 1914–1918 mentality, which consists in regarding the whole role for which the Army is being prepared as a repetition of its tasks in the last war.'[44]

Hore-Belisha's hostility to the continental commitment reflected, of course, the advice given to him by Basil Liddell Hart.[45] Reacting to his own experiences as an infantry officer during the Great War, Liddell Hart was passionately opposed to sending 'millions of men' to face a new bloodbath on the western front. He accused the British military of advocating 'a large scale expansion of the Army for the bigger professional opportunity it presents to them, without due regard for the interests of the country as a whole'. In November 1936 Liddell Hart had argued with Deverell and Haining over their insistence that the despatch of a British army to France was 'essential to maintain their [French] morale'. When Haining told Liddell Hart that the French would not be able to hold their frontier against Germany without British land support, given Germany's larger population, Liddell Hart responded with his by now familiar argument that superiority in manpower no longer mattered 'in view of the superiority of modern defence on land'.[46] Liddell Hart reiterated this theme in frequent memoranda to Hore-Belisha during 1937, warning the secretary of state that a British pledge to despatch an expeditionary force would only encourage the French to repeat their folly of August 1914 by launching an offensive against Germany. At midnight on 16 November Hore-Belisha phoned Liddell Hart to inform him that the prime minister was 'delighted' with Hore-Belisha's 'proposals for the reduced role of the Army', but that Deverell (shortly to be removed from his office by Hore-Belisha) was 'almost in tears – and kept on harping on about France and the importance of sending the E.F. there.'[47]

The air staff fully supported Inskip's proposals, as well they might since they promised increased funding for the Royal Air Force. The air staff's opinions were supported by a few air-minded senior army officers such as General Sir John Burnett-Stuart, the General Officer Commanding Southern Command until 1936, who angered the army general staff by writing to *The Times* to voice his opposition to the continental commitment, advocating its replacement by a strong Royal Air Force, which 'is a far reaching instrument of great destructive and punitive power'. In his opinion, to despatch 'the British Army to a Continental War in its then condition would be to condemn it to disaster.'[48]

His views were shared by the former Conservative minister, Leopold Amery, who was convinced that the use of the Royal Air Force in France 'would be far more decisive and more immediate than that of the handful of divisions which, short of conscription, is all that we can send for many months.'[49] In vain General Sir Ronald Adam, then Commandant of the Staff College at Camberley, pointed out to Liddell Hart that in a few years' time France might have to fight on three fronts – German,

Italian and Spanish – and then 'even our small force might make a difference.'[50]

It was difficult to see how the decision to downgrade the expeditionary force could be reconciled with the chiefs of staff's warning at the end of 1937 that they 'regard the present internal conditions in France and Russia, and the consequent effect on the military strengths of these countries, as factors which increase the dangers of war.'[51] The logic of this warning was that the despatch of the expeditionary force to France was, as Adam suggested, more, not less, essential if the French were to withstand a German attack. Furthermore, there were doubts in British military circles about whether the Maginot line was as impregnable as the French suggested. Inskip wrote to Hankey at the end of January 1938 that War Office opinion was not confident that the line would hold out for long against a determined German assault: 'It bears on the eternal question of the size and role of the Expeditionary Force & I wonder if we ought to try & assess the value of the Maginot Line'. This view was not shared by Hore-Belisha, who returned from a visit to the Maginot line in September impressed by the strength of its fortifications, and reported to Chamberlain in November that this had convinced him that the British army need not be sent to the continent at all.[52]

Later, Inskip told Hankey that the French military attaché, General Albert Lelong, did not believe that the line would delay a German advance for ever – 'but of course he has an axe to grind.' Hankey thought that an enquiry about the strength of the Maginot line would be useless since all that 'we shall get' was 'two different versions according to the circumstances of the expert giving them'.[53] Inskip hoped 'that I may not be accused of a suspicious mind in suggesting that the existence of a gap between Lille and the sea might be a deliberate inducement to compel us to intervene in order to safeguard an area which we have regarded as vital for several centuries?'[54] Shortly before the visit of French ministers to London in April 1938, Hankey asked the prime minister to encourage the French to extend the Maginot line to the sea, since it was in France's interest to do so. 'Incidentally it is a strong British interest, but it would advisable not to say so, or else the French might ask us to pay!'[55] Clearly Hankey, who had advised Inskip in preparing his report, no longer supported the continental commitment – his advice was that the existence of the Maginot line made it unnecessary for a large expeditionary force to be sent to France.[56]

Eden, while expressing some doubts about Inskip's recommendations about the future role of the British army, urged Inskip that the French should be fully informed about the decision, since 'It is of supreme importance to us to maintain a close and confident relationship with the French Government and to co-ordinate our efforts to safeguard the stability of Europe.' With Halifax's recent visit to Germany evidently in mind, he cautioned against 'opening the floodgates of territorial change by open and express acquiescence' in Axis expansion. While Europe remained in a state of armed truce, Eden suggested that the policy of 'so-called "cunctation"' be continued – this was the price Britain and the League had to pay for their inability to assert effectively the principles of international order against aggressors since 1931.[57] 'Cunctation, or waiting on events', was not a policy which appealed to Chamberlain and it led Eden into a confrontation with Chamberlain when the latter wanted to press ahead immediately with negotiations with Italy, while Eden preferred to delay.

On 16 December 1937, and again on 1 January 1938, Eden suggested to Hankey that now that negotiations with Germany for a new Locarno had completely collapsed, Britain should fulfil its pledge to France and Belgium of 15 April 1936, that in the event of the failure of the five-power talks, there should be further trilateral staff talks to put into effect Britain's undertakings to defend these two countries. He also wrote to Duff Cooper on 17 December pressing for naval conversations with the French.[58] Strang was anxious that, while

> on the one hand, there are the obvious advantages of close collaboration between the two Powers, whose interests, in the present state of the world, are largely coincident, if not identical; on the other hand there is the possible objection that the wider and more intimate the arrangements for Anglo-French military collaboration, the more these are likely to be given an anti-Italian interpretation, and so strengthen and perpetuate the Berlin–Rome connection.

E.M.B. Ingram of the Southern Department was also concerned that any Anglo-French staff talks about North Africa, 'seeing that they are with the French, cannot be kept secret', and that leaks to the British press about them would upset the Italians.

Sargent pointed out that Chamberlain, at the recent Anglo-French ministerial talks, had agreed that there should be exchanges of information between their respective attachés on aircraft production, and Eden told the cabinet on 22 December that 'the time has come, I consider, that we should tell the French about the scope and purpose of our re-armament in more detail.'[59] Eden informed the secretary of state for air, Lord Swinton, on 31 December 1937, that he did not believe that, in a protracted conflict, the Maginot line would hold, while Germany would soon overrun Belgium.

He wanted the British air expeditionary force to be based in northern France to meet Britain's obligations under Locarno. He continued:

> From a psychological point of view I attach very great importance indeed to the presence of British uniforms on French, and, if necessary, Belgian soil. I believe that this would make the whole difference to the stubbornness of French resistance to a German onslaught ... If, of course, the British Air Force in France could be covered by a British mechanised division, so much the better, but this I should have hardly have thought essential.[60]

Swinton rejected Eden's appeal, arguing that, when Britain's bomber squadrons were equipped with long-distance machines, they would operate from bases in the United Kingdom. Not only would it be too expensive, it would also be 'undesirable' to establish a British air expeditionary force on French territory.[61]

The chiefs of staff met on 1 February 1938 to consider Eden's request for staff conversations. They repeated their previous opposition to such talks, adding for good measure that 'the very term "staff conversations" has a sinister import', since it suggested to 'interested countries' 'mutually assumed military collaboration'. In any case the chiefs argued that, since the despatch of the expeditionary force to the continent had been virtually ruled out by the cabinet, there would be no point in holding discussions with the French on the subject. They should merely be informed of the 'new situation'.[62]

Predictably, Vansittart rejected the chiefs of staff's arguments. He pointed out that German and Italian ground forces outnumbered those of the French by three and four to one, while France now had to defend two frontiers. Like Eden he did not accept that the Maginot line would be 'impregnable' in a long war. He agreed that Britain's military contribution to France would necessarily be a small one, at least initially, but feared the deleterious effects on French morale when they discovered that Britain would probably not be sending any troops at all to their aid.[63]

At their 1 February meeting, the chiefs of staff, while acknowledging Eden's argument, that, given that Britain's air contribution to France in war would now be important in the absence of an army expeditionary force, air staff talks would be 'desirable', proceeded to reject them on the grounds that the French would turn 'conversations to their own political advantage', by leaking them to the press 'to flaunt an Anglo-French accord in the face of Germany', thus undermining 'Britain's efforts to reach a detente with Germany'. 'From the military standpoint ... we should not appear to have both feet in the French camp.' The chiefs also turned down naval conversations about French fleet dispositions in the Mediterranean if Britain had to despatch its Mediterranean fleet to the Far East in an emergency. They also rejected conversations about joint action against Italy. Britain could easily defeat Italy without French assistance, and, if France did come in, Germany would intervene on Italy's side, 'with the consequent risk of a world conflagration, the outcome of which we should view with much less confidence'.[64]

Neither Chamberlain nor the chiefs of staff wanted to risk upsetting Mussolini as a result of French-inspired leaks about possible Anglo-French military cooperation against Italy. Chamberlain had long been anxious to negotiate a *modus vivendi* with Italy to reduce tensions over Spain, the Mediterranean and the Middle East. For its part the Admiralty wanted friendly relations with Italy in the Mediterranean so that the British fleet would be able to sail to the Far East in the event of hostile moves against British interests in that theatre by Japan – planning for a naval war with Japan had become an obsession with the first sea lord, Chatfield.[65] These considerations led the British government to play down France's security concerns in the Mediterranean and Spain. In January 1937, Halifax told the cabinet that Britain must not view Spain 'through French spectacles'.[66]

Nevertheless, from the British perspective, 1937 saw a further improvement in Anglo-French diplomatic relations. Eden was pleased that 'the French played up much better than any of us expected in the naval help they gave' at the Nyon Conference in September. 'Actually the French are contributing almost as much as we ourselves ... their whole attitude, indeed, has been the reverse of that which obtained in Laval's day.'[67] However, Neville Chamberlain's advent as prime minister, the appointment of Nevile Henderson as British ambassador to Germany and the replacement of Clerk by Phipps at the Paris embassy were to have important consequences for British attitudes towards France in 1938. Already, by the end of 1937, Chamberlain had presided over the virtual abandonment of the continental commitment. In August he had praised Hore-Belisha's activities at the War Office, which had 'already shaken the old dry bones [in the army] up till they fairly rattle'. He foresaw a fierce struggle with the War Office before he could rebuild military policy 'on sounder foundations' and described as 'incredible' 'the obstinacy of some of the Army heads in sticking to obsolete methods ... and I believe that with H. Belisha I shall get something done.'[68]

Hitler's forward moves in Central Europe in 1938 and Chamberlain's search for a settlement with Germany together were to result in a further and more serious weakening of French security and morale, although admittedly France allowed this process to take place by its unwillingness to defend what it had hitherto considered its vital interest in Central European stability. By the end of 1937 the French government had conceded that it lacked the military capability to defend Czechoslovakia against German aggression. It was distracted by the Italian threat in the Mediterranean, while its morale was undermined by a deteriorating economy and financial chaos. French weakness, as Martin Alexander has shown, convinced British Conservatives that little was to be gained by cooperating too closely with the unreliable and unstable French.[69]

THE ECONOMIC AND FINANCIAL CRISIS IN FRANCE IN 1937

Francophiles in the United Kingdom looked on in despair as France's economic and financial troubles threatened to tear apart a social fabric which was already damaged by bitter political divisions. During 1936 France's gold reserves had fallen dramatically as a result of unsuccessful interventions by the Bank of France to preserve the value of the franc on the international exchanges. On 26 September 1936, when Vincent Auriol, the finance minister, was finally forced to devalue the franc, an Anglo-French-American agreement was reached whereby the value of the franc was readjusted to that of the pound sterling and to the dollar and allowed to fluctuate within certain limits on the exchanges. The three governments also promised to relax the existing quota and exchange control system in an effort to revitalise international trade.[70] However, in November, Rowe-Dutton reported that, despite this agreement, confidence in the franc had failed to revive and as a result he could see no grounds for optimism about the present or future financial situation of France. Roderick Barclay, a second secretary in the Central Department, surmised that confidence would not be restored while the Blum government remained in office.[71]

In January 1937 there were signs of a slight improvement as strikes and labour disputes began to diminish. Clerk reported that the industrial situation was better than it had been at any time during the last two years, and Vansittart commented, 'This is *much* better.' Although this improvement appeared to confirm Clerk's opinion that France possessed an underlying strength that would ultimately enable the country to overcome its internal problems, Sargent regretted that 'the outward & visible signs which she at present displays are those of weakness rather than strength.' Eden added that 'even my colleagues in the government feel this, and I confess it is difficult sometimes to deny the accusation.'[72] This apparent dichotomy was noted by Frank Ashton-Gwatkin, a counsellor in the Economic

Section of the Western Department, who on reading the Paris embassy's economic report on France for 1936, commented that, while it 'gives an impression of muddle and mismanagement running through the whole of the French economy from Government finance downward ... we know that next to the United Kingdom and the United States of America, no country has greater resources of all kinds.'[73]

Towards the end of January 1936 renewed financial troubles led Blum to appeal to Chamberlain to help France obtain a British loan of £40 million, which Blum believed was being blocked by the Bank of England. Eden urged Chamberlain to support this loan since failure 'might even affect the life of the French Government and the last thing any of us want is a political crisis in France at this moment'.[74] Chamberlain persuaded Montagu Norman, the governor of the Bank of England, to ensure that the loan was supported by City of London bankers.[75] The loan was floated successfully, but it did not lead to any improvement in France's financial fortunes. On 5 February, Ashton-Gwatkin noted that the French equalisation fund was selling gold 'at a tremendous rate',[76] while Lloyd-Thomas told Sargent that the financial situation was 'very grave'. Inflation generated by the shorter hours and the wage increases decreed by the Popular Front government in the summer of 1936 was fuelling demands for yet another round of wage increases. He reported that 'all observers' feared the injuries the inflationary spiral would inflict on France's already divided society.[77]

On 10 February Neville Chamberlain informed the American treasury secretary, Henry Morganthau, that the London loan to France was now exhausted, and that unless the French government took vigorous action to restore confidence, there would be a flight from the franc, the imposition of strict exchange controls and the breakdown of the tripartite agreement.[78] Sargent thought that 'we should do all we can to help France through her present difficulties. But the remedy, I fear, lies with the French themselves, since fundamentally it is a matter of faith in the future, and it is precisely this faith which is so completely lacking in the French financial world at the present time.'[79] On 20 February Rowe-Dutton also described the French financial situation as 'thoroughly alarming', and warned London that if the drain of gold continued at the present rate, the exchange equalisation fund would soon be exhausted, leading to a panic which would result either in the imposition of exchange controls or a further devaluation of the franc.[80]

A French request for a British declaration of solidarity to help restore confidence was rejected by Chamberlain on the 19 February. Gladwyn Jebb commented:

> the real trouble is that, for internal political reasons, the French Government can never be induced to take salutary economic action without some high sounding declaration on the part of other friendly powers to the effect that such action is part of a world scheme for saving democracy and peace.[81]

Morganthau and Chamberlain concluded that there was little the United Kingdom or the United States could do to help France. On 1 March Sargent complained that the Foreign Office had heard nothing from the Treasury about the crisis:

> In view of the very serious consequences which a French financial collapse or indeed the collapse of the Blum Government would undoubtedly have on British foreign policy, it is very important that we should be kept regularly informed of what is happening by the Treasury, and what they think can be done, and ought to be done, in order to save the situation, assuming that the latter is still in danger.[82]

On 5 March the French council of ministers introduced various deflationary measures in an attempt to ease the financial situation, including the reduction of the public works programme and the raising of a national defence loan of ten and a half milliard francs.[83] On 11 March Eden was informed that the loan had been fully subscribed and the financial position had stabilised.[84] At the same time Rowe-Dutton was trying to counter French right-wing accusations that Blum had only introduced these orthodox financial measures to please the British.[85]

On 6 April Rowe-Dutton reported that capital had begun to return to France. But he remained pessimistic about the future. Left-wing riots in Clichy on 16 March followed by a half-day general strike in Paris against the cuts demonstrated the opposition Blum faced in trying to reduce public expenditure. Productivity was not increasing, there was a shortage of skilled labour, the trade gap continued to widen while the upsurge in wages was unabated.[86] On 3 June Phipps reported that the French government's financial difficulties had not been eased by the recent austerity measures. Since tax yields had fallen, a 20 milliard franc loan was now essential to bridge the gap, but this was unlikely to be secured from the Bourse, which had no confidence in the economy or in the government's ability to manage it.[87] On 14 June the French Chamber of Deputies passed a bill which gave the government decree powers to deal with the financial situation until 31 July 1937,[88] but gold continued to flow out of the country.

One reason for British, and especially City of London, reluctance to help the French was lack of confidence in the competence and integrity of the French financial community – indeed British financial experts regarded French financiers and bankers with ill-concealed contempt. In February Nigel Law, a former Foreign Office official,[89] who was now employed in the City, wrote a memorandum for the Central Department on the subject, which Vansittart described as 'very wise and entertaining', pointing out that the City's attitude towards France was 'governed by an ancient and enduring hostility towards all things French'. This feeling had been reinforced by war-time contacts with the French by British bankers who had served as officers in France. He continued:

> everywhere you hear it said that whereas the pre-War German (not so much is said of the post-War German) was a straightforward honest man of business, the Frenchman was, and still is, shifty, unreliable and greedy.

City of London criticisms were directed at the mismanagement of the French public finances, with no attempt being made to balance the budget, and at the French government's allegedly profligate social reform expenditure. City of London gossips claimed that 'the French never paid their taxes or their railway fares' and 'they add that the French must be the most unpatriotic nation in the world because they don't trust their bankers and the bankers don't trust their Government.'[90] Phipps agreed with this assessment. He told the Foreign Office in June that 'Latin standards of business are very different from those prevailing in the City of London. The long spoon is essential for any British banker who sups with Latin colleagues.'[91] Peter Borneau reported in April that 'the French Govt. – excepting the brilliant Blum – are even more stupid in dealing with their [financial] problems than the Baldwin Cabinet in handling theirs. Blum stands out as an oasis in a desert of incompetence.'[92]

Léon Blum resigned on 21 June when the French Senate refused to allow him to impose exchange controls under the recent decree laws. The Popular Front government was reconstructed, with Camille Chautemps as president of the Council of Ministers, Blum as vice-president and Georges Bonnet, recalled from a brief stint as French ambassador in Washington, as finance minister. Barclay described Bonnet as 'not of a heroic mould'. He was a right-wing radical deputy from the Dordogne and a financial expert who had served in a number of French governments since 1926.[93] Chautemps was granted the full powers which the Senate had denied Blum, but this did nothing to alleviate the financial crisis. On 20 September, in a message to Chamberlain, Chautemps confessed that the pressure on the gold reserves was now so severe that it was impossible to maintain the value of the france any longer and that the authorities would have to let it find its own level in the financial markets.[94] Britain and the

United States sent messages in support of the French efforts to restore confidence, but neither these, nor new austerity measures introduced by Bonnet, did anything to stabilise the financial situation. The Foreign Office was now resigned to the imminent fall of the Chautemps government because of its inability to solve the country's economic problems, while in September, Sir Richard Hopkins, a second secretary in the Treasury, thought that there could be no prospect of a French financial recovery until a government of a different complexion was formed.[95] However Chautemps managed to survive for the time being.

A Foreign Office memorandum on 29 September assessed the potentially severe consequences of the flotation of the franc on the British economy. A further heavy depreciation of the franc would have a damaging effect on British trade, and if exchange control was also introduced by the French government, the effect on Britain's balance of payments would be even more serious. The memorandum continued:

> But of even greater moment to His Majesty's Government is the question of the possible effect of any further deterioration in the financial and currency situations on the present international standing of France. In the present state of tension in Europe with the ever present risk of a trial of strength between the Fascist Powers and the Western Democracies, it is of the highest importance that France should be as strong and steady as possible. A falling currency and general financial instability might in course of time lead to political demoralisation which would not only seriously weaken the country if a crisis developed, but would also constitute an invitation to possible aggressors to take advantage of her disorganised state.

The memorandum attributed the lack of any return of confidence in France to the continued presence of Blum and his socialist colleagues in the cabinet. They might force Chautemps and Bonnet to adopt further inflationary measures such as far-reaching public works schemes or old age pensions. The Foreign Office now began to favour the formation of an all-party national government in France, but of this there appeared to be little prospect in 1937. The memorandum ended on a gloomy note:

> We seem, therefore, to be between the devil and the deep blue sea. Either we let the franc slide in the hope that its descent into the abyss will pull the French together and result in the formation of a strong government and financial reconstruction; or we bolster up the franc … in the hope that the French Government will pull themselves together and that the franc will attain a de facto stabilisation of around about

> 150 … The danger of the first alternative lies in the fact that the franc's plunge might result, not in a National Government, but in civil disturbance. In any case the Dictators might profit by a period of confusion and despondency to perpetrate some 'coup,' whether in Spain or elsewhere. The dangers of the second course are obvious: we might lose our money and the situation will be as bad or worse for all our pains. On the other hand such action might give the Dictators the temporary impression that the situation had been saved, and in any case it would represent a useful demonstration of Anglo-French solidarity.[96]

Strang sent this memorandum to Sigismund Waley, a principal assistant secretary at the Treasury dealing with overseas finance, on 5 October, asking him whether

> the financial and, and therefore, the political stability of France, who, for better or worse is our chief partner in a disturbed and dangerous Europe, is important enough to justify financial sacrifice on our part in an attempt to preserve it; and whether, supposing we are prepared to make the sacrifice, it would in fact be of any avail …

Waley ruled out either a long-term British loan or the purchase by Britain of depreciating francs, concluding that 'nothing will be any good till French capital regains confidence in the French Government.' Gladwyn Jebb accused Waley of not realising 'how grave the international situation is, and what a really desperate situation we should be in supposing things went seriously wrong in France, e.g. the Army was affected.' Jebb's remedy was to tell the French that if they introduced exchange control, 'we may have to revise our whole policy towards Germany', but, on the other hand, 'we will grant a stabilisation loan if a National Government is formed.'

Strang did not accept Jebb's suggestion: 'I don't think we can do much to save the French financially and she can only be saved by herself.' He could only hope that the French government would 'keep things fairly steady … If we tried to impose political conditions for financial support we should become undesirably involved in French internal affairs and risk raising a political storm here.' Vansittart did not agree. He sent a telegram to Eden, who was in Brussels for the nine-power conference, complaining that Treasury reluctance to help France was 'regrettable politically' and he hoped the foreign secretary would persuade Simon to change his mind.[97] However, no action was taken.

The destabilising effects of the financial crisis on France's domestic situation alarmed the Foreign Office. In June the Paris correspondent of the *Daily Herald*, Jack Sandford, 'a moderate right wing socialist' according to Phipps, gave Phipps a memorandum he had written on the subject. In this memorandum Sandford blamed Popular Front social and economic policies for the increasing destruction of what he regarded as the backbone of French society: the craftsmen, small shopkeepers and peasants. After reading this, Sargent lamented:

> Much as we sympathise with the French Government in many matters, and approve of their policy in a great many particulars, it is well to bear in mind ... that their policy is likely in its ultimate results to bring about a general proletarisation of the French nation. This might well have serious and far-reaching repercussions on this country – & on Europe.

Vansittart added, 'Not might but will most certainly have such repercussions.'[98]

In November, on the eve of the visit by Chautemps and Delbos to London, Phipps attempted to put a more favourable gloss on the French internal situation. He could not deny that France still faced great internal problems which were much discussed 'in a country where rumour has it that a crisis is round the corner and that the Government is about to fall. But that is the normal in France and if the normal is healthy, it is a sign of health rather than of disease.' He pointed out that Germany and Italy were facing more severe economic and financial difficulties than France, that France had survived the war and the world economic crisis, and that it had maintained a high standard of living with a minimum of real poverty and destitution. In his view, its social structure had been virtually unimpaired by all these vicissitudes:

> ... she has preserved complete theoretical liberty of personal thought, speech and action within a framework of democratic institutions which have shown themselves sufficiently elastic and vigorous to deal with problems which elsewhere led to dictatorship. She has maintained an immensely powerful army, the second, perhaps even the first, in Europe, highly efficient and free from political influence ... It would be foolish to deny her abiding vitality or to under-rate her fundamental strength.[99]

There seemed little in the French economic and political climate in 1937 to justify this optimistic assessment of France's underlying health. Industrial unrest continued to plague French industries until the end of the year, while, on the eve of a new world recession, French gold reserves had fallen to 81 milliards of francs in December.[100] General Edmund Ironside who was, in 1937, General Officer Commanding, Eastern Command, summed up the general impression of France in Britain when he remarked in December, 'Out of sight out of mind is particularly applicable to a people come to such straits as France today.'[101]

None of this augured well for 1938, when France faced its gravest challenge with Germany's threat to Czechoslovakia, France's only reliable ally in Central Europe, and the cornerstone of the French security system in that region.[102]

4 Britain and France in the Year of Munich, 1938

... if only we can find a solid and coherent France.

(Winston Churchill, 12 April 1938)[1]

We have many common interests, but we have many that are not common.

(General Edmund Ironside, 25 March 1938)[2]

Chamberlain was anxious to follow up Halifax's November 1937 discussions with Germany's leaders by putting forward a new peace initiative to Berlin, which he outlined to the cabinet committee on foreign policy on 24 January and 3 February 1938. He intended to propose the conclusion of a comprehensive agreement between the two countries, which would include the restoration of some of Germany's former colonies, a peaceful resolution of Germany's grievances about Austria and the Sudetenland Germans, an agreement on the limitation of bombers, and Anglo-German collaboration to ensure the future peace of Europe. He insisted that only limited information should be given to the French about these soundings, since, although Chautemps and Delbos 'had shown that they were ready to play their part in any attempt to get an agreement with Germany on broad comprehensive lines', he remained sceptical about France's discretion. While Chamberlain now accepted that France was

> deeply attached to her understanding with us, [France) has been in a terribly weak condition being continually subject to attacks on the franc & flight of capital together with industrial troubles & discontent which seriously affects her production of all kinds & particularly of arms & equipment.[3]

What little the British did tell the French about the proposed initiative alarmed Delbos, who complained to Phipps on 18 February that even the suggestion that Britain was prepared to discuss Austria would encourage German ambitions there.[4]

When informed of these French reservations, Nevile Henderson wrote to the Foreign Office to urge that, 'however unpalatable this may be to the

French', any opportunity to reach agreement with Hitler over Austria should not be missed. Sargent rejected this suggestion on the grounds that, 'we should not run after Hitler at the moment'. But Cadogan and Strang thought that it might be worth following up: 'neither we nor the French possess the offensive power sufficient to prevent Germany from working her will in Central Europe- and in order to prevent her, it is *we* & the French who would have to take the offensive.'[5]

These exchanges coincided with Eden's resignation on 20 February 1938 (Vansittart had been made chief diplomatic adviser and replaced as permanent under-secretary by Sir Alexander Cadogan on 1 January) following a disagreement with the prime minister over Chamberlain's insistence on entering into immediate conversations with Italy. Pownall was pleased by Eden's departure: 'Thank goodness all this F.O. policy has at last come to a head.' He was glad 'to see the back of Van ... with his pro-French tendencies so strongly developed that he detests every other nation.' Britain could now inaugurate a more sensible foreign policy 'with a realist like Chamberlain and a decent man like Halifax, who has had experience of tempering ideals with realities.'[6]

Pro-British sections of the French press and French ministers were dismayed by the departure of the supposedly pro-League and Francophile Eden. Phipps reported that Delbos, Chautemps and Léger had summoned him to a meeting at which they warned him that, if the recent personnel changes in London foreshadowed a radical change in British foreign policy without France being consulted, the effect on French opinion would be 'quite disastrous'.[7] The French press even compared the fall of Eden with that of Delcassé in 1905, that is, as a German victory in its efforts to divide Britain from France.[8] On Phipps's advice,[9] Chamberlain assured Chautemps that the resignations would not result in any change in the direction of British foreign policy.[10] However thc appointment of Lord Halifax as foreign secretary, with R.A. Butler as his parliamentary under-secretary, and Henry Channon as Butler's parliamentary private secretary, both pro-German and anti-French, on 1 March 1938, increased French doubts about the future.[11]

French anxiety prompted Phipps to appeal to the Foreign Office to keep the French government closely informed about any Anglo-German discussions with Germany, as, if it came into the open that Britain was negotiating with Germany without telling the French, the ensuing press and parliamentary outrage at British behaviour would force the weak Chautemps–Delbos government out of office. Strang commented: 'It is a familiar gambit of French Foreign Ministers to tell us that unless we agree to do something or the other, the French Government will fall. We need not pay any particular attention to it on this occasion.' The Central Department hoped that, if the Chautemps government did fall from power, it would be replaced by a government of a wider political complexion than the existing radical and socialist one, with Chautemps instead of Delbos at the Quai d'Orsay, since the former 'is much more in sympathy with and has greater understanding of, British policy than M. Delbos'.[12]

On 10 March 1938 Chautemps resigned, but his replacement did not meet the Foreign Office's requirements in any way. The new government was yet another popular front administration, with Léon Blum once more prime minister, and Joseph Paul-Boncour as foreign minister. Paul-Boncour, a socialist pro-Leaguer, was even more distrusted by the Foreign Office than Delbos, since the former was considered to be a fervent supporter of the French alliance with Czechoslovakia at a time when Britain wanted to weaken the ties between the two countries.[13]

Halifax immediately turned down a request from Blum for a Anglo-French ministerial meeting, since, as Sargent put it, 'we don't want Paul-Boncour to get the kudos' of a meeting with his British counterpart. Phipps told Edouard Herriot, the influential radical socialist deputy, former prime minister and currently president of the Chamber of Deputies, that 'such meetings seemed to me quite useless until the days of transitory French Governments were over: when a strong and durable Government appeared they would, on the other hand, be very useful.'[14] Cadogan and Sargent now began to encourage Phipps to interfere in France's internal political affairs, thus creating a precedent which Phipps was to use for his own purposes during the September crisis over Czechoslovakia.[15] In a minute of 15 March, Sargent described the Blum administration:

> as the most deplorable Ministry that could possibly be imagined in present circumstances. A typical Front Populaire administration, composed of little men in wrong places…The appointment of Paul-Boncour to the Quai d'Orsay is particularly bad. We can only hope that they will fall soon …
>
> I am not at all sure that the moment may not be coming when we will have to convey tactfully to the French that if they expect us to enter into closer co-operation with them in order to deal with the international crisis, we in return expect to be able to deal with an administration which really represents the true strength of France and not merely ephemeral combinations of parliamentary groups – an administration, in fact, of "concentration nationale" which will give us satisfactory guarantees of authority and durability.

Cadogan agreed: 'until France can pull together under a strong Govt., she is really rather a broken reed.' Sargent urged Phipps to do all he could 'to embarrass and weaken the present French government' in the hope that it would collapse and be replaced by 'a gouvernment de concentration nationale', with which 'we shall be most glad to arrange a meeting'. In another minute on this subject on 17 March, which was not placed on the Foreign Office political files, but was sent to Phipps 'not as an "instruction"' for 'officially you have not seen it', Sargent wrote:

> M. Paul-Boncour at the Quai d'Orsay is a disaster and an invitation to him [to visit London] would only strengthen his position, whereas it must be our sincere wish to see him out of office as soon as possible. In fact I would go as far as to say that anything we can do to weaken the present French Government and precipitate its fall would be in the British interest.[16]

In his annual report on leading personalities in France in 1936, Clerk had given his jaundiced opinion of Paul-Boncour, describing him as 'a vain and somewhat futile man with an unattractive personality. He studiously cultivates a resemblance to Robespierre by wearing long hair. He may possibly be sea-green but it is to be doubted whether he is entirely incorruptible.'[17]

Phipps and the Foreign Office were alarmed when, in the middle of this French ministerial crisis, Lloyd George and Winston Churchill visited Paris on separate occasions in March. Both men embarked on a series of meetings with French politicians. Lloyd George, who stayed in Paris from 17 to 19 March, saw Paul-Boncour, Paul Reynaud, Georges Mandel, Georges Bonnet, Léon Blum and Edouard Daladier. The former British prime minister was accompanied to a restaurant to dine with French politicians by his private secretary, A.J. Sylvester, who was, Phipps reported, carrying 'two enormous maps of Europe', which were used by Lloyd George to demonstrate, by means of arrows, how France would be encircled if General Francisco Franco and the Spanish nationalist forces were not defeated. Lloyd George told the French journalist 'Pertinax' that France should intervene militarily in Spain to help the republicans.[18] Phipps hoped 'that this visit will not have too bad an influence on some of the light-weights in the present French Cabinet.'[19] The ambassador immediately

> impressed upon Léger that he should let all the French parties know that Mr Lloyd George represents very little more than himself in the England of to-day, and that they would do well to realise that they should take what he said with a considerable amount of salt.[20]

Phipps was equally critical of Churchill's activities in Paris. At a dinner on the 25 March with Edouard Herriot and, on the following evening with Blum and Paul-Boncour, Churchill called for a solid Anglo-French bloc and for a grand alliance with the Central European and the Balkan states against Germany, to include air, military and naval staff talks. As with Lloyd George, Phipps laid 'great stress in talking to French ministers about Churchill' that 'he only speaks for himself'. Phipps poured 'liberal sprinklings of salt on what he says'. On the 28th, Phipps reported that Churchill's stay 'has continued in an increasingly kaleidoscopic manner. Nearly every facet of French political life has been presented to him at and between meals.' At nearly all conversations at which Phipps was present Churchill continued to advocate a close Anglo-French alliance. Consequently Phipps suggested that 'If and when a strong French Government is formed I feel it will be very useful for you and the Prime Minister to come over here and put things into somewhat better proportion than they have been left by Winston.' Halifax read this letter to the cabinet, telling Phipps that several ministers 'were disposed to be a little critical of my having encouraged you, as I think I did, to show hospitality to him and keep an eye on his movements. I still think it was better so, and the P.M. was on the whole of the same opinion.'

Halifax thought that Phipps should tell the French politicians who had met Churchill that the British government was the 'right source' of British policy 'rather than Winston's exuberant interpretations of it'.[21] Even Churchill was concerned about the effects of French governmental instability on Anglo-French relations, writing to Phipps soon after his return from Paris to ask 'How can they expect us to open these serious matters [staff conversations] to Ministers who expect to quit at any moment?' In an article in the *Daily Telegraph* on 14 April, Churchill complained that 'All the Heil Hitler brigade in London exploit and gloat over what they are pleased to call "the Parliamentary impotence of the French democracy."'[22]

Meanwhile, Phipps continued his campaign to undermine the Blum government, informing Paul Reynaud on 12 March that he was disappointed that the *Anschluss* had not resulted in the formation of a strong French government.[23] On 27 March the ambassador informed Herriot that Herman Goering had advised the Berlin correspondent of the *News Chronicle* that Britain would do well to enter into close collaboration with Germany since France was no longer a 'great power'. Herriot assured Phipps that Edouard Daladier, a radical socialist former prime minister, who had been minister of national defence and war in the successive popular front governments since 1936, would soon form a government of national concentration.[24] Herriot's forecast was correct: Daladier replaced

Blum as prime minister on 10 April, forming a government composed mostly of members of the radical socialist party. The Popular Front had been finally extinguished.[25]

Phipps described Daladier as 'simple and direct and not as conceited as most French politicians', but not 'a real strong man, despite his determined aspect'.[26] Georges Bonnet became foreign minister in the new government after Phipps had informed Daladier 'indirectly' that it would 'be most unfortunate' if Paul-Boncour remained at the Quai d'Orsay, 'not only because of his mad hankering after intervention in Spain, but because it seemed highly desirable for France to get on better terms with Italy' – Paul-Boncour was opposed to negotiations with Fascist Italy. Phipps told Sargent that he had taken 'a certain risk' in interfering, but 'if any questions were asked in Paris, he would disown any role in sending the warning to Daladier'. Halifax 'warmly approved' what Phipps had done. While agreeing that Bonnet was not 'ideal', the foreign secretary thought that 'his weaknesses are more the result of personal ambition than of misguided principles.' Phipps did not think that Daladier's government would last for more than three months, which was unfortunate because 'we cannot do better than the existing Daladier–Bonnet combination.'[27]

On 24 March the ambassador wrote a gloomy appreciation of the state of France and of its new government. Recent political developments had given 'the friends of France ... legitimate cause for anxiety', since Daladier had 'no clear body of support and [had] ministers in wrong places', while Bonnet, despite having 'moderate and sound views on foreign affairs ... is so personally ambitious as to be a somewhat unreliable colleague'. Meanwhile the French economy remained in a precarious state, with excessive public expenditure, falling production, rising unemployment, a rising cost of living and intense pressure for increased wages.[28] Pressed by Phipps to make some gesture to demonstrate British confidence in the hard-pressed Daladier government, Halifax and Chamberlain agreed to meet Daladier and Bonnet in London on 28 and 29 April.[29] Chamberlain was 'glad to see the French are pulling themselves together again'.[30] Cadogan impressed on Halifax 'that French come over here for two reasons – (1) to boost themselves (2) to tighten our leading string. We must look out for (2).'[31]

The British delegation at the Anglo-French ministerial talks comprised Chamberlain, Halifax, Vansittart, Cadogan, Sargent, Strang and Frank Roberts, a second secretary in the Central Department. Daladier, Bonnet, Corbin, Roland de Margerie, Léger and Charles Rochat, assistant director of the European Department at the French Foreign Ministry, represented France. At their first meeting the two delegations discussed the forthcoming Anglo-French air conversations and the conversations about joint purchases of food and petrol in time of war, which the cabinet had recently authorised.[32] Halifax repeated the by now familiar formula that the air staff talks must be strictly limited to technical matters, and that they did not imply any political undertaking by Britain to France. Since Britain did not envisage the extension of a war to other powers, Germany was to be regarded as the only potential aggressor. Halifax said that it 'would be no surprise to the French Government that any British assistance would be chiefly in the air and at sea.' Since naval cooperation could be concerted 'very quickly after the outbreak of war', he said that the Admiralty did not consider that naval conversations were necessary. Halifax then explained the War Office view that, since only two ill-equipped British divisions might be despatched to France in the event of war, further army staff talks were equally unnecessary. Any undesirable reactions from Germany and Italy about the air and economic talks, he said, would be forestalled by Britain informing the German and Italian ambassadors in London that the conversations were being held on the same bases as those laid down in March 1936. During the afternoon session on the 28th, Daladier, while paying tribute to the 'great moral importance' of Britain's two divisions, urged that, since the two armies and air forces had to work closely together in wartime, staff conversations should be extended to include army cooperation as well. He also requested naval conversations on the grounds that 'it was wrong to regard national defence as something which could be cut up into sections.'

While accepting the last point, Chamberlain reminded the French prime minister that a Royal Air Force 'of a very formidable character was being built up', which was making heavy demands on British industry. Britain's military advisers had informed the government that, at the outset of hostilities, Germany would strive to inflict a knock-out blow on its adversaries to avoid a long war, and the only way to resist such an attack was from the air, which was, after the Royal Navy, receiving priority in British defence expenditure. Chamberlain then said that the British government was not committed to sending even two divisions to the continent in the event of hostilities. Thus he reiterated that army staff conversations on such a hypothetical basis would be a waste of time.

Daladier countered that, since Germany could open an offensive without warning, this was an additional reason why the entente should coordinate its armed forces well in advance. He admitted France's weakness in the air but insisted that progress in increasing aircraft production was being achieved. But he did not believe that aviation could win a war by itself. The army remained 'the predominant factor'. Contacts between the army staffs well in advance of hostilities was essential in order to make arrangements for the disembarkation of the two British divisions and their accommodation in France. He did not believe that it would be difficult for 'a great industrial country like Great Britain to motorise these [two] divisions and so to economise in men'. Chamberlain reminded Daladier that, while Britain and France were still proceeding with their rearmament programmes, they both remained 'extremely vulnerable' to a German offensive, and they should therefore do nothing to excite German and Italian suspicions 'that we were now devising fresh military, naval or aerial conversations to injure these two Powers'. After further pressure from Daladier, Chamberlain eventually gave way and agreed that there should also be contacts between the Anglo-French naval staffs, but not immediately, since, as Halifax put it, Britain did not want to upset Italy 'when the sealing-wax was scarcely dry on the Anglo-Italian agreement'. Returning to the question of the commitment of the British army to the continent, Chamberlain declared that 'the British public were ... very nervous about a land commitment', since this would restrict Britain's power to use its forces in other overseas theatres. To equip two divisions for a continental war rather than for 'general purposes' would imply a commitment the government was not prepared to make.

The third meeting, on the morning of the 29th, was taken up with a gloomy account by Halifax of the inability of the entente to take any military action in support of Czechoslovakia. Neither France nor Britain, he said, was strong enough to resist a German attack on Czechoslovakia, and the British chiefs of staff had already written off Czechoslovakia's ability to defend itself. Soviet Russia, weakened by 'internal unrest' and the military purges, could do little or nothing to assist Czechoslovakia, and it was doubtful that any assistance would be forthcoming from Poland. Thus nothing could be done to save Czechoslovakia from a German attack while, even at the end of a victorious war over Germany, the entente would not be able to reconstruct Czechoslovakia in its existing form. The logic of all this was that Anglo-French pressure should be applied to Czechoslovakia to reach a settlement of the German minority problem by direct negotiations with the Sudetenland Germans. In the meantime nothing should be said by London or Paris to encourage the Germans to think they could impose a settlement on the Czechs by force or threats thereof. In response, Daladier asserted that 'the ambitions of Napoleon were far inferior to the present aims of the German Reich', and that capitulation by the entente in the face of another threat from Germany would merely encourage the Germans to undertake further aggression, probably against Romania since Germany's conquest of that country would provide Germany with the petrol and wheat supplies it required in order to fight a long war. He rejected the chiefs of staff's assumption that the Czechoslovak army should be written off, and insisted that Russia, despite the purges, possessed both the strongest air force in Europe and great potential war resources. He insisted that France would stand by her obligations to the Czechs, while supporting reasonable concessions to the German minority which, however, must not result in the break-up of Czechoslovakia.

Chamberlain promised that no settlement of the Sudetenland question would be acceptable if it threatened the independence of the Czechoslovak state. He dismissed a suggestion by Daladier that the entente should warn Germany not to go too far as 'what the Americans in their card games called bluff'. He repeated that Czechoslovakia was indefensible, but admitted that 'it made his blood boil to see Germany getting away with it time after time and increasing her domination over free peoples. But such sentimental considerations were dangerous.' Furthermore, British public opinion would not allow its government to go to war for the sake of Czechoslovakia. Chamberlain doubted if Hitler really wanted to destroy Czechoslovakia or to seize Romania. He was convinced that the recent improvement in Anglo-Italian relations would help to keep Central Europe and the Balkans out of the German orbit. He reiterated that Britain would only go to war 'in the very last resort'.[33] Daladier insisted that, while everything possible should be done to avoid war, France would live up to its treaty obligations. If the entente failed to stop 'the disturbing manifestation of the dynamic force of Germany', once Germany controlled the resources of Central and Eastern Europe, 'how could any effective military resistance be opposed to her?'

It appeared by lunchtime on the 29th that the conference would end in deadlock over Czechoslovakia. It was, of course, unclear whether Daladier's firm language was the sincere expression of his views, or merely intended for the record so that Britain, not France, would be saddled with the blame for any subsequent disaster which overtook Czechoslovakia.[34] Chamberlain later confided to his sister Ida that 'Fortunately the papers have had no hint of how near we came to a breach over Czecho-Solovakia [*sic*].' However, after private conversations over lunch, and the British concession about holding naval staff talks, Daladier accepted a compromise put forward by Halifax whereby the British would approach the German government to find out what kind of peaceful settlement of the Sudetenland question would be acceptable to Germany, and at the same time remind Hitler of Chamberlain's speech of 24 March in which he had issued a warning that Britain would not necessarily remain aloof if war broke out over Czechoslovakia. Britain and France would also press the president of Czechoslovakia, Dr Edvard Beneš, to make the 'maximum concessions' to the Sudetenlanders.[35]

The prime minister did not

> find Daladier as sympathetic as Chautemps, but he seems simple and straightforward, though perhaps not as strong as his reputation. Bonnet I have known since 1932: he is clever but ambitious and an intriguer. The French are not very fortunate in their Foreign Secretaries.[36]

Cadogan suspected that Vansittart had been behind Daladier's strong language about German ambitions in Europe. He described Vansittart as 'a French agent, and the French know it and play upon his nerves'.[37] Oliver Harvey noted that the French had left the conference 'in high spirits', having achieved the promise of naval staff talks, a joint Anglo-French approach to Beneš and a British warning to Hitler.[38]

If the British had adopted their usual grudging tactics in dealing with the French, these were mild by comparison with Hitler's treatment of Chamberlain's offer of comprehensive negotiations earlier in March. Owing to the changes in the German government in January, with Joachim von Ribbentrop replacing Constantin von Neurath as German foreign minister, Henderson was unable to meet Hitler to put forward Chamberlain's proposals for a general settlement until 3 March. To Chamberlain's intense disappointment this received no positive response. Hitler indulged in one of his stage-managed diatribes, telling Henderson that Germany wanted a free hand to settle the Austrian and Sudeten German problems. Nor did Hitler show any enthusiasm for aerial disarmament. As for colonial concessions, which lay at the heart of Chamberlain's initiative, Hitler brushed these aside – he told Henderson he was in no hurry for the return of German colonies.[39]

Clearly the failure of Chamberlain's search for a general settlement with Germany and increasing tension in the Sudetenland boded ill for the future peace of Europe – Halifax commented that 'we must certainly admit that our constructive efforts have suffered a pretty severe setback.'[40] The cabinet committee on foreign policy met twice during March to finalise its policy towards Czechoslovakia. The prime minister, at a meeting on 18 March, feared that if France became involved in war with Germany over Czechoslovakia, it would do so because it reckoned that Britain could not afford to see France destroyed and would have to come to its aid. Halifax accepted that, 'whether we liked it or not we had the plain fact that we could not in our interests afford to see France overrun.' British policy, he thought, should be to keep both France and Germany 'guessing as to our attitude' by refusing to say whether Britain in any particular case would come to France's aid: a carbon copy of Eden's non-policy of 'cunctation'.

Oliver Stanley, the president of the board of trade, disagreed. He wanted Britain to declare that it would stand by France if it was attacked by Germany as a consequence of France fulfilling its treaty with Czechoslovakia. He thought that such a declaration would make Germany think twice before attacking Czechoslovakia. Halifax and Chamberlain opposed this suggestion on the grounds that Britain was not strong enough to risk war with Germany. Chamberlain stated that 'No doubt France's army was good and would fulfil expectations but in other respects e.g. finance, air, the domestic political situation, France was in a hopeless position. Her relations with foreign countries, Germany, Italy, Nationalist Spain, were bad, while her influence in Central and Eastern Europe was declining.' Under these circumstances France should support Britain's efforts to find a peaceful solution to the crisis.[41]

On 20 March Chamberlain confessed to his sister that the state of Europe was weighing on his mind, 'with a French Government [Blum's] in which one cannot have the slightest confidence and which I suspect to be in closest touch with our opposition'. He was depressed by Franco's recent victories in Spain, Russian intrigues to involve Britain in a war with Germany, and a Germany 'flushed with triumph' after its annexation of Austria on 12 March 1938.[42]

The cabinet foreign policy committee met again on 21 March to discuss Czechoslovakia. Halifax repeated his objection to giving France a guarantee of British support if it went to the assistance of Czechoslovakia. The dominions secretary, Malcolm MacDonald, thought that Britain's refusal to intervene on France's side would be 'a terrible blow' to France, while Oliver Stanley declared that its effect on France would be 'catastrophic'. Halifax agreed that 'no doubt France would be shocked but he could not see how in any case this could be avoided. Because France would be shocked was no reason why we should refrain from pursuing a policy the correctness of which we were fully satisfied.' He complained that 'the French were never ready to face up to realities, they delighted in vain words and protestations.'

When the committee came to examine the draft of a Foreign Office despatch informing the French that no British guarantee of their alliance with Czechoslovakia would be forthcoming, Malcolm Macdonald complained that its contents 'sadly lacked the warmth and friendly sentiments which might in all circumstances have been expected, in particular it might well have referred in warmer and more friendly terms to our existing commitments to France.' Halifax was prepared to adopt this suggestion but Oliver Stanley objected that even such a half-hearted and limited statement 'might cause a great collapse in France and lead to the severance of our relations with her'. He wanted to offer France a more concrete guarantee, which, while promising British support for France in resisting aggression 'in certain well defined circumstances', would also enumerate the obstacles in the way of helping Czechoslovakia. Stanley thought that 'the phraseology of the document seemed to him cold and unsympathetic and if he had been a Frenchman he would have said that it forecasted the adoption by H.M. Government of Lord Beaverbrook's policy of isolation.' Eventually Chamberlain admitted that he found the proposed communication 'stiff and unsympathetic', and declared that he did not, 'at the present juncture, wish to offend France beyond what might be absolutely essential'. The prime minister then suggested that Phipps should make a verbal and not a written communication to French ministers 'on warmer and more friendly terms'.[43]

The cabinet met on 22 March to consider the foreign policy committee's recommendations. Halifax said that, while British policy would be 'unpalatable to the French ... however upset the French Government might be, he did not see what other alternative was open to them but to acquiesce.' The essential features of the first draft were retained. The French were to be informed that they should not 'assume that His Majesty's Government would at once take joint military action with them to preserve Czechoslovakia against German aggression, especially as the two countries would be in no position to prevent a German takeover of the country.' The cabinet instructed Phipps to 'emphasise our strong desire to maintain the closest possible relations with France but to urge that nothing could be more detrimental to those relations as to leave the decision on peace and war to France alone.'[44]

Those ministers who wanted nothing to do with France's alliance with Czechoslovakia were also influenced by Britain's continuing military weakness. At the end of November 1937, in one of their characteristically gloomy reports on the relative military strengths of Great Britain, France and Belgium by comparison with Italy and Germany 'as at January 1938', the chiefs of staff emphasised the numerical superiority of the Italian and German armies over those of Britain and France. However they did not think that the *Wehrmacht* would be strong enough to launch a land offensive against France until 1939 or 1940, and even then the Maginot line and the mountains on the Franco-Italian frontier would prevent a rapid German or Italian breakthrough. They estimated that France could maintain 40 divisions in the field over a long period, but that Britain 'will be in no position to render her material assistance either in the form of troops or equipment', since only an 'Intermediate Contingent' of two divisions would be available 'for despatch to a theatre of war'. Moreover, Germany and Italy were vastly superior in the air to Britain and France, especially in long-range bombers, while German air defences were also 'in a very advanced state compared with those of France and Great Britain'. In view of the 'deplorable' disorganisation of the French air industry, German and Italian output of aircraft would be greater than that of the entente for several months after the outbreak of war. This depressing recital of the entente's relative military inferiority vis-à-vis the Axis Powers was only slightly redeemed by the fact that the Anglo-French navies were quantitatively superior to the German and Italian navies.[45] After reading this report, Eden had to admit that 'it appears that we are not in a position to fulfil our Locarno obligation to France and Belgium, as far as land warfare is concerned.' Under the circumstances he could only suggest the continuation of 'the unheroic policy of so-called 'cunctation' i.e. the continuation of the present armed truce 'without a general settlement, but without war.' This recommendation was anathema to Chamberlain, who wanted to embark on an active diplomatic effort to persuade the two dictators to agree to a peaceful settlement of outstanding differences in Europe, in the hope that this would lead to a reduction in armaments.

In this quest he was supported by the chiefs of staff, who, as has already been discussed,[46] had turned down staff conversations in February as likely to offend Germany. The air staff's opposition to air talks was contested by the British air attaché in Paris, Group Captain Douglas Colyer, who, in a memorandum of 14 January, pointed out that 'the French Air Ministry wished to take full advantage of what they took to be the Prime Minister's implied offer to discuss military questions with the French' at the Anglo-French ministerial conference in November 1937. He noted that 'it is now perhaps some of the Service Departments which might be inclined to hang back, partly from a desire to keep free of any engagements to another country and partly from an inherent distrust of the French character and the present French Government'. He thought it impossible

> that Britain would not support France in the event of a Franco-German war ... Leaving out of consideration the respective merits and demerits of the French and German peoples, the aspirations, situation and relative geographic positions of FRANCE and GREAT BRITAIN would appear to place them almost automatically on the opposite side of the fence from GERMANY whose policy is directed by her present rulers.

Germany, he continued, could attack France 'without warning and in such circumstances that we shall have to take our place beside FRANCE without a moment's delay'. Air forces could not be improvised 'at a moment's notice', since arrangements for their accommodation and operational efficiency in a foreign country 'need very careful working out and cannot be arranged in a few hours'. Joint planning on targeting, and the roles of the two air forces in war, even if based on hypothetical cases, were essential if British help was to be 'of the greatest possible value'. He could not understand how Britain 'had anything to lose by discussing the matter with the French now'.[47]

Phipps and the Foreign Office fully supported Colyer. Cadogan described the chiefs of staff's rejection of staff talks as 'astonishing', protesting that the service departments were 'hanging back on *political grounds*', in which they 'are exceeding their functions'. He could not 'see the harm, from the political point of view, in discussing these matters with the French on a hypothetical-technical basis, making it clear that it involves no commitment'.[48]

Vansittart pressed Eden to insist that the service departments agree to immediate and comprehensive staff conversations with the French, since, if war broke out in 1938, 'the cumulative effect' of failing to arrange for prior cooperation with France, especially in the air, 'may well be fatal to us'.[49] Eden replied that 'it is certain that we must have staff conversations with France'[50] and wrote a trenchant minute to Chamberlain on 31 January:

> I cannot help believing that what the Chiefs of Staff would really like is to clamber on the band wagon with the dictators, even though that process meant parting company with France and estranging our relations with the United States. I believe, moreover, that there is a tendency among some of our colleagues to under-estimate the strength of France. The recurrent political crises in that country seem to them evidence of fundamental weakness.

Eden dismissed the latter contention: 'French politicians in opposition have not the same sense of restraint as we and no doubt to English people whose tendencies are strongly "Right," co-operation with a Left Government is not very sympathetic.' However 'the French Army is fundamentally sound … [and] we must avoid … the temptation of being led astray by any exaggeration of the weakness of our friends and an unduly high estimate of the strength of the totalitarian states.' He challenged the 'disinclination on the part of the Chiefs of Staff to discuss military matters with the French' and urged Chamberlain that at the very least there must be discussions with the French to coordinate the two countries' air plans.[51]

In rejecting the charge of interference by the chiefs in political matters, Hankey pointed out that defence and foreign policy were so closely linked that it was impossible for the chiefs to differentiate between the two, although he admitted that the chiefs' mention of 'leaks' to the press by the French did have a political dimension. He justified this on the grounds that if leaks about the conversations were to occur and Germany was offended, 'plenty of people in Britain would happily blame the Services, as after 1906, and the Chiefs had to mention this to protect their staffs.'[52]

The chiefs of staff's February report on the staff conversations was examined by the cabinet on 16 February 1938. The cabinet agreed with its rejection of military and naval talks, but, in order 'to keep faith with the French', as Chamberlain put it, it authorised limited technical Anglo-French air staff talks between the respective attachés, and agreed that RAF officers might be allowed to make occasional visits to French airfields.[53]

After further Foreign Office protests about the limitations which the cabinet had placed on the air talks, the cabinet returned to the issue on 6 April. Halifax, now foreign secretary, thought that Germany's recent annexation of Austria made it imperative that army staff talks with the French should be authorised. While Chamberlain would not agree to the widening of the staff talks to include discussions about naval and army cooperation with the French, he agreed that air talks were essential since the speed of Germany's occupation of Austria made it essential for Britain to concert its air preparations with France well in advance of any hostilities with Germany. The French should be told firmly that it was unlikely that a British expeditionary force would be sent to the continent, because the prime minister thought it unreasonable to keep the French 'in the dark' about the future role of the British army. 'To him it seemed disloyal to the French and unfair on ourselves to do so. If the French were bound to receive a shock sooner or later, surely it be sooner the better.' No conclusion was reached at this meeting and the issue was referred to the committee of imperial defence.[54]

At this meeting, held on 11 April 1938, Chamberlain and Inskip complained that, in recent reports, the chiefs of staff had referred to the possibility that two infantry divisions might be available for despatch to France in an emergency. They pointed out that this statement contradicted the cabinet's decision in December 1937 that land assistance to Britain's allies was to be the lowest priority in Britain's defence agenda, and that, in future, the expeditionary force would be equipped only for a colonial theatre. The home secretary, Samuel Hoare, insisted that in the event of a war with Germany, both the Royal Air Force and 'all available troops' would be needed to defend London against German air attack: none could therefore be spared for France. Chamberlain agreed that Britain could hardly send troops to defend the Maginot line while London was being subjected to heavy German air attack. Duff Cooper, the first lord, reluctantly accepted that in these circumstances army staff conversations would serve no useful purpose, but added that 'it was impossible to contemplate France with her back to the wall and three million men in this country in plain clothes.' Finally the committee recommended that only the air staff conversations should be held with the French.[55]

On 13 April the cabinet approved the committee of imperial defence's recommendations. Air staff talks were authorised but they were to be restricted to the fulfilment of Britain's Locarno obligations to defend France and Belgium against a German attack. Since 'the probability of our being able to send an Expeditionary Force to France is so slight ... Military Conversations are unnecessary.' The cabinet also ruled out naval conversations on the grounds that if Germany found out that they were taking place it might use them as a pretext to repudiate the 1935 Anglo-German naval treaty.[56]

Halifax dissented from the cabinet's decision to reject army conversations, writing to Chamberlain on 14 April to protest that, 'owing to the pressure of time', the cabinet had not fully understood that any communication to the French telling them about Britain's army dispositions in war-time would 'have a discouraging effect' on them, especially if they concluded, 'which I should have thought was premature, that assistance on land was likely to work out at zero'. The bad effects of this disclosure could, he thought, be alleviated, if Britain also informed the French at the same time that it was ready to hold military staff conversations. He continued:

> I fully recognise and share your anxiety to avoid what may grow into a large commitment, but I think it would be dangerous, and academic, at this juncture to carry the suggestion of the negative further than may be warranted by need or events.

He reminded Chamberlain that Britain wanted 'to induce in the French a most collaborative disposition' towards Czechoslovakia and this would not happen if there was 'any unnecessarily bad effect upon them with this communication in regard to military co-operation'.[57]

At a further cabinet meeting to discuss the conversations on 27 April, Halifax managed to persuade the ministers to agree to the opening of army conversations if the French pressed strongly for them. Naval conversations were authorised if and when the prime minister and the foreign secretary thought these were necessary. The scope of the conversations was to be strictly limited to technical matters, and were not to include any discussion of war plans, and they were to be handled only through the service attachés. Chamberlain now supported this decision since 'to refuse a request for Conversations under severely limited conditions would seem rather churlish'. Simon disagreed: he thought that even limited army conversations might encourage the French to assume that Britain was committed to send two regular divisions to the continent. While 'other Ministers' shared Simon's apprehensions, they were eventually overruled: Chamberlain's support for the conversations ensured this.[58] Pownall complained that, when the French were notified about the army conversations, they immediately leaked the information to the French press – 'The French saw to that for they use it as a means of lining us up as definitely as possible on their side and against Germany.'[59]

The air staff remained unhappy about the prospective air talks. Any press publicity about them might lead to accusations that Britain was 'planning an offensive war against Germany', while the air planners had not yet decided between 'the various courses of action open to us' for the deployment of the advanced air striking force against Germany.[60] The Admiralty also wanted 'to stave off any further enquiries by the French Naval Staff as to our proposed war dispositions of Naval forces'. The director of plans at the Admiralty, Captain V.H. Dankwerts, assumed that the object of the conversations

> is a political one, to meet the very strongly expressed wishes of the French, presumably with a view to allaying their feeling of insecurity as regards their Atlantic sea communications, and that the object is certainly not to prepare a combined 'British-Naval' war plan for a war with Germany.

Hence Dankwerts was relieved that the talks were to be restricted to technical exchanges of information and the provision of details of naval forces available in home waters:

> It may be considered that the above suggestions represent a very meagre exchange of information. Moreover it is less than is presumably done by the Air Staff ... It seems unlikely, however, that it will satisfy the French in their present mood.

Although Chatfield agreed that 'we start with the *minimum*: and try to restrain the French when they ask for more', Duff Cooper overruled him:

> Personally I incline to the view that if we are to have the conversations the fuller and franker they are the better. The only argument against having them was that they would upset the Germans and Italians. This they will do however restricted they are.[61]

The conversations between the Anglo-French military, naval and air attachés took place at various times during the summer. At the army talks, the French were reminded that only two infantry divisions would be available for overseas duties at the onset of war, and that Britain was not committed to send them to France.[62] During the Anglo-French naval conversations the French were given details of the dispositions of the British fleet as at 31 May, divided into ships ready for service at 14 days' notice and ships ready for service at more than 14 days' notice, together with a list of defended ports. The French supplied the Admiralty with similar information about the French fleet. The French wanted these exchanges to be followed by discussions about strategic plans, but Dankwerts rejected this since it

> would imply the existence of an absolute obligation to collaborate, a conclusion which must be avoided ... A hard and fast line must be drawn beyond which we cannot go without morally committing ourselves to act with France in war, and it appears that this line has almost been reached ...

In any case he thought that discussions of naval plans were unnecessary, since, in the event of an Anglo-French war with Germany, no major redisposition of the two fleets would be required as British naval forces would control the North Sea and the Channel, while French naval forces would control the western Mediterranean.[63]

In June 1938 Group Captain John Slessor, the deputy director of plans at the Air Ministry, reluctantly agreed to a French Air Ministry request to provide 'special facilities' for the French air attaché at forthcoming British air defence exercises. The attaché was to be shown the operations room (usually forbidden to foreign air attachés), but Slessor insisted that 'he should be taken round in plain clothes and secretly and [he is] not to tell any of his foreign colleagues' about what he had seen. The air staff also opposed discussion of air plans because

> A nation cannot undertake the discussion of war plans with a potential ally without in fact incurring a moral commitment, no matter what disclaimers of liability and responsibility are stipulated as a basis of the conversations.

In this connection the air staff referred to 'the moral commitment' incurred by the Royal Navy to defend French western coasts and ports in 1914.[64]

In any case the British could not see what they would gain from air conversations with the French in view of the parlous state of the French air force and the French aircraft industry. As a result, there might not be a viable French air force with which the Royal Air Force could cooperate in the event of a war with Germany. Vansittart complained to Corbin in November 1937 about the conflicting and misleading statistics about French aircraft production with which he had been provided by the French Air Ministry. These varied from 25 to 90 planes a month. The permanent under-secretary commented that 'Nothing but an increase in production – and a large one – can save them. And we are directly affected by their present plight.'

While Eden suspected that 'the estimates given are all ... from sources hostile to the French Government',[65] the British industrial intelligence centre [IIC] confirmed in February 1938 that the rate of French aircraft production was depressingly low, endorsing Chautemps' estimate to Chamberlain at the Anglo-French ministerial conference in November 1937 that the French aircraft industry was manufacturing no more than 60 aircraft a month. The IIC reported that French aero-engines were poor, in both quality and power, that skilled French aeronautical labour was in short supply, that the French appeared to be incapable of either designing or producing improved models and that the industry was still not equipped for mass production. Central Department officials described this report as 'a discouraging picture'(Barclay), 'catastrophic' (Strang) and 'as bad as ever' (Vansittart).[66]

While the cabinet was still wrangling about authorising even limited air staff conversations with France in April 1938, Inskip added to the uneasiness of those ministers who were concerned that any conversations with the French might saddle Britain with a commitment to go to their aid in war-time, when, on the 17th, he requested cabinet authorisation for Anglo-French discussions about the joint purchase of food, coal and oil in neutral markets in the event of war, which had been mentioned at the Anglo-French ministerial talks in November 1937. Simon and 'several other Ministers' protested that the extension of Anglo-French talks to cover trade and economic cooperation between the two countries would only increase German suspicions that Britain and France were combining to make defensive preparations against Germany at a time when the prime minister still hoped to reach a settlement with Germany. Furthermore they argued that talks of this nature would encourage France to believe that

Britain would support its anti-German policies. Halifax rejected these arguments and insisted that Britain must be 'brutally frank' to Berlin that nothing was to be gained by German military action against Czechoslovakia, while knowledge of Anglo-French trade and economic discussions might be a useful signal to Germany not to go too far. When Chamberlain supported Halifax, Simon reluctantly fell into line behind the prime minister. However, Kingsley Wood, the minister of health, cautioned against 'drifting back' to the 'old' position whereby Britain always consented to everything asked for by the French while rebuffing Germany's approaches.[67]

Discussions with the French about coal and food supplies in war-time began in May, while those on petroleum supplies commenced on 13 June 1938.[68] Then, on 6 July, Inskip asked the cabinet to approve an extension of these talks to cover non-ferrous metals and minerals, raw materials, textiles and shipping tonnage. He admitted that there was a danger that the widening scope of these talks might lead the French to claim that they had relied on the British to put any agreements reached into effect when war came, while press leaks about them might adversely affect Britain's efforts to improve relations with Germany. He also referred to naval staff fears that the naval conversations might lead the French to redistribute their fleet on the basis of the dispositions of the Royal Navy revealed to the French during the conversations. Such a redistribution might place the French at a disadvantage if Britain decided not to enter a European war. The cabinet agreed to the extension of the economic talks providing it was made absolutely clear to the French that they were on a purely hypothetical and noncommittal basis, while the French should be informed that their fleet dispositions should only be made on the basis that war without British support 'was the graver danger for France', a formula suggested by Duff Cooper.[69] Vansittart protested in vain to Halifax about the last stipulation – 'It can only have a damaging effect on Anglo-French relations, and that at a moment when they are in no condition for further strain.'[70]

When the Anglo-Italian negotiations were nearing a successful conclusion at the end of March, the British rejected a French request to participate, and Phipps told Herriot on the 26th that France should reach its own agreement with Italy. Herriot replied that he regarded Italy as a lost cause, since it was tied hand and foot to Germany. Instead he wanted Britain and France to draw nearer to Russia as a counterweight to Germany. Phipps reminded him of the appalling effects of the recent purge of senior officers in the Red Army on Russia's military efficiency. Herriot denied that this was necessarily the case. He reminded Phipps of 'the wonderful efficiency of the French revolutionary armies at a time when French generals were being guillotined' and he called for an Anglo-French-Soviet alliance, comprehensive staff talks and the formation of two or three mechanised British divisions to be sent to the western front in the event of war.

Herriot's remarks produced an angry minute from Strang, who described Herriot's attitude as 'quite deplorable' and hoped that Phipps had told Herriot 'that his policies would at practically every point be in direct conflict with those of His Majesty's Government.' Cadogan added that 'With M. Herriot in control, an Anglo-French policy will be difficult to conduct ... But M. Herriot is an awful windbag: if he were in power his views might moderate.' Vansittart had no patience with these opinions. He asked,

> *is* there anything dreadful or silly in what M. Herriot says in the Russian section? ... Might not the extent of the executions have been exaggerated in the West? ... Is he not right in saying that it is 'absurd to ignore her?' [Russia] Is he not right in thinking she is a 'useful counterweight to Germany'? If Germany and Russia with their not far different systems, ultimately coalesce, Britain and the smaller countries of Europe would be very vulnerable ... In all this M. Herriot seems to me to be talking plain common-sense; and I do not see where it cuts across our own policy, which does not profess to be biassed by 'ideologies'.

Halifax minuted that 'It is perhaps a question of method. ... if we were to "draw nearer" to Russia in such fashion as to draw further away from Germany.'[71]

Phipps described Herriot as 'foolish and even dangerous ... He weeps with Boncour over red Spain; he revels in Soviet bloodbaths and feels convinced that they enormously increase the efficiency of the beloved Red Army.'[72] The ambassador assured Sargent that 'we need not take this too tragically, however, as long as the "Jelly Fish," (as Ramsay MacDonald used to call him) is not at the Quai d'Orsay. If and when he is we will have to put water in his wine.'[73] The Anglo-Italian agreement was signed in Rome on 16 April 1938, promising British recognition of Italy's annexation of Abyssinia when Italy withdrew its 'volunteers' from Spain.

There was no resolution of the Sudetenland issue during the spring and summer of 1938.[74] In May 1938 there was a momentary panic in London that war might be imminent over what turned out to be false rumours of an impending German attack on Czechoslovakia. Simon wrote in his diary on 22 May:

> We are endeavouring ... to make sure that France will not take some rash action such as mobilisation (when has mobilisation been anything but a prelude to war?) under the delusion that we would join her in defence of Czechoslovakia. We won't and can't – but an open declaration to this effect would only encourage German *intransigence*.[75]

Given the uneasy relations between Britain and France since the spring, the Foreign Office welcomed the apparent success of a visit by the King and Queen to France in June. Halifax accompanied the Royal party and Phipps reported that Bonnet had invited the Foreign Secretary to lunch with him and Daladier on the 29th, where he wanted Halifax to stress to Daladier the importance of keeping the Pyrenees frontier closed. Daladier, Phipps feared, tended to listen to Mandel, Reynaud and Herriot 'who sing pro-Soviet and anti-dictator ... songs to him'.[76] Nevile Henderson hoped that the Royal visit would be used 'to convince the French nation ... of the closeness of Anglo-French relations', which might in turn 'enable it to view Germany with less fear and jealousy',[77] while Ronald Campbell, who had been appointed minister in Paris after Lloyd-Thomas's death in February, thought that 'the visit has shown the earnestness with which all Frenchmen look to Anglo-French co-operation both as guaranteeing at a dangerous moment in history, the preservation of the ideas of personal liberty, and of freedom of thought and speech.'[78]

Whatever might have been its impact on Parisians in public relations terms, the image of Anglo-French solidarity conveyed by the Royal visit did nothing to improve diplomatic relations between the two countries, which remained troubled throughout the summer. On 11 August, Campbell reported that 'for the last week or two I have felt that the atmosphere of Anglo-French relations has lost something in mutual confidence.' The French, he wrote, continued to suspect secret dealings between Britain and Germany, and there had been much French press and parliamentary speculation about what had transpired during a visit by Captain Fritz Wiedemann, Hitler's aide de camp, to London in mid-June.[79] Campbell warned the Foreign Office that if the French were taken into the fullest confidence about such contacts,

> we are more likely to be able to keep them in what we consider the straight path, and also to prevent them taking initiatives which interest us without our knowledge ... The French press sometimes speak of the initiative in policy having passed from Paris to London. If we wish to maintain French acquiescence in this state of affairs, we must be careful to *manager* the French Government ... If, on the other hand, the

Foreign Office now wish in general to be 'cagey' with the French, would you let me know and we will act accordingly.

This letter led Cadogan to circulate the various Foreign Office departments dealing with relations with the French for their reactions to Campbell's accusations. This produced an admission by the Western Department that they had recently been forced to exercise a certain amount of restraint about giving information to the French about Spain, because much of what the French had been told previously about British policy towards the civil war had been leaked to the French press. The Southern Department regretted that it had not been possible to persuade the French to enter into negotiations with Italy. The Far Eastern Department replied that 'the French on the whole have played up exceedingly well in all matters relating to the Far East ... We do therefore make every effort to keep them informed of what we are doing (when we know what we are doing) and will continue to do so.' In the end, Campbell received scant satisfaction: Sargent told him that it was impossible to lay down a general rule that France should be told everything about the state of Anglo-German relations, and he refused to promise that such reticence would not continue.[80]

With no settlement of the Sudeten issue in sight during the summer, Simon, in a speech at Lanark on 28 August, tried to dissuade Hitler from resorting to force over Czechoslovakia, by adopting what Simon described as 'a firm tone' about Britain's possible involvement in a Franco-German war. Simon confided to his diary on 31 August that, 'It is quite certain that this country would never "go to war for Czechoslovakia," but France is bound by treaty if she is attacked (though I have no idea how this promise could be fulfilled) and if Germany and France came to blows, no one can say whether we will not be drawn in.'[81]

Increasing French military weakness, especially in the air, reduced the already slim possibility that France would adopt a resolute stand over Czechoslovakia. On 30 August the prime minister told the cabinet that 'the strategic situation seemed to him to be somewhat worse than in May, France being weaker and the position vis à vis Italy having deteriorated.' Lord Maugham, the lord chancellor, suggested that, given Britain's unpreparedness and the risk of Italian and Japanese intervention on Germany's side in a European war, Britain should 'hesitate for a long time before subscribing to the view that if France was at war with Germany we were inevitably bound to come to her assistance.'[82] In early September 1938, Guy La Chambre, the French air minister, informed the Chamber of Deputies that the French Air Force possessed only 21 machines equal in speed to most *Luftwaffe* aircraft, causing Frank Roberts to exclaim that 'This is even worse than we had supposed and fully explains the French reluctance to be drawn into a war in which they have to take the offensive to achieve any useful results.'[83] An Air Ministry memorandum of 19 September, 'The French Air Force: Efficiency and Readiness for War in Comparison with the German Air Force', revealed that France currently possessed 1350 front-line planes, 900 of which were obsolescent, and that the German aircraft industry was producing 600 planes a month and the French 100. Furthermore, German fighter aircraft were faster than the French, while France's anti-aircraft artillery capability was virtually non-existent. The memorandum concluded:

> the French Air Force is not only heavily inferior in total strength in the air and on the ground in relation to the German Air Force but is weak also on the state of its organisation, tactical training and technical efficiency. Its relative vulnerability is higher and its relative potential for expansion much lower.[84]

Moreover, France's financial situation showed no signs of improvement. During August there were further heavy losses of gold and Daladier appealed to the prime minister for an Anglo-French meeting to discuss the situation, since otherwise there might be 'incalculable consequences' – a business collapse in France and falling national income – at a time when the western democracies needed to maintain their influence in Europe. The Treasury suspected that the French were seeking a demonstration of Anglo-French financial solidarity to impress Germany, and refused to help, especially as Britain was also facing an outflow of sterling. Chamberlain could only advise the French to introduce a programme of sweeping financial reforms.[85]

Given these unfavourable air and financial indicators, as the Czechoslovak crisis deepened in early September, the British conviction that France would not fight hardened. On 13 September Inskip wrote that 'Everything showed that the French didn't want to fight, were not fit to fight and wouldn't fight.' Phipps informed Halifax on the following day that Bonnet 'was in a state of collapse', while Daladier was adamant that Germany must be stopped from moving 'at all costs'.[86] Maugham informed the cabinet on 14 September that France had 'cold feet'.[87] Nor, apparently, was there any British public support for involvement in a war for the sake of Czechoslovakia. Sir Leo Chiozza Money, who had been a junior minister in Lloyd George's coalition government, and was now a Labour Party financial expert, echoed the opinions of most informed Britons when he wrote to Lloyd George on 14 September that:

> The decline of France, the friend, right or wrong, goes far ... Is it not high time some authoritative voice warned our unfortunate people of the consequences of a war waged in company with Paris and Moscow? *The only possible victory is a Russian one*.[88]

Neville Chamberlain, Halifax and Horace Wilson met a Labour Party delegation on the evening of 17 September, at which Chamberlain pointed out that 'the real difficulty is the weakness of France ... Within the last few days French resolution has crumbled ... Bonnet in particular was appalled [by French weakness in the air] and was now very weak...' while 'Daladier [was] likewise irresolute now.'[89] At a cabinet meeting on the same day, only Chatfield wondered whether 'we were in danger of being accused of truckling to dictators and offending our best friend.'[90]

Reports by Phipps in early September that Gamelin was planning to 'wear down' the Germans by a series of offensives, instead of remaining on the defensive behind the Maginot line,[91] puzzled the chief of the air staff, Air Chief Marshal Sir Cyril Newall, who considered it a dangerous departure for a nation which he had assumed 'always acts on a basis of logical thinking and hates last hour improvisation'. It was clear to Newall that Gamelin was relying on British military assistance being forthcoming to enable him to launch such offensives. The chief of the air staff therefore suggested that army staff conversations with the French should now be extended to include exchanges of war plans, so that the British could prevent the French army from doing anything 'unwise', thereby committing Britain to 'an unsound plan of campaign'.[92] General Lord Gort, the chief of the imperial general staff, who had replaced Deverell in December 1937, rejected this suggestion as he did not think it 'politically opportune' to discuss war plans at the moment.[93]

Chamberlain's failure to inform the French in advance about Plan Z – his dramatic visit to Hitler at Berchtesgaden on 15 September (although he did not tell the British cabinet of his intention until 14 September) – left them understandably aggrieved, since Daladier had earlier suggested a joint Anglo-French approach to Hitler to try to settle the Czech crisis. Chamberlain justified his summit diplomacy on the grounds that Bonnet was 'panicking', Daladier had '*very* little backbone' and that, as a result, dramatic action on Chamberlain's part was essential to avert a war for which the French were manifestly unprepared.[94]

Daladier and Bonnet flew to London on Sunday 18 September, where they were given details of Chamberlain's meeting with Hitler at Berchtesgaden. With Chamberlain were Halifax, Sir John Simon and Sir Samuel Hoare (Chamberlain's inner cabinet during the crisis),[95] together with Sir Horace Wilson and a retinue of Foreign Office officials. Inskip learned that 'the whole morning passed in the two sides trying to avoid any commitment until the other side had declared their intentions.'[96] Chamberlain made much of Hitler's promise that he would not order immediate military action against Czechoslovakia if the entente agreed to the cession of the Sudetenland to Germany. Chamberlain had already persuaded the cabinet on 17 September to accept Hitler's demand for 'self-determination' for the Sudetenlanders, and he did not think that he would encounter much difficulty in persuading the French to agree either.

It was not to be as easy as the prime minister anticipated. Daladier warned the British ministers of the dangerous consequences for the future security of south-eastern Europe if Czechoslovakia disintegrated as a result of allowing the Sudetenlanders to secede from Czechoslovakia and join Germany. While Halifax said that he shared 'to the full M. Daladier's doubts and misgivings' about Hitler's proposal, and with the 'anxieties and preoccupations M. Daladier had expressed', he nevertheless recommended that the Chamberlain–Hitler agreement be accepted. Daladier's response to this casuistry was to remind the prime minister that at their April meeting both countries had agreed that Czechoslovakia's independence must be maintained: the succession of the Sudetenland would place that independence in jeopardy. Cadogan listened cynically to Daladier 'with voice trembling with carefully modulated emotion, talking of French honour and obligations'.[97]

Daladier then followed his display of determination with an appeal to the British to find 'some means of preventing France from being forced into war as a result of her obligations', and finally Daladier and Bonnet accepted the Berchtesgaden proposals, after Chamberlain agreed to a French request for an international guarantee of the remainder of Czechoslovakia. The Sudetenland was to be handed over to Germany after a short, but decent, interval. Daladier thanked the British ministers for understanding 'the great sacrifices France would be making in agreeing to the territorial concessions contemplated'. All that remained was for the conference to agree to the draft of a joint Anglo-French telegram to Prague, which the British drew up, informing the Czech government of the decisions Britain and France had reached.[98]

Simon considered that 'Chamberlain handled them [the French] admirably', noting that the French had accepted 'the proposal (as well they might) [for an international guarantee] with the greatest show of gratitude that I have ever seen in a spokesman of France'. He concluded that the decision to sever the Sudetenland from Czechoslovakia and hand it over to

Germany 'involved the reversal after twenty years of one of the very worse rearrangements made in the Peace Treaties'.[99]

Chamberlain was provided with ammunition in dealing with Duff Cooper and the few other ministers who were unhappy about the Berchtesgaden proposals by a series of telegrams from Phipps describing the disintegration of French morale as the prospect of war came closer. As a result, Phipps was convinced that France would not fight for Czechoslovakia under any circumstances. In support of this conviction, however, he relied exclusively on the opinions of defeatist French politicians, like Bonnet, with whom Phipps had struck up a close friendship, Joseph Caillaux, a former French prime minister and chairman of the Senate finance committee, whose record in and out of government office had long marked him out as pro-German, Flandin and Laval.[100] The ambassador's communications to London after 10 September became increasingly hysterical as he described the collapse of Bonnet's nerve and the latter's increasing desperation as he struggled to find a 'way out of this impasse without being *obliged* to fight'.[101] Chamberlain read out extracts from Phipps's telegrams and despatches describing the defeatist spirit in Paris to the cabinet in order to reinforce his arguments for the acceptance of Hitler's demands.

In the process Phipps destroyed his previous reputation in the Foreign Office as an anti-appeaser and as an 'objective' observer of France and the French. To pro-French officials like Vansittart and Sargent, Phipps had betrayed them by acting as a mouthpiece for the opinions of the French defeatists. One particular telegram, in which Phipps stated that 'All that is best in France in against war, *almost* at any price' and attributed support for war to a 'noisy and corrupt war group here', a telegram which Chamberlain read to the cabinet on 24 September, caused the Central Department the most anguish.[102] Vansittart had already complained to Halifax that the Foreign Office only knew about the reactions of the French government to the crisis from what Bonnet told Phipps. Phipps had revealed little or nothing about the views of Daladier and the French cabinet as a whole, and, consequently, Britain might be saddled with the responsibility for adopting a particular policy towards Czechoslovakia without knowing where France really stood.[103]

When Chamberlain returned to Germany on 22 and 23 September to inform Hitler at Godesberg that Britain and France had accepted the Berchtesgaden demands, Hitler told the prime minister that these were no longer adequate as a solution to the problem and that he now wanted the Sudetenland, including areas of mixed nationality which were in dispute, to be occupied immediately by German troops – there was now to be no decent interval before Germany took over.[104] Although irritated by Hitler's hectoring tone, Chamberlain was prepared to accept the latest *dictat*. Halifax was not. Cadogan had decided that the Godesberg demands went too far and were unacceptable – 'I *know* we and they [the French] are in no position to fight: but I'd rather be beat than dishonoured.'[105] Cadogan's arguments reinforced Halifax's own increasing doubts about Hitler's latest demands. On Sunday 25 September, at a cabinet meeting at 10.30 a.m. to discuss the Godesberg proposals, Halifax declared that he could not accept Hitler's demands, and that if Czechoslovakia rejected them, 'France would join in and if the French went in we should join them.'[106] Chamberlain, angered by Halifax's *volte face*, scribbled a note to the foreign secretary at the meeting that 'It remains to see what the French say. If they say they will go in, thereby dragging us in, I do not think I could accept responsibility for the decision.'[107]

Daladier and Bonnet arrived in London for another meeting with their British counterparts at 9.30 p.m. on that day. After Chamberlain had given them an account of his two interviews with Hitler at Godesberg, Daladier informed the group that the French council of ministers had rejected the Godesberg terms. Then Simon, using his dialectical skills as a lawyer, subjected Daladier to a lengthy catechism about French military plans if war now broke out, 'not with the object of putting anybody in a difficulty but because we, as close friends of France, were necessarily interested in what took place.' He recorded that Daladier 'did not like' these 'direct questions'.[108] Simon hoped to undermine French ministers' confidence in the military capability of the French army so that Chamberlain could subsequently demonstrate to the cabinet that France would not fight for Czechoslovakia. This time, however, Daladier did not budge. He insisted that if war broke out the French army would launch an offensive against the Siegfried line and bomb German factories and military centres from the air. Chamberlain countered this by dwelling on the poor condition of the French Air Force, painting a vivid picture of 'a rain of bombs' descending on Paris and on French military and industrial installations, pointing out the unreliability of Russia and referring to recent reports by Phipps about the lack of bellicosity in the French press.

Daladier asked whether the British government were prepared to accept the latest German demands without a shot being fired, not only handing over 31 million Sudeten Germans to Hitler but 'everything else as well'. Germany would then be master of Europe – 'after Czechoslovakia would come Rumania and then Turkey. He might even turn to France and take Boulogne and Calais. He might even afterwards land in Ireland.' While accepting that the French Air Force was inferior to the *Luftwaffe*, he believed that France could still mobilise an effective air force, while

France would have the support of a Russian air force of 5000 modern planes. The meeting ended in deadlock and was adjourned until the following day, when Gamelin was to come to London to explain French military and air plans in the event of war.[109]

Gamelin spoke to a meeting of defence ministers and the chiefs of staff in the morning of 26 September 1938. He claimed that once it was fully mobilised the French army could field one 100 divisions (consisting of 5.5 million men) with the bulk (about 60 divisions) concentrated on the frontier with Germany. He insisted that he had no intention of sitting behind the Maginot line waiting for a German offensive but would march immediately into Germany on the outbreak of war, and continue to advance until he met serious resistance, when his forces would withdraw. He would also bomb German military objectives by air. He thought that the German general staff opposed war and that their intermediate commanders were weak. He wanted to know what British army formations could be expected to arrive in France at the outset of hostilities, and the arrival dates of subsequent British reinforcements. The chiefs refused to answer this question without reference to the cabinet.[110] Pownall summed up the general British impression of Gamelin's plan – 'there was little enough ... merely an advance to the Siegfried line and then withdrawal to the Maginot. That wouldn't have helped the Czechs much.'[111] Simon 'did not believe, and do[es] not believe, that the French really intended any offensive operations against Germany at all'.[112]

In a final effort to prevent a war which now appeared almost inevitable, despite Simon's doubts about French determination, Chamberlain told the cabinet at midnight (the third meeting on that day) that he was sending his close aide, the chief industrial adviser, Sir Horace Wilson, immediately to see Hitler to convey a personal appeal by Chamberlain to agree to the setting up of an international commission to determine which Sudeten areas should be transferred to Germany.[113] Wilson would also convey a verbal warning that if the prime minister's appeal was rejected, Britain would side with France and Czechoslovakia. Simon helped draft this declaration, which, he claimed, was 'a definite promise to go to war with Germany if France goes to war with Germany over this business.'[114]

On the 27th Wilson delivered Chamberlain's new offer and the verbal warning to Hitler. Neither made any impression on the German leader, who gave the British until 2.00 p.m. on 1 October to accept his demands.[115] Britain began preliminary naval and civil defence measures on 26 September, when the first sea lord, Admiral Sir Roger Backhouse, wrote to Cadogan demanding immediate exchanges of senior British and French naval officers between the British and French Admiralties. 'I wish to emphasise that it is of the highest importance that we should get in touch with the French, or we shall not be able to use our two Fleets mutually to the best advantage.'[116]

When the British ministers met Daladier and Bonnet again on the morning of the 26th, Wilson had only just set off on his mission to Hitler. Daladier had already approved Chamberlain's initiative and the two countries could now only await Hitler's reply. The Anglo-French conference ended with 'Mr Chamberlain ... very happy to note that they had found themselves in complete agreement' and with Daladier pronouncing that 'it was always a pleasure to meet men as frank and loyal as the British Ministers.'[117]

As has been well documented elsewhere, war was narrowly averted when, on 28 September, Hitler, claiming that Mussolini had persuaded him to postpone German mobilisation for 24 hours, invited Chamberlain, Mussolini, Daladier and Chamberlain to meet him the following day at Munich to arrange a settlement of the Czech issue. The Munich conference convened at 12.30 p.m. on the 29th. Hitler now agreed to extend the time scale for the German occupation of areas in the Sudetenland in which Germans predominated from 1 October to 10 October and to the setting up of an international commission to supervise plebiscites in mixed areas. The agreement was signed at 2.00 a.m. on the 30th.[118] The conference ended with a private meeting between Hitler and Chamberlain at which they discussed disarmament and south-east Europe, and Chamberlain persuaded Hitler to sign the famous Anglo-German declaration pledging peaceful relations between the two countries in the future.

This was the high noon of Chamberlain's appeasement policy. He returned to London to be greeted by cheering crowds: Daladier, who was not told of the Anglo-German declaration until later, was also, much to his surprise, greeted enthusiastically by the Parisian populace. In Czechoslovakia, sacrificed to Chamberlain's determination to avoid a general war, there was of course no such rejoicing as the Czechs were forced to yield first to the Munich *dictat* and then to Polish and Hungarian territorial demands.[119]

A few British dissidents like Churchill were of course plunged into deep despair over the Munich agreement. Colin Coote, a journalist on *The Times*, wrote to Eden castigating the 'squalid scuttle' at Godesberg:

> Already the rubber stamps who exist to supply Mr Chamberlain with a Cabinet are explaining that they were forced to surrender because France would not fight, and Neville himself told the Labour people that France let him down. It is true that there were shiverers also among the

> French – Bonnet and Chautemps among them – but no attempt was made on our side to correct those shivers. On the contrary we eagerly collected every sign of them, and then told the French we should only back them if they were successfully invaded. So they feel pretty sore.[120]

Lord Robert Cecil equally condemned 'the policy and conduct of the British Government [as] ... utterly deplorable', but he thought that the French government's behaviour had been even more culpable:

> it [British policy] is not quite as bad as that of the French Government; what they can be thinking of passes my comprehension. I believe it is true that they made no resistance to the British proposal to surrender to Hitler – on the contrary they were much relieved of it![121]

5 Britain and France from Munich to the German Occupation of Bohemia

… no one, I imagine, would now suggest that concessions could be made to Germany, or deny that the main purpose of our rearmament programme is to discourage the aggressive nations from making war.

(William Ivo Mallet, 13 December 1938)[1]

After the signature of the Munich agreement and the Anglo-German declaration which accompanied it, Hitler did not, as Chamberlain had hoped, make any proposals for a general European settlement. Moreover, in his public speeches after September 1938 Hitler adopted a truculent and disparaging tone about the British, and attacked British politicians like Winston Churchill and Duff Cooper for their opposition to the Munich settlement. These attacks caused much resentment in Britain. Nazi Germany's reputation overseas was further undermined by the anti-Jewish pogrom – *Kristallnacht* – on 10 November 1938, which outraged British and American opinion, even those circles that hitherto had been sympathetic to Germany.

These factors were partly responsible for the waning of the initial enthusiasm in Britain for the Munich settlement, a decline assisted by increasing feelings of guilt amongst erstwhile Chamberlain supporters about the forcible methods which had been employed to destabilise a small Central European state, feelings exacerbated by the subsequent seizure of Czechoslovakian territory by Poland and Hungary. Chamberlain was not to be deflected from his vision of an Anglo-German settlement, although he admitted that he was disappointed that Hitler had not made 'even the slightest gesture of friendliness' after Munich.[2]

Nor would he listen to advice from Halifax and others to broaden the political base of his cabinet in order to give it a more resolute aspect in the face of continuing uncertainty about Hitler's future intentions. Chamberlain refused to invite Eden to return to the Government,[3] because Eden 'would do what he did before, always agree in theory, but always disagree in practice.' The prime minister 'wanted more support for his policy [in the cabinet] and not further strengthening of those who did not believe in it' – a swipe perhaps at Halifax's insubordination.[4]

In any case Eden would not have acquiesced in Chamberlain's continuing search for appeasement if he had re-entered the cabinet. Eden believed that, as a result of Munich, France, 'now our only surviving ally in Europe, has become a second class power'; later he complained that 'there is no sign of any real speeding up or increase of [the rearmament] programme, such as the international situation calls for.'[5] Others in the administration, such as Halifax and Walter Elliott, were also appealing to a reluctant Chamberlain to inject more urgency into British rearmament efforts. Warren Fisher wrote to Chamberlain on 1 December:

> the events of the past few months may well prove for civilisation the writing on the wall unless we – and likewise the French – put such time as may still be allowed us to much more effective use than has been done since the commencement of the Hitler regime in 1933.[6]

However, Fisher had lost any credibility he may have had with Chamberlain, mainly as a result of the Treasury secretary's opposition to Munich: Chamberlain preferred to confide in Sir Horace Wilson, who took Fisher's place as chief secretary at the Treasury when the latter retired in February 1939.[7] Pownall noted the increasing mistrust of Hitler in Britain and also the widespread demand for increased rearmament. He was now convinced that the 'main lesson' of the Munich crisis was 'that we must *expect* to have to send troops to help the French'.[8]

Chamberlain was, of course, not without supporters. One of these was Sir Eric Phipps, who, well aware that the Foreign Office no longer trusted his judgement, confined his views on French politics to private letters to Chamberlain, Halifax and Horace Wilson. In these he continued to laud the virtues of the French 'peace party', and to condemn those French politicians such as Paul Reynaud and Georges Mandel who sought a more determined stance against the Axis Powers by the Daladier government. Unfortunately for Phipps, some of his letters to Halifax found their way into the Foreign Office official files, thus reinforcing the officials' convictions about Phipps's unreliability.[9]

Sir Maurice Hankey, who had retired as cabinet secretary in July 1938, visited Paris early in October, where he stayed at the embassy with Sir Eric and Lady Phipps, friends of long standing. Phipps told Hankey that 'attempts have been made continuously by our F.O. and the Quai d'Orsay to *saboteur* both the Chamberlain peace policy and Phipps himself', while 'Phipps is being called a defeatist [by the Foreign Office] because he repeats things as he gets them from the best-informed quarters. His secret despatches are quoted to opposition French newspapers.'[10] On 4 October Hankey wrote to Sir Horace Wilson painting a painful picture of a beleaguered British embassy in Paris,

> engaged in a difficult struggle against warmongers inside & outside the [French] Cabinet & and against a press that has been corrupted by Soviet money to an extent unparalleled even before the war ... They have a very uncomfortable sense of being thwarted by intreaguers [*sic*] not only in Paris (where they expect it) but equally in London.

Hankey thought that Vansittart was at the centre of this anti-Phipps intrigue, using his influence with *The Daily Telegraph* 'to give a sinister twist' to its news reporting of events in France during the Munich crisis and leaking to the French left-wing press details of Bonnet's panicky behaviour during September. Hankey was convinced that Vansittart was trying to discredit Bonnet and at the same destroy Phipps's influence. As an example of this Hankey quoted to Horace Wilson extracts from Cadogan's letter to Phipps protesting about the ambassador's one-sided reporting of French political opinions in September, which, Hankey believed, was inspired by Vansittart, 'peevishly questioning Phipps's reports of wide-spread anti-war feeling in France etc.'[11] Early in 1939 Phipps complained repeatedly, but without much success, to Cadogan, Halifax and Horace Wilson about leaks to the press of official information derogatory to Phipps, which he was convinced emanated from Vansittart or from the Foreign Office News Department. Cadogan replied to one such accusation that he could find no evidence that the information leaked came from London: 'Are you sure it didn't occur at your end? What Bonnet says isn't always evidence!'[12]

Indeed the Foreign Office regarded Phipps and Bonnet as being too closely identified in their defeatist attitudes to enable Phipps to act as a reliable interpreter of the opinions of the wider French political community. Duff Cooper, who had resigned from the government in disgust at the Munich settlement and was now a backbench MP, wrote to Phipps in December: 'if M. Bonnet is our strongest rampart against Hitler then indeed I feel inclined to despair.'[13]

When, in early December, Phipps wrote to Halifax that a friend of Caillaux had told him that the French 'war party', paid for by Russia with Mandel as its 'most dangerous leader', was 'again raising its head', Phipps once more attracted much opprobrium in the Central Department for his one-sided and tendentious reporting. Frank Roberts exclaimed that at least Mandel was 'a patriot', a 'doubtful' description if applied to Caillaux:

> M. Mandel has a great reputation for energy and is one of the most active and influential members of the French Cabinet. He represents the group that is opposed to M. Bonnet's foreign policy and has always favoured a more vigorous policy of opposition to German and Italian pretensions.

Sargent added:

> ... the so-called 'war party' happens also to be the Anglophile party – a fact which Sir E. Phipps seems to forget. And ... the fact that they are denounced by Caillaux and his followers is, I should have thought, from the English point of view, a strong recommendation in their favour – French separatism surely cannot be a British interest.

Vansittart wrote to Halifax to remind the foreign secretary that this latest attack on the so-called French war party parallelled Phipps's infamous '"all that is best in France"' telegram during the Munich crisis.[14]

After Munich the Foreign Office tried to encourage and support French Anglophiles against those French politicians who hankered after a separate agreement with Germany. Its officials were initially concerned that there might be recriminations between 'certain quarters in France and in this country', with the French government excusing its betrayal of Czechoslovakia because of the 'defeatist attitude' of British public opinion. The Foreign Office possessed enough evidence

> to make the position of certain members of the French Government extremely unpleasant. Any washing of dirty Anglo-French linen would of course be very gratifying to the German Government and might do us a great deal of harm in the United States of America.[15]

Such recriminations would, of course, threaten the very existence of the already weakened Anglo-French entente. However, the enthusiasm with which Daladier was greeted by the French crowd when he returned from Munich put an end to fears of this kind. Phipps wrote to tell Chamberlain about this ecstatic reception, and his effusion provided ample evidence of Phipps's pro-Chamberlain and defeatist leanings:

> This [Daladier's reception] shows how surrounded he [Daladier] has been of late by the war-party – the mad and criminal war party – who, having missed every preventive train since Hitler's accession to power that might have led to the terminus of not too expensive victory, wished to embark on a train at this late hour that could have only led to utter destruction and chaos.

> The evil forces working for war combined with foolish and misguided, although patriotic, forces and I have had the distinct impression lately that these forces, both here and in England, were working their hardest to undermine your efforts.
>
> The true France knows what you have done and will give you the greatest welcome ever accorded to a foreign statesman if and when you come to Paris.[16]

The Foreign Office's determination not to strain France's loyalty to the entente any further after Munich was reflected in its rejection, early in October, of an Air Ministry suggestion that the impending visit of a British air mission to France be cancelled in order not to offend Germany so soon after the signature of the Munich agreement. William Ivo Mallet, a first secretary in the Central Department, thought that cancellation

> would have a bad effect on the French ... [and] would be an indication of a belief that now everything is going to be easy and that we can sit back again and enjoy our leisure. Any such belief would be disastrous.

Cadogan, Halifax and even Chamberlain agreed with Mallet. The air mission arrived in Paris on 10 October.[17] However the air staff still wanted to discourage '*periodical* liaison of a routine nature' between French and British air officers, since Britain might be drawn thereby into 'more definite commitments'.[18]

Later in the year the Foreign Office began actively to encourage British ministers to visit Paris 'in view of the importance of neglecting no occasion for keeping the French sweet' – previously, as has been shown, visits of this nature had been discouraged, or at least carefully supervised, by Phipps to ensure (not always successfully) that nothing should be said by British visitors to suggest that the British government was committed to France.[19]

After Munich there was some disposition on the part of Central Department officials to accept that France, having lost Czechoslovakia, should relax, if not sunder, its ties with Poland, the little entente and the Soviet Union, in order to avoid the possibility of France becoming involved in a war with Germany for the sake of these remaining commitments, a war in which Britain might well become embroiled. France's eastern alliances had, of course, long been regarded by British isolationists and imperialists like Lothian as a potential danger to European peace and as a provocation to Germany. When, on 12 October, Bonnet told Phipps that he wanted to revise these alliances to deprive them of automatic mutual commitments to go to war, Sargent, who had opposed the Franco-Soviet pact when it was signed in 1935, commented:

> it is curious that it should have taken 2 and a half years for a *realistic* and *logical* people like the French to appreciate such an obvious fact. If they had accepted it sooner and acted on it frankly and courageously instead of trying to evade the issue and shelter behind us neither they nor Czechoslovakia would have been in the false and eventually untenable position which has now ended in the destruction of Czechoslovakia.
>
> The coming change in France's position and policy in Europe is bound to affect this country also. Till now we have always claimed and exercised the right to intervene actively in the problems of Europe both domestic and international whenever we felt it desirable to do so. For this purpose we have collaborated with the French – or to put it crudely we have used the French army and the French system of alliances as one of the instruments with which to exert our influence on the continent. It is sometimes said that this policy of cooperation with France has meant in practice that we have been tied to French 'apron strings'. If looked at another way it may with equal truth be said that we have used France as a shield, behind which we have maintained ourselves in Europe since our disarmament.

He concluded that if France decided to opt for a passive role in Europe, Britain would have to adapt her policy accordingly. As a result, Britain would no longer be morally bound to support France against Germany or Italy, which meant that a British expeditionary force would no longer be needed on the continent.

Cadogan minuted that, as a result of Munich, Britain and France would have to remain on the defensive for a number of years, and 'during that time we shall not be able (we may never again be able) to direct affairs in Central & Eastern Europe as we attempted to do in the "Covenant" years.' Vansittart firmly challenged these assumptions, which were probably the product of the disillusionment of Central Department officials with the passive French response to the crisis over Czechoslovakia. (What had struck Sargent in October had been 'the absence of any self-reproach [in France] for the abandonment of France's ally or pity for the refugees created by the secession to Germany of the Sudetenland territories.') Vansittart thought that 'Circumstances will probably decide differently for us, and we must be prepared for them. If we and the French are really to fall apart into some form of isolation, we shall not even be second-class powers.'[20]

On 22 October Sargent returned to the charge, urging that Britain advise the French to abandon their treaty with the Soviet Union since, 'if they did get involved in a war with Germany in defence of Russia they clearly could not count upon the collaboration of Great Britain as they were able to do in the case of Czechoslovakia.' Cadogan, however, rejected this suggestion on the grounds that the French 'are already aware of the implications of our commitments, such as they are', and that the repudiation of the Franco-Soviet alliance, by reducing French security even further, 'would put a greater burden on us, or at least render it less unlikely that we shall have to implement our guarantee to France.' Halifax preferred 'to see whether Franco-German relations develop formally – before taking any action ourselves'.[21]

Halifax was as pessimistic as Sargent about the future direction of French foreign policy. When, in October, following a warning by Oliver Harvey that one of the dangers of Munich was that pro-German elements in France might be encouraged to reach agreement with Germany 'behind our backs and at our expense', Halifax thought it

> inevitable that recent events and German strength will affect French policy in the sense of making it more restricted and more defensive on narrower lines. But if the ultimate choice for France is between that and an attempt, probably not very successful, and potentially very dangerous, to obstruct German expansion in Central Europe, the French may think the first is the wiser.[22]

The foreign secretary outlined his policy towards France and Europe in a letter to Phipps on 1 November:

> The greatest lesson of the crisis has been the unwisdom of basing a foreign policy on insufficient armed strength ... It is one thing to allow German expansion in Central Europe, which to my mind is a natural and normal thing, but we must be able to resist German expansion in Western Europe or else our whole position is undermined.

He was worried that France 'may in certain political circumstances turn so defeatist as to give up the struggle of maintaining adequate defences even for the safety of metropolitan France'. If this occurred, 'we might have to face alone the weight of German military power in the West.' It was therefore essential that Britain exploited every opportunity to encourage the French to rearm as soon as possible. He thought that, since Poland was falling more and more into the German orbit, he could not advise France to denounce the Franco-Soviet Pact 'as the future is too uncertain!'[23]

In any case Foreign Office disillusionment with the pacts was a passing phenomenon – when Bonnet repeated his desire to 'slacken' both the Polish and Soviet pacts in a conversation with Phipps on 31 December, Roger Makins, a second secretary in the Central Department, minuted, 'There is undoubtedly a strong feeling in Paris in favour of cutting adrift from Eastern Europe – a policy not less short-sighted than other French policies in recent years.'[24] But Conservatives like Leopold Amery, who had turned against appeasement after Munich, continued to support the abandonment of France's eastern pacts. He thought that Britain and France should in future concentrate on the security of Western Europe, since, while Germany's control of the resources of Eastern Europe would make Germany 'undoubtedly ... much stronger materially ... psychologically and strategically, France and ourselves will now be in a much simpler defensive position.'[25]

French threats to abandon its eastern pacts, frequent reports in the French press and parliament about French unreadiness for war, and rumours of a possible Franco-German deal at Britain's expense, alarmed British officials, who regarded them as serious manifestations of increasing defeatism and demoralisation in France. On 2 November, Jacques Kayser, a former vice-president of the radical Socialist Party, and described by Phipps as 'un homme de confiance' of Daladier, warned a member of Phipps's staff that if Germany offered France a non-aggression pact, defeatist French ministers like Bonnet, Camille Chautemps, the deputy prime minister, Charles Pomaret, the minister of labour, and Paul Marchandeau, who had succeeded Paul Reynaud as minister of justice on 1 November after the latter's transfer to the Finance Ministry, would recommend acceptance.[26] All this prompted Halifax to write to Phipps in November asking him to assess the reliability and steadfastness of France in the face of future German aggression. In his reply Phipps exuded much more confidence in French staying power than he had done in his private correspondence with Chamberlain in September. He was able to assure Halifax:

> I do not see any prospect of France turning so defeatist as to abandon the necessary defences for the safety of metropolitan France. I am convinced, moreover, that the French will fight like tigers to maintain their independence.[27]

In his annual report for 1938, Phipps continued in this optimistic vein: 'France has shown that she retains her hard core of patriotism and common sense ... There is every reason to believe that the country, if called upon to do so, would respond to a major emergency with as great reserves of strength and determination as she has in the past.'[28]

However, there had been little but gloom in a despatch Phipps had sent to the Foreign Office in November about France's economic situation in 1938. A wave of strikes had followed the government's efforts to extend the 40-hour week decreed by the Popular Front in 1936. Inflation was increasing while output was declining in all sectors of the economy. French industrial production was now the lowest of all the great powers. The report concluded that 'France is living upon her capital; she is exhausting her reserves; her building trade is so reduced that at the present rate four centuries would be required to replace existing dwellings.'[29]

In an effort to revive French confidence in the entente, Chamberlain and Halifax invited themselves to Paris between 23 and 25 November 1938.[30] Halifax had earlier pointed to the necessity, 'without giving offence', of persuading the French to put their national defences in order,[31] while Chamberlain had also referred to this as one of the main purposes of the visit. He wanted to

> give [the] French people an opportunity of pouring out gratitude and affection – to strengthen Daladier and encourage him to do something at last to put his country's defences in order and to pull his people into greater unity – to show France and Europe too that if we were more anxious to make friends with Germany & Italy we were not on that account going to forget our old allies.[32]

Corbin warned Strang that the French agenda for the Paris talks contained no reference to future entente policy towards Germany and pointed out that

> The German Government had of late adopted an attitude of hostility towards Great Britain and an attitude of friendship towards France, and their attitude was clear. They desired to separate Great Britain and France and he was afraid that M. Daladier and M. Bonnet, who were both weak men, might be tempted further along the path of *rapprochement* with Germany than was desirable. It would, M. Corbin thought, be disastrous if, in the present situation of the world, France should choose this moment to come to an understanding with Germany. The world would not understand what France was coming to.[33]

Halifax decided to raise it under 'the General Situation after Munich' on the agenda for the talks.[34]

The visit of the British ministers to Paris seemed to be even more necessary after Colonel William Fraser, who had replaced Beaumont-Nesbitt as British military attaché in Paris in August 1938, relayed to Phipps a warning he had been given by the French deputy chief of staff,

General Henri Dentz, on 18 October, that German propaganda directed at France was inciting the French people to believe that Britain would leave French soldiers to do all the fighting in the event of a war with Germany. Dentz said that this kind of propaganda could only strengthen the French 'peace at any price' party in France.[35] This report and other French grievances about the paucity of British military assistance to France in a future war with Germany were all part of an orchestrated campaign in French government, press and army circles, which gathered momentum in the months ahead, to persuade Britain to increase the size of the field force and to introduce conscription as a means of restoring French morale after the loss of the Czechoslovak army. For example, Gamelin's staff officer, Colonel Jean Petibon, also told Fraser that the French chief of staff wanted to see a large British expeditionary force in France as soon as possible after the beginning of war, since Gamelin though that it was unlikely that the French army could, without British help, hold the Germans for the nine months which it would at present take Britain to raise and train its armies.[36]

Frank Roberts agreed that only some 'spectacular decision involving national service will convince the world that we really mean business' and weaken 'those forces in France making for a composition with Germany at our expense'. Roger Makins also thought that such a measure 'would be an outward and visible sign of an inward determination & a resolute spirit would be of the greatest possible advantage to our foreign policy'. Sargent agreed –' spectacular measures of rearmament' would have 'a most important psychological effect'. In their absence 'it will strengthen and crystallise the already existing doubts and suspicions ... as to our intentions and capacities to deal with the new world situation in which we find ourselves.' It was left to Cadogan to point out the 'difficulties there may be in the way of '"spectacular measures of rearmament"' in the existing financial and political climate in Britain. He believed that Britain had already 'done something "spectacular" in Naval matters, and what we are doing in the air, if not "spectacular," is a good deal better than what France will be capable of for some time to come.'[37]

Many high-ranking British army officers, of course, supported the campaign for a larger British land commitment to the continent. General Sir W.H. Bartholomew, a former director of military operations, and now General Commanding, Northern Command, wrote to Hankey in December:

> We cannot choose the way we will go to war and I feel [we] must be prepared to intervene in France & Belgium and we cant [*sic*] do that without some army. I do not ask for a large one but larger than

> we have. Something should be done to kill the idea that we can take as little of the war as we like relying only on a navy & air force & Home Defence, all due to the myth created by Liddell Hart, ex-soldiers & others.[38]

In fact, following the change in the strategic balance in Germany's favour as a result of the Munich settlement, Liddell Hart no longer opposed the despatch of an expeditionary force to France. The loss of the Czechoslovakian army had left France to face both Germany and Italy alone, and now Liddell Hart believed that Britain would have to send an army to help defend France.[39] Nevertheless Liddell Hart still maintained that the size of a British expeditionary force should be limited, telling Anthony Eden on 30 January 1939 that, while a British 'land reinforcement' of France had become 'a necessity', it could not be on the scale of Britain's efforts in 1914–18. By the summer of 1939 Liddell Hart had, however, reverted to his pre-Munich opposition to the despatch of the expeditionary force to the Continent.[40]

In the aftermath of Munich, Lothian also abandoned his isolationist and pro-German sympathies, having 'been driven by hard facts to believe it is imperative to adopt universal compulsory service to preserve our liberties'. He was now convinced that the fascist powers were seeking world predominance, and to counter their ambitions, Britain must address its military weakness since it might be called upon at any time to 'send absolutely indispensable reinforcements to the Maginot Line'.[41] Pownall agreed. He hoped to 'use the Military attaché in Paris to press the French to demand that Chamberlain and Halifax agree to despatch the BEF to France when they visited Paris', as 'now that France's political system has broken down ... she is left without effective allies in Eastern Europe.'[42] Pownall accordingly told Fraser 'to have a nice chat with Petibon and make hints, in the form of questions, that such questions might be raised during the discussions'. Hence Pownall was upset to hear Chamberlain declare, before he left for France, that he would be firm with the French and 'give them no more than we had promised'. Pownall noted that 'Chamberlain's colleagues agreed ... What a lot they are!'

Pownall was even more disgusted when he heard that Chamberlain had told Hore-Belisha that 'as our Army was so small was it worth worrying whether it was ready or not?'[43] On 21 November the chiefs of staff confirmed that only two infantry divisions and the advanced air striking force would be available for despatch to France by April 1939. Even then the two divisions would be equipped with obsolete infantry equipment, tanks and artillery.[44]

In a brief for the two ministers before the Paris talks, Sargent pointed out that the whole system of French guarantees in the East and West had suffered 'a disconcerting blow' with the loss of Czechoslovakia and he feared that even the vague French guarantee to Britain was not 'necessarily exempt' from the virtual collapse of the French security system. Since Britain's defence plans were based on the Delbos guarantee of 4 December 1936, it was vital that France reaffirm this guarantee even 'in the changed situation' after Munich. He alluded to 'certain disquieting factors' in France, which might undermine the Delbos guarantee – 'the almost universal pacifist sentiment' which 'in its extreme form refuses to contemplate military action except in defence of an actual invasion of French soil', and which might result in French neutrality in the event of a German attack on Britain alone. Furthermore there was

> the lack of a resolute government in the present state of French politics … For the present we have to deal with a French Prime Minister incapable of taking a decision, and with a Foreign Minister who is completely untrustworthy, and even when the present office-holders go there is no reason to suppose their successors will be any different.

Under these circumstances, Britain should prepare for the possibility that in another crisis France might offer Britain only benevolent neutrality, justifying this on the grounds that France could not launch an offensive against Germany with Italy and Spain on its flanks, that the French Air Force could not defend France from a German aerial offensive, and that French morale would not stand up to the strain of such a war. Cadogan and Halifax noted these 'gloomy possibilities which we cannot afford entirely to ignore', and accordingly placed the renewal of the Delbos guarantee and the need to give effect to it in staff conversations firmly on the Paris agenda.[45]

The talks took place on 24 November 1938. The British side were well prepared, even to the extent of taking with them a copy of a 15-page memorandum, leaked to a British journalist by Roland de Margerie, the counsellor at the French embassy, and which the embassy had prepared for Daladier's use at the meeting. This put defence and the strengthening of the British army as the principal French subjects for discussion.[46]

Chamberlain and Halifax were accompanied by Cadogan and Strang, with Phipps and Valentine Lawford from the British embassy, and Daladier and Bonnet by Corbin and Léger and other Quai d'Orsay officials. After Daladier had described the terms of the relatively anodyne Franco-German agreement, which was to be signed by Bonnet and Ribbentrop in Paris on 6 December, he plunged into his main concern –

the need for 'intensive collaboration between France and Great Britain with regard to defensive measures'. He confirmed that France would come to Britain's assistance if Germany attacked Britain and not France (Bonnet reaffirmed the Delbos guarantee in a statement to the French Chamber on 14 December). The French prime minister then demanded more British land support for France in view of France's geographical vulnerability in the face of a possible three-pronged Axis attack and its weaker population base. Chamberlain responded that London's vulnerability to German air attack meant that she had to give priority to anti-aircraft defences over the expansion of her land forces. It was no good, the prime minister said, raising more troops if they could not be properly equipped. Britain could send only two regular divisions to France.

The visit did nothing to reassure the French that Britain was prepared to do anything more to strengthen its army than it had before Munich, although towards the end of the meeting Chamberlain, probably pressed by Halifax, made a vague promise to Daladier about the holding of further Anglo-French staff talks.[47]

The prime minister said nothing to the French about his forthcoming visit to Rome in January 'for fear of inevitable leakage', and was somewhat embarrassed when it was revealed in the *Daily Mail* and the *Daily Express*. However, Chamberlain thought that 'there is such genuine confidence between us that I imagine the French will have no fears that their interests will be in any way prejudiced.' In fact, Daladier and Bonnet were concerned about the British visit to Rome, suspecting that the Mussolini would take the opportunity to divide Britain from France.[48]

By this time Halifax, especially after what he had seen of French demoralisation during his visit to Paris – and after further warnings by Colonel Fraser and Phipps that 'there is always latent in France the idea that Great Britain is willing to fight her battles in Europe with French soldiers'[49] – was thoroughly converted to the view that if Britain did not reassure the French by the promise of more assistance on land, France might abandon the entente and make the best terms with Germany it could get. Gort and Hore-Belisha (the latter having changed his mind and now supported a more effective continental commitment) were also pressing for more expenditure on the army on the grounds that 'present arrangements will not permit the Army to meet satisfactorily or safely the responsibilities it may be called upon to discharge.'[50]

On 2 December, Gort wrote, in a memorandum to the cabinet, that limited liability was no longer an acceptable option for Britain, especially as the French were now demanding British assistance on land. He feared that without such a promise France might not go to the assistance of

Belgium if Germany attacked that country. As a result the Germans might be able to outflank the Maginot line through the Low Countries and seize northern France and the Channel ports. Britain's very existence would then be directly threatened. Nor did Gort believe that the Maginot line could be held indefinitely against a German assault, although much depended on the 'numbers, morale and efficiency of its defenders'. He reassured cabinet ministers that the general staff were not contemplating the creation of a British army 'on the Continental scale', but wanted the formation of 'an efficient and well-equipped' expeditionary force which 'may again play a decisive part in stabilizing the situation and so gaining time to develop the strength of our Empire. We can win a long war.'[51]

On 15 December 1938, at a meeting of the committee of imperial defence, Hore-Belisha pointed out that 'every member of the Committee could not but recognise that the present situation of the Army was most serious, and he hoped they would agree that steps should be taken to put matters right.' The first and second contingents of the expeditionary force were deficient in men and equipment, while the territorial army had hardly any equipment at all. At this meeting Halifax again voiced his fear that

> although he was the last to want to see a large British army involved in the Continent, he was bound to point out that a time might come when the French would cease to be enthusiastic about their relations with Great Britain if they were left with the impression that it was they who must bear the brunt of the fighting and slaughter on land.

Hoare countered that 'whatever the French might think, their interests were so bound up with ours that they could not afford to stand aloof from us.' Halifax rejected this argument, repeating his warning that France might reach agreement with Germany to stand aside if it received no satisfaction for its request for more land assistance from Britain. The committee decided to refer the future of the field force for further consideration by the chiefs of staff.[52]

The indefatigable Vansittart was also busy lobbying Halifax and the prime minister about the expeditionary force, repeating the by now familiar arguments that France would be heavily outnumbered by Germany and Italy, and that, even with the Maginot line, which 'no professional soldier' believed was 'eternally impregnable', France could not maintain its frontiers 'for long against these odds'. He supported French complaints about the inadequacy of the field force, and the lack of British naval support in the western Mediterranean if the main British fleet went to Singapore. He considered that it would be easier for France than for

Britain 'to make her terms with Berlin ... for in such matters as the recent Jewish, and the impending ecclesiastical, persecutions there will always be a louder and more vehement protest from the sentimental English than from the more cynical French.' He pointed out 'that there are just as many Anglophobes in France as there are Francophobes in England. Indeed perhaps there are more', and that only 'a small but energetic and influential minority' of Frenchmen had tried to promote friendly Anglo-French relations. As a result, the 'Germans are going to find a fruitful terrain for agitation' against Britain in France.[53]

In January, Vansittart again appealed to Halifax to tell the cabinet

> that Anglo-French relations will be in severe danger and [the] capacity of French resistance will be rapidly exhausted unless we greatly increase our military contribution ... This is a fantastic and impossible situation. It may not be possible to accelerate the date at which our infinitesimal army will be properly armed because, owing to the lack of foresight, capacity has not been created in time, *but what we can do is to see to it here that our larger military contribution which would have to be in the nature let us say [of] at least 20 divisions, should not be put in the same position, and that the capacity for equipment, including guns and tanks, should be authorised and initiated at the beginning of February 1939.* I have no doubt this proposal will encounter all the usual technical objections, but when it is a case of saving one's skin, where there's a will there's a way.[54]

The chiefs of staff held two long meetings on 21 December 1938 and 18 January 1939 to consider whether to recommend the re-equipment of the expeditionary force so that it would be ready for combat on the continent immediately war broke out. Backhouse strongly supported Gort's request for the money to be made available to achieve this, since France might withdraw from the unequal struggle with Germany if British troops were not sent to the continent. Gort believed that the definite commitment of the expeditionary force would enable the French to release ten French divisions to defend Belgium. Newall objected – even four British divisions sent to the continent would lead eventually to an unlimited commitment and this British public opinion would not accept. He insisted that Britain could not afford to maintain a strong Royal Navy and Royal Air Force and, at the same time, spend more money on the army. 'If we tried to be strong everywhere we should be strong nowhere.' Eventually, after a further argument with his colleagues, he softened his stance slightly by agreeing that Britain would have to send some ground forces to France, but insisted that two infantry divisions and two mobile divisions of the expeditionary force, fully equipped for war, should be the maximum British contribution. Furthermore the French should be warned in advance that even this might not be sent to the continent. Backhouse insisted that such a tiny contribution would not be sufficient to prevent the French from abandoning the struggle. 'It was not', he said, 'in our best interests that France should cease to be a Great Power' since Germany would then dominate the continent. Gort also rejected the idea that Britain could fight a war on the basis of such a limited commitment. The next war would, like the last, be a fight to the finish, while the moral effect on the French of a British promise that they would be given the utmost British support on land would be very great. With Newall isolated, the chiefs, at their January meeting, finally recommended the provision of equipment 'to enable the Army to carry out its allotted role'.[55]

Seeking to reassure Italy, before his visit with the foreign secretary to Rome, that Britain had no hostile intentions towards that country, Chamberlain, on 12 December, announced to the House of Commons that Britain had no specific treaty obligation to France to send military assistance if France was attacked by Italy alone. Phipps reported that this statement had been greeted with a 'chill of disappointment' in the French press.[56] On the 20th, Bonnet assured the Chamber of Deputies that if either Britain or France were subject to unprovoked aggression, the other would come to its assistance, implying that, contrary to Chamberlain's recent assertion, Britain would go to France's assistance if it was attacked by Italy alone, and vice versa.

Halifax thought that this contradiction should be raised with the French government. While aggression by Germany on either France or Britain was covered by the existing guarantee, 'such action by Italy (Germany standing out) should be in a different category – it might well be, I imagine, that in such an event both France & we should prefer the other to stand aside & not bring Germany in? Improbable but possible.' Halifax asked Vansittart for his opinion, but the latter discouraged any approach to the French on the subject because 'unless it were done with the utmost skill & on a good wicket, it would undermine confidence & play the German game of wedge-driving against Public Enemy No 1 (us).' Vansittart was certain that if Italy attacked France, Britain would be automatically involved, and in any case thought it 'improbable' that the French would wish Britain to stay out. Britain should not 'niggle in any way, when the French will say (& many will feel) that they have just made a warm and "generous" statement that we ourselves solicited.'

Halifax was not entirely convinced, however, and replied:

> I agree ... that if Italy attacks France, we should make it plain to France that we should immediately be in, if Germany joined Italy. If she didn't, I imagine the French would sooner we stopped out than, by joining in, bring in Germany. But as I said before, this contingency is no doubt reciprocal. Did I not see a telegram a day or so ago saying that the French were well satisfied they could manage Italy alone as no doubt they can!

Nevertheless Halifax decided to defer discussion of such 'dangerous, delicate and academic (probably)' matters until after the ministerial visit to Rome on 11 and 12 January 1939.[57]

The French need not have worried about Chamberlain's visit to Italy, which was devoid of any positive results. Mussoloni was now too closely tied to Germany to consider changing course, while on the way to Rome Chamberlain and Halifax met Daladier and Bonnet briefly in Paris, where the former categorically rejected any suggestion of French concessions to Mussolini to achieve a *rapprochement*.[58]

In January and February 1939, rumours began to circulate in London and Paris that Germany was planning either to attack Holland or launch a pre-emptive air strike on London. These probably came from anti-Nazi sources in Germany, although Pownall suspected that the French were behind the rumour about a German invasion of Holland 'to put a bit of ginger into us. More power to them!'[59] This was a propitious moment for the French to redouble their pressure to secure a larger continental commitment from Britain. This included lobbying Colonel W.S. Pilcher and Kenneth de Courcy, newspaper proprietor and secretary of the imperial defence league, when they visited Paris in January. The two men reported their alarming impressions of French morale, and how this could be improved, to the secretary of the committee of imperial defence on their return to London:

> In our opinion we believe that the life and death of France as a first-class power depends on our decision in respect of the Army. It is impossible to over-estimate the place this question takes in the thought of most French politicians to-day ... There is a fundamental anxiety that things are much more serious than they are prepared to admit and a great many highly patriotic French men are playing with the idea that to take a second place is better than to fight a war if it means that the French Army will have to sacrifice 1,000,000 men while Great Britain contents herself with engaging her sea and air forces and the United States with the application of moral indignation and economic sanctions ... There is a streak of defeatism in France which might prove highly dangerous.

Cadogan commented on this report that, however justified the French were in their demands, Britain's war industries were not capable of producing enough military material to equip a large conscripted army, whereupon Vansittart demanded the creation of 'industrial capacity for 15–20 divisions *before it is too late. There is not a day to lose.*' R.A. Butler commented, with typical insouciance, that 'Mr de C[ourcy]. would be much flattered by the formal battery of minuting his sloop attracts.'[60]

During a visit by Hore-Belisha to the Maginot line in early January, Gamelin and General Pierre Héring, the military governor of Strasbourg, also impressed on the war minister that without the assistance of British ground forces, the French army would not be able to hold out for long against a determined German attack on France.[61] Hore-Belisha's report on this visit, and a stream of similar warnings by the British military attaché in Paris, prompted Strang to ask the chiefs of staff for their views as to whether France could defend itself successfully against either a direct German attack across her border or through the Netherlands and Belgium, on the assumption that no extra British land assistance than that already planned would be available. What, he asked, would be the position if Italy joined Germany against France?

The chiefs of staff replied on 1 February that they doubted a German offensive directly across France's border would be decisive, since both sides were evenly matched with about 60 divisions each. However, France's weakness in the air would enable Germany to stop or delay movement of French reserves to threatened sectors and to bomb French population and industrial centres. The chiefs did not believe that the poorly trained and ill-equipped Dutch forces would be able to resist a German offensive for long, and, although the Belgian army was in slightly better condition, with 18 infantry divisions and three mobile divisions with modern equipment, high morale and strong fortifications, it possessed no modern tank units and little heavy artillery. It would probably be able to hold up a German advance for about 14 days. France would be less able to withstand a German attack across the Franco-Belgian frontier since its defences there were weak. Italy could field 18 divisions against France, but the French frontier with Italy was well fortified. However, there was the danger that Germany and Italy might outflank French defences by attacking France through Switzerland.[62]

Thus the weight of professional military opinion believed that unless Britain increased the number of divisions to send to France in the early days of a war France would not be able to hold out for very long. Strang's response was to restate the obvious fact that 'The defence of the West is vital to us, and if France is overwhelmed we have no chance of maintaining our present position in the world', and Halifax circulated the chiefs of staff's report to the cabinet. Vansittart now made two demands, neither of which was likely to appeal to Chamberlain or Simon:

> (A) That we should accelerate our pace in men and materials regardless, for the next year or two, of the cost. (The Treasury are always preoccupied with the problem of *how* we are to live five years hence, and not whether we shall be alive one year hence).
> (B) That the French will not make the timorous muck of their Eastern connections that they did in 1938; but should on the contrary find out now, and precisely, what if anything they could hope from Russia and/or Poland on the Day ... I would strongly urge both *at once* ... We may be in need soon and on this lay out – there is nothing new or unexpected in it – the chances for us are very black indeed.[63]

The ministers who attended the cabinet foreign policy committee on 23 January were at least united in agreeing that Britain would be forced to intervene if Germany invaded Holland and Switzerland, with Kingsley Wood and Hore-Belisha insisting that it was 'essential to get into as close an intimate relationship as possible with the only country which was in a position to render us assistance at the present time.' The chiefs of staff also attended this meeting. Newall explained that the chiefs of staff's report in November had been written in a different atmosphere from that which now prevailed, and the chiefs wanted comprehensive staff talks with the French to work out the entente's plans for war in all likely theatres.[64] The cabinet on 8 February concluded that it was essential that the French agree to send military support to the Low Countries in the event of British intervention on the side of Holland, and this would necessitate regular and wide-ranging staff conversations with France and Belgium.[65]

The Foreign Office and the chiefs of staff were now supported by influential politicians in campaigning for an expansion in the size of the British army. Sir Horace Wilson learned that Hore-Belisha 'personally believes that, on a long view, this country will have to modify its military tradition and embark upon the maintenance of a large army available to fight on the Continent.' Indeed, Hore-Belisha's newfound zeal for a larger army prompted Simon to protest to him in February: 'I *really* think you might drop the method of representing that all your troubles are due to "the opposition of the Chancellor." It is so *personal*. It is so *unfair*. No other Minister ever does it.'[66]

Hankey told Hore-Belisha that he too had come round 'more and more to the view that we ought to have a bigger army'.[67] The former military attaché to Paris, Colonel Beaumont-Nesbitt, now deputy director of military operations and intelligence at the War Office, had heard that 'a considerable body of French opinion ... begins to regard the English connection as a liability and not an asset',[68] and Ivone Kirkpatrick, a first secretary in the Central Department, took up this theme in a minute on 4 February:

> We are faced with the serious danger that unless we can hold out the hope of assisting France on land, the French Government will refuse to show the firm front which is essential at the present moment ...[69]

Roger Backhouse was concerned that 'we are playing with fire to drift on in the way we are doing now. I do feel really anxious about our position which in many ways is worse than it was in 1914.'

Vansittart was, of course, in full agreement with those who criticised the government's inadequate response to the French pleas for a greater British military effort, and complained to Halifax in early February that the cabinet had failed

> to grasp the condition of French thought at this moment. That is not intended as a reproach, because it would be unnatural if men who have occupied all their lives with their own politics and their own countrymen were able easily to enter into another nation's mind, shirt and shoes. But the inevitable fact is that this has got to be done ... In the long run the French will not hold their position and we will not be able to hold the French with a contribution of less than 15 divisions. But here we find the Cabinet boggling at the possible provision of 8. Let us at least have the eight or one over the eight.

Halifax minuted that he would 'certainly press the case'.[70]

The chiefs of staff now recommended that all four divisions of the regular expeditionary force should be provided with equipment and reserves for continental warfare and that the mobile division should be split into two smaller divisions. They proposed that the embarkation dates for the expeditionary force should be brought forward, but they made no definite proposals about the territorial army, beyond pointing out that the inadequacy of even four divisions as a support to the French army.

The chiefs' recommendations were seized on by Hore-Belisha, Halifax, Oliver Stanley and Walter Elliot to demand, at the 8 February cabinet meeting, the end of the restrictions which had been placed on industrial production for the army. The prime minister opposed this on the grounds that it would impose too heavy a burden on the country's finances. He wanted the French to be reminded of the gigantic efforts Britain was making to expand its naval and air forces. Given Chamberlain's opposition, no decision was reached at this meeting, and the issue was referred for further consideration to a ministerial committee consisting of Chamberlain, Hore-Belisha, Simon, Chatfield (who had replaced Inskip as minister for coordination of defence in January) and W.S. Morrison, Chatfield's deputy in the House of Commons.

At this meeting, held on 10 February at 10 Downing Street, Chatfield 'raised the question whether it would be better to use our financial strength now to an even greater extent than hitherto or whether it would be better that we should wait and see and use it after the war started.' Chamberlain retorted that he had argued 'from the beginning ... that it was impossible for us to find either the money or the man-power to embark in land operations on the same scale as in the last war. He still adhered to that view.' The French should be told that Britain would prepare an army of a certain size whose deployment would be determined if and when war came. They would not then base their plans on false expectations of British support. Simon added that 'it would, of course, be in the interest of the French Government to press us to undertake to send as many divisions to France as early as possible. We shall have to resist this pressure.' The committee recommended that the four regular infantry divisions and the two mobile divisions should be equipped for war, but the chiefs of staff's recommendation that the second contingent of two divisions should be ready to embark in 40 days after the outbreak of war was extended to 60 days, in order to save £1.4 million. Four territorial army divisions should be readied for despatch to the continent within six months of the outbreak of war.[71]

Halifax was not satisfied that even this expanded military contribution would be enough to restore French morale, and, in a note to Chamberlain on 17 February, he argued that 'In view of the vital interest of this country in the defence of the West, and of the fact that if France is overborne we should have no prospect of maintaining our present position in the world', Britain would have to assist the French on land on a larger scale and within a shorter time than now contemplated, otherwise the French, faced with the prospect that they would have 'to make a disproportionate sacrifice in blood ... may slowly swing over to a policy of complete surrender'.[72] Halifax's arguments notwithstanding, the cabinet, on 22 February, approved the ministerial committee's recommendations after Simon stated that these increases in army strength were as much as could be achieved given the pressures on British finances.[73]

Meanwhile arrangements for the holding of comprehensive staff conversations with France began after the cabinet had approved them on 8

February. General Hastings Ismay, the secretary to the committee of imperial defence, told Newall, 'it seems pretty certain that the Cabinet expects detailed joint plans, which go just as far, and possibly further than the pre-1914 plans, to be worked out; and to risk the element of commitment this would involve.'[74] However, it was not long before Vansittart was complaining to Halifax about 'the leisureliness' with which the chiefs of staff were dealing with the conversations: 'It seems clear that the machinery here contemplated will involve the maximum delay and the accumulation of papers. We surely do not want any more written "European appreciations". We have been snowed under with papers from the CID for years.' Halifax agreed that 'the layout sounds leisurely – but I think the Cs of S are alive to the urgency & will not allow themselves to be suffocated by intellectual debris!'[75] He spoke to Chatfield, who assured him that the chiefs would waste no time in dealing with the talks.[76] In fact, it was the French who were responsible for delaying the talks by their slowness in replying to the British *aide-mémoire* on the subject.[77]

Phipps gave the *aide-mémoire*, which had been drawn up by the joint planning staff, detailing the proposed contents of the talks, to Léger on 25 February 1939. The British remained sensitive about press leaks, since, as the chiefs of staff put it earlier in the month, 'the French might seize the opportunity to make major political capital out of important Staff meetings', and leaks to the press might provoke Hitler into precipitate military action on the pretext that Britain and France were preparing to go to war with Germany.[78] They insisted that the service negotiators on both sides wore civilian clothes and not military uniforms. The talks were to be held in London where greater control could be exercised over the press than in Paris.[79] Finally, 'anything as spectacular' as the suggestion of a visit to London by Gamelin must be avoided.[80]

These precautions were unsuccessful – much to the embarrassment of the Foreign Office, articles appeared in *Le Figaro* and the *Daily Telegraph* on 16 February speculating about forthcoming Anglo-French staff talks.[81] The efforts to keep knowledge of the talks secret prompted Vansittart to write in a scathing minute:

> This displays all the old fundamental errors of thought. Last year, thanks largely on the mistaken information and judgement of Sir Nevile Henderson, we carefully refrained until it was too late from making the slightest gesture or saying any word that might have irritated Herr Hitler. And look at the result! This, as I urged at the time, is not the way to deal with Dictators, and we should never recoil from any step which we may consider necessary or even advisable for our own defence

> through any fear they may criticise it. They will certainly criticise us whenever they so choose and they will even go further if they deem fit, but they are far more likely to respect and fear us and so to avoid clashes with us if they realise that we reserve to ourselves exactly the same liberty as they claim and practise ... I feel sure that we should rid ourselves of this obsession of refraining from this or that practical action because we might be afraid of totalitarian criticism.[82]

The chiefs of staff's continuing lack of confidence in French discretion was further illustrated by the fate of 'the European Strategical Appreciation', which they had intended to send in its entirety to the French military authorities in March. This would have enabled the French to study the document in advance of the staff talks. However, after further reflection, the chiefs decided that the appreciation should not be sent to Paris after all as 'it was rather too explosive a document to send out of the country' and might fall 'into the wrong hands'.[83] In fact, there was little in the appreciation which could have occasioned any surprise to a potentially hostile power, let alone to the French. It merely repeated the information contained in previous chiefs of staff reviews of this kind: the increasing strength of the Axis Powers on land and in the air, the conviction that the Maginot line would nevertheless hold during the initial stages of a war, and the importance of propaganda in undermining the morale of the Axis peoples.[84]

The decision to withhold the appreciation from the French would, the joint planners recognised, 'cause, to say the least, great disappointment to the French and may well have the effect of starting the conversations in the wrong atmosphere.'[85] It also contradicted a statement by the chiefs of staff on 25 February that:

> we are now ... entering into an entirely new and frank phase of our relations with France on questions affecting the joint defence of the two countries. We are indeed assuming a mutual commitment which is even more close and binding than those existing with some of our Dominions.[86]

Finally, Chatfield agreed that written extracts from the document should be given to the French military, naval and air representatives at the London talks to avoid creating 'an atmosphere of suspicion'.[87] Sargent commented that 'however great our confidence in the French soldiers may be, this confidence certainly does not extend to French politicians or the Quai d'Orsay.'[88] Subsequently, the committee of imperial defence agreed that the French staffs be provided with the fullest information about

Britain's military capabilities, including developments in chemical warfare, since 'the alternative policy of reticence would be bound to create an atmosphere of suspicion and distrust.' According to Vansittart, the committee 'thought ... that the risk of leakage in science was less than the leakage in politics'.[89]

Since January 1939, British policy towards France, particularly in the defence sphere, had undergone a complete metamorphosis. Leading ministers, officials and senior service personnel, who had been previously wary of too close an association with the French Republic, were now converted to the conviction that Britain's future existence was entirely bound up with France. Since Munich, Halifax and Hore-Belisha, hitherto supporters of both limited liability and of Chamberlain's search for agreement with Germany, had come to the conclusion that Hitler's behaviour in September 1938 and subsequently demonstrated the impossibility of any settlement with that country except on terms which would result in German predominance in Europe. At the same time they had watched France becoming increasingly demoralised after Munich, especially as the loss of the Czechoslovak army reduced its security even further. This, together with the rumours of an imminent German invasion of Holland, convinced them that Britain would have to increase the size of its expeditionary army and enter into comprehensive staff talks with the French. Chamberlain was not convinced that appeasement was dead. He and Simon continued to resist expanded armaments expenditure, until they were forced by cabinet and chiefs of staff pressure to give way after January 1939, and then reluctantly. Hitler's take over of Bohemia in March 1939 galvanised public opinion to support a policy of resistance to further German expansionism, although Chamberlain continued to believe that Britain's increasing military, naval and air strength would not only deter Hitler from further adventures, but might convince the German leader that it would be more sensible to reach a comprehensive agreement with the democracies, in which Germany's remaining Versailles grievances could be addressed.

6 Britain's Perceptions of France from March 1939 to the Fall of France

... there is no altruism about Anglo-French co-operation. It is a stark necessity because it is one of the essential ways of saving our own skins, and it will continue to be necessary for the rest of our lives and probably for another 100 or 200 years time, when perhaps it may be merged into a European federation.

(Orme Sargent, 30 March 1940)[1]

Angry parliamentary and press reaction to Germany's occupation of Bohemia on 15 March 1939, which the Foreign Office noted 'will ... strengthen Germany's prestige, increase Herr Hitler's already overweaning self-confidence and thus augment the chances of an early conflict with the Western Powers',[2] forced Chamberlain to take a number of initiatives in foreign affairs which would have been unthinkable before that date. On 31 March 1939, the British government issued a unilateral guarantee of the independence of Poland, now regarded as the next likely candidate for German aggression. After Italy's seizure of Albania on 7 April, guarantees were given to Greece, and, on French insistence, to Romania on 13 April 1939. The French were anxious to prevent Romania, with its oil and other raw materials, falling entirely under German control and hoped that the guarantee would stiffen Romanian resistance to Germany's pressure.[3]

The worsening international climate increased French and parliamentary pressure for the introduction of conscription in Britain. Chamberlain remained opposed to this and adopted a suggestion by Hore-Belisha on 28 March to double the territorial army as an alternative, overruling Treasury objections that Hore-Belisha's proposal had been 'invented in the space of a few hours' and was 'an important new step towards a commitment to fight the next war, like the last, in the trenches in France'.[4] On the 29th Hore-Belisha announced that the territorial army would be increased to 340,000 men, much to the consternation of the general staff, who had not been consulted beforehand.[5]

Neither this, nor an earlier announcement by Hore-Belisha that an expeditionary force of 19 divisions would eventually be raised for continental service, satisfied the pro-conscription lobby in London and Paris. Ronald Campbell reported that French press and politicians were unanimous in calling for the introduction of conscription in Britain. The Foreign Office was convinced that:

> If we cannot take this decisive step there is always the danger, though it may perhaps be remote ... that the French will prefer to submit rather than risk having to hold the fort almost unaided while we presumably would be endeavouring somewhat belatedly to raise a conscript army.

Ivone Kirkpatrick agreed: 'if we do not have compulsory service we shall suddenly find ourselves without an ally.'[6] On 19 April, Daladier, in a conversation with Phipps, called on Britain to adopt conscription,[7] and two days later Phipps saw anti-British posters in Paris stating that France was being duped by other countries to fight for them. The ambassador warned the Foreign Office that these sentiments were being exploited by German propaganda and by the French defeatists.[8] Hankey became tired of this campaign, complaining to Phipps in April that the French

> are overdoing the pressure about National Service. They are actually doing harm. Serious people are beginning to say 'What right have these people to talk? They have spent all their money on funk-holes (the Maginot Lines) and grossly neglected the main offensive weapon, the Air Force. Their present output is about *one seventh* of ours and they are coming to us for equipment!

Nevertheless, whatever 'serious people' thought, faced with unrelenting pressure in the cabinet, the press and the Conservative Party, Chamberlain was forced to announce to the House of Commons on 29 April the introduction of six months' compulsory military service for men aged 20. Later in the debate, in justifying this decision, he referred to 'that jibe that Britain was "ready to fight to the last French soldier" [which] is one that is being bandied about from capital to capital'.[9]

This decision was, of course, welcomed by Daladier, but not by the War Office, which was faced with shortages of equipment, accommodation and instructors for the influx of conscripts.[10] It also concerned the chancellor of the exchequer, who had already written to Chamberlain in mid-April that the recent increases in the size of the army were adding 'to the uncomfortableness of the Exchequer', and he predicted national bankruptcy if military expansion continued at the existing rate:

> What is really happening is that we are assuming a great change in the role of the Army and acting on that assumption without having really discussed and decided it. Is it possible to maintain a great Fleet, an immense Air Force, requiring a vast labour force behind it, to sustain the dislocation of continuous bombardment from the air, to provide munitions at the rate contemplated for allies as well as ourselves, and at the same time to fight with an unlimited army on the continent backed by an unlimited supply of materials? Of course the difficulties of purchasing abroad when the war starts will be far greater than last time, for we have already lost so much gold, and the foreign securities held in this country are a mere fraction of what we requisitioned in 1914.[11]

The first series of Anglo-French staff conversations were held between 29 March and 4 April.[12] On the morning of the 29th, the British and French naval, air and army representatives gathered at the War Office for a welcoming speech by General Sir R.F. Adam, the deputy chief of the general staff. He reminded them that:

> At the Conversations held in London [in 1936] the head of the French Delegation had remarked that the Conversations reminded him of a football match, and he constantly expected the referee to blow his whistle for off side, as the delegations had been very closely tied down by their Governments and the scope of the Conversations had been strictly limited. In the present discussions he hoped there would be little need for the blowing of a whistle as the Conversations would proceed with the utmost frankness. We had moved a long way since 1936, perhaps in some ways tardily, and the Dictators might force us to move faster.[13]

The main French preoccupation at the army talks continued to be the inadequate size of the British expeditionary force and the length of time it would take to reach France. The War Office planned at that time that the first two divisions would arrive in the assembly areas in France 30 days after mobilisation and the third division three months after mobilisation, with the rest, if they were sent at all, arriving much later. At the second meeting of the joint army staffs on 29 March, the French delegation 'expressed dismay at the present situation of the Field Force and the greatest anxiety with regard to the future programme'.

General Lelong, the French army representative, demanded that the arrival of the first echelon in France should be accelerated, but Brigadier

Kennedy, the British army representative, rejected this. Lelong pointed out that France would have to bear the main burden of defence until British reinforcements eventually arrived and he left it 'to British imagination how strongly the French felt on the subject'. He continued to complain about this at subsequent meetings down to the seventh on 3 April, but could not extract a satisfactory answer from Kennedy.

On 21 April, Chatfield wrote to the prime minister urging him to give the French 'such encouragement for the future as we can' about the timing of the despatch of the Field Force.[14] Eventually the chiefs of staff agreed to accelerate the timetable, with the first echelon of the field force (two divisions) now embarking on Z (mobilisation day) + 21 days, the second echelon on Z + 40 days, four territorial divisions by Z + 4 months and four further territorial divisions by Z + 6 months, with the rate of production of equipment stepped up accordingly. This decision was announced to the French at the tenth meeting on 25 April.[15]

Anglo-French dissension also emerged during the naval staff talks. Strang feared the 'bad effect on the French' when they discovered that the Admiralty was still planning to send the Mediterranean fleet to the Far East to deter Japan if war broke out in Europe. He thought that 'there were people in France who already thought that the British connection was a liability rather than an asset, and we ought to do nothing that would strengthen this tendency.'[16] The chiefs of staff had assumed that in a European war in which both Germany and Italy were involved, France would be Britain's ally and its fleet would be prepared to defend Britain's interests in the Mediterranean against Italy, enabling the British Mediterranean fleet to sail to Singapore. Indeed, the Dominions' representatives had been promised, at the imperial conference in June 1937, that the despatch of the British fleet to the Far East was 'the basis of Britain's Far East strategy'.[17] The chiefs of staff's *European Appreciation for 1939–40* of February 1939 reiterated that, 'if Japan joined our enemies … a British Fleet would have to be despatched to the Far East and only very reduced British light forces would remain in the Mediterranean',[18] although it added that this 'must depend upon our resources and the state of the war in the Far East theatre'.[19]

When, at a committee of imperial defence meeting on 24 February, the prime minister raised this question, Chatfield insisted that the fleet must go to Singapore even if this meant the abandonment of the eastern Mediterranean to the Axis Powers. Lord Stanhope, the first lord of the admiralty, challenged this strategy. He did not wish to see the Mediterranean denuded of British capital ships and suggested that a smaller fleet be despatched to the Far East.[20] Backhouse wrote to Ismay in April: 'I have felt for a long time that the Singapore policy has been over-stressed by the particular people who have been mixed up with it. The Admiralty Plans Division is absolutely soaked in it.'[21]

The Foreign Office, which had earlier supported the despatch of the British fleet to the Far East, now reversed itself, painting a nightmare scenario of the loss to the enemy of Egypt and Palestine and also Arabia and East Africa if the Royal Navy abandoned the Mediterranean. To Cadogan, the outcome of war would be decided in Europe, and when the entente defeated Germany and Italy there, it would then be a relatively easy task to deal with any hostilities that may have broken out in the Far East. Halifax entirely agreed: 'the strategic effects may be disastrous & I think we must point this out with full vigour.'

Bonnet reinforced these Foreign Office concerns when, on 10 April, in a conversation with Phipps, he declared that 'the French Government considered the Royal Navy's strategy as "catastrophic."' When it was presented with these protests on 2 May, the committee of imperial defence ruled that it was impossible to determine in advance the size of the fleet which could be sent to the Far East in the event of war with Japan or when it could be sent there. This was based on the argument that Britain could not abandon the Mediterranean after its recent guarantee to Greece and alliance with Turkey.[22] However, no firm decision about the ultimate distribution of Britain's naval forces was made before the outbreak of war either by the committee of imperial defence or at the Anglo-French naval staff talks in London and Singapore during the summer, although by that time it looked almost certain that Italy would remain neutral.[23]

By comparison with the arguments over naval strategy, the air talks with France went fairly smoothly. Conversations between Wing Commander Kingston McCloughry and Commandant Bailly at the Air Ministry in London on 1 May ended in an agreement on the stationing of the advanced air striking force in 12 aerodromes in France.[24] However, the weakness of the French Air Force continued to disturb the British. In March Colyer reported that the French air industry was still producing only 90 machines a month, and, as a result, Sargent and Cadogan pressed the British air representatives at the joint air talks to 'bring home to the French our dissatisfaction, not to say alarm, at their continued inability to put their aircraft industry in proper working order'.[25] The prime minister expressed his concern about the inadequacy of French aircraft construction 'forcibly' (according to Cadogan) to Bonnet during a visit by the French foreign minister to London on 22 March, '(and have since got the usual come-back about conscription)'.[26]

At a meeting between Kingsley Wood and Guy La Chambre and their respective air force advisers at the Air Ministry in London on 4 April, Kingsley Wood offered British air experts and British assistance to the French to advise them on large-scale air production. He agreed to supply modern British aircraft to France, and also suggested that the two countries discuss standardisation and joint specification of machines. However when, in August, Guy La Chambre asked for Rolls-Royce Merlin engines for France's new bombers, the chief of the air staff insisted that the Royal Air Force needed all it could get to re-equip its own bombers.

There was also a fundamental disagreement between the two countries about their respective air strategies. Air Marshal A.S. Barratt, the designated commander of the advanced air striking force (an assortment of obsolescent British bombers which were to go to France on the outbreak of war), visited French air installations between 18 and 20 April 1939. He criticised French concepts about the use of air power, which were 'entirely bound up with the use of land forces', and thought that the Royal Air Force should educate them 'to more enlightened views on the subject of the use of air forces in war'.[27]

In July, the British and French air staffs were drawing up plans for air attacks on German forces advancing into Belgium and on railway communications behind the German army's lines.[28] But as Barrett had suggested, there was no meeting of Anglo-French minds over the use of air power. At a chiefs of staff meeting on 30 August 1939, Group Captain Slessor, the director of plans at the Air Ministry, said that the French were disappointed that the Royal Air Force would do nothing to assist Poland when war broke out. He had tried to explain to the French that the Royal Air Force did not intend to fritter away its strength on targets which did little to harm Germany. The French wanted to attack German aerodromes, but the air staff believed that these were too dispersed across Germany to make economical targets. Gort hoped that the two air forces would restrict their activities to reconnaissance and leaflet dropping over Germany, which would bring the war 'into the heart of their country'.[29]

The chiefs of staff instructed the British staff representatives at the staff conversations to join the French in planning for a long war. The chiefs were confident that the entente would ultimately prevail because of its greater economic staying power vis-à-vis Germany and Italy. The planners envisaged a war which would be fought in three phases. During the first phase, a naval blockade would be imposed on the Axis, while entente land forces would remain on the defensive. If, however, the Low Countries were invaded by Germany, Anglo-French forces should form a front as far forward into Belgium as circumstances permitted, although, during the conversations, the French pointed to the difficulties of advancing into Belgium given Belgium's refusal to make prior arrangements for co-operation with the entente. When the Foreign Office suggested to Beaumont-Nesbitt that the British approach the Belgians through diplomatic channels to arrange staff talks, the director of military operations dismissed it as a waste of time: 'Those people in Belgium who at present control the policy of their country are living in a fool's paradise.'[30] Under these circumstances the French declared that they might advance only as far as the Scheldt River if Belgium was invaded.[31]

In the second phase of the war, the entente would remain on the defensive against Germany – although bombing attacks on its economic and industrial infrastructure would be undertaken to weaken its resistance. Britain and France would concentrate on knocking out Italy by offensives into north and east Africa and a possible offensive against continental Italy if forces could be released from the western front for this purpose. During the third, and final, phase of the war, an Anglo-French offensive would be launched into Germany to destroy the *Wehrmacht* and Germany's industrial infrastructure.

Despite the progress made at these talks in agreeing on a common overall strategy for ultimately winning the war, the British remained doubtful that France possessed the 'economic staying power' to enable it to ride out a lengthy period on the defensive. In March, Desmond Morton's Industrial Intelligence Centre (IIC) forwarded to the Foreign Office a lengthy account of France's inadequate material resources and industrial capacity, factors which would seriously impair its ability to withstand a long war. The IIC asked whether France's population of 41 million, which included two million foreigners, mostly refugees, would be sufficient to provide simultaneously for its fighting forces and industry and to sustain its national life, especially as a third of its population was involved in agricultural production. Even more worrying was the fact that the bulk of France's heavy industry and mineral resources (for instance, 75 per cent of its coal mines and 95 per cent of its iron ore) was concentrated in the highly vulnerable area between the German and Belgian frontiers and the Seine. France was already deficient in coal and if it lost its northern departments and Lorraine to the enemy, France would then become almost wholly dependent upon Britain and the United States for its coal supplies. France also depended on uninterrupted seaborne trade to make up for its deficiencies in foodstuffs, fuel, copper, tin, zinc and other raw materials. French industry was also short of machine and precision tools. Nor could the French chemical industry provide the necessary resources to sustain a long war. Given these depressing statistics it was clear to the IIC that French industry would not be able to maintain for any lengthy period the large army which France intended to raise on the outbreak of hostilities. The French navy would also be in dire straits, since the shortage of skilled dockyard labour in wartime would make it impossible for France to expand its warship construction. Finally, the ICC pointed out that the output of French aircraft still amounted to a derisory 80–100 machines a month.[32]

Despite these chilling statistics, the British believed that they could overcome France's deficiency in raw materials by ensuring that shipping, food, coal, non-ferrous metals and minerals were fairly apportioned between the two countries before war began. Coal was, of course, particularly important to the joint war effort, and the French, cut off from German and Polish supplies in war-time, would need to import British coal to make up the deficiency. In December 1938, in a memorandum for the committee of imperial defence entitled 'Estimated requirements of France for Coal Supplies from the United Kingdom in time of War', the president of the board of trade stated that his department would shortly be consulting the British coal industry to find out what Britain could do to meet French coal requirements in war-time. Strang agreed that 'We ought to do our utmost to help the French, although it is fair to ask them to keep up their purchases here *in peace time*, if only to make *war-time* supply easier.' However, he hoped that the French should not be pressed 'too strongly' to maintain their peace-time coal output during the war, since Britain was going to leave France '*almost entirely*' alone to defend its frontier against Germany. Because France would have to mobilise practically its whole manpower for military purposes, 'any suggestion from us that they should keep their men in the mines rather than in the ranks would not be well received and should be carefully avoided.'[33] In subsequent negotiations between the British coal industry and the French mines department, Britain agreed to provide France with the extra coal it would require in war-time.

By June 1939, a comprehensive system of Anglo-French coordinating boards and joint purchasing missions had been established, and schedules of French and British requirements of raw materials in war-time had been drawn up.[34] However, in July, John Nicholls, a Foreign Office economic specialist, complained to Ismay that there was no provision for the overall coordination of these various bodies in war-time. 'It all boils down to a question of higher *economic* command in war: and, as that is a subject on which I tend to become a bore, I'll leave it at that!'[35] This problem was not properly addressed until after the war had begun.

Despite the bleak IIC picture of the likely strains on the French economy and social structure in the event of war, there were encouraging signs in 1939 of a French economic revival. On 1 January the Chamber of Deputies voted to allow the French government to effect economies by decree. Paul Reynaud, the French minister of finance, introduced a budget which attempted to staunch the financial deficits which had long plagued France. Norman Young, the new British financial adviser at the British embassy in Paris, commented that, since France's financial weakness had 'been exploited abroad, and has been an element of weakness in the European situation', Reynaud's vigorous efforts to solve the problem 'must be a source of encouragement to France and to the friends of France'. Barclay was pleased that Reynaud had strengthened 'the general stability of France and that is clearly of great advantage to us from the political point of view'.[36]

On 21 April 1939, Reynaud issued 39 decrees under the budgetary law, inaugurating a two-year financial and defence programme with 15 milliard francs allocated for defence, and introducing measures to combat tax evasion, an excess profits tax on armaments manufacturers, cuts in public works and road building, an increase in working hours and a reduction in overtime payments. Young was relieved that these unpopular measures had been accepted by the French public with comparative equanimity, presumably because of the increasingly threatening behaviour of Germany and Italy. By July confidence in the franc had been re-established.[37]

The state visit to London of the president of the French Republic and Madame Lebrun at the end of March – nicknamed 'Frog Week' by Henry Channon – was intended to demonstrate to the British and French peoples, and to potential enemy powers, the close and harmonious relations which existed between the entente partners. On 24 January, Halifax asked the Speaker of the House of Commons, Captain E.A. Fitzroy, that 'in view of the special nature of the relations between France and this country ... we should do rather more than is customary'.[38] Lebrun was invited to a reception in Westminster Hall as a guest of both Houses of Parliament, with the Speaker and Lord Chancellor presenting addresses of welcome. The Lord Chancellor, Lord Maugham, could see no objection to this, 'provided that the reactions of Germany and Italy will not be so unfavourable as to outweigh the advantages which may be gained by so remarkable a demonstration of our solidarity (a hateful word) with France.' Consideration for Axis feelings no longer troubled Halifax, who commented, 'I don't think the totalitarian reaction w[oul]d be worse to this reception than to the visit as a whole!'[39]

There was also a banquet at the Foreign Office on 23 March, followed by an entertainment in the India Office which Vansittart organised. Halifax asked Vansittart to 'try his literary hand at' writing the King's speech for the banquet. Vansittart insisted that the speech should be delivered in English and not French, since 'we have had a long struggle since the war to establish the equivalence of English as an international language … I would like for once in a way to get away from our eternal and nauseating diplomatic jargon, and let the King say something in English and good English. And I would like it to be short.'[40]

Chamberlain thought that

> The visit of the French President … was … highly opportune and there is no doubt that the good impression was mutual. Lebrun reached a very high level of (apparently) natural eloquence in his speech in Westminster Hall, delivered without a note & with admirable emphasis and gesture.

The prime minister 'really enjoyed the dinner at the F.O. and the performance afterwards in the court of the India Office … I laughed … [at] Guitry[41] & Seymour Hicks and Cicely Courtneidge[42] and got hiccups.'[43] On the other hand, Channon did not think it 'too well done' and commented sourly that at the rehearsals in the morning for the entertainment, Harold Caccia, an assistant private secretary to Halifax, 'had gone on so long … about the Entente and our wonderful Friendship with France'.[44] Halifax and Chamberlain discussed relations with Poland, Romania and the Soviet Union with Bonnet, who accompanied the Lebruns to London. Bonnet agreed that it was time to call a halt to German aggression, but took the opportunity to re-emphasise that France could not bear the burden alone and that Britain must increase the size of its expeditionary force.[45]

The British hoped that Italy could be persuaded to remain neutral in the event of a European war, but Daladier, whose anti-Italian stance was highly popular with the French electorate, rejected repeated British appeals for a French initiative to improve Franco-Italian relations as a means of achieving Italian neutrality. At a cabinet meeting in April, Chamberlain 'expressed the view that the French were not doing their share in smoothing out their difficulties with Italy'.[46] The Foreign Office was alarmed at rumours that Daladier intended to dismiss Bonnet, who, whatever his other faults, was at least anxious to achieve a Franco-Italian *rapprochement*. Halifax commented: 'I hold no particular brief for Bonnet, but we don't want Daladier to develop into another Poincaré!' In May, Halifax was still complaining about the failure of the French to negotiate with Italy, especially as 'we had done a great deal for France lately, indeed far more than France has done for us.' By the outbreak of the war Daladier had done nothing to improve relations with Italy, despite a personal appeal from Chamberlain.[47] The prime minister complained that when 'the French for their part continue to keep up a quarrel with every one with whom they might make friends, Italy, Spain, Turkey and we inevitably get tarred with the same brush.'[48]

During the spring and summer the entente was equally unsuccessful in negotiations with the Soviet Union for a political and military agreement. (This subject has already been explored thoroughly in other works and it is not intended to deal with it here in any detail.)[49] The French were more enthusiastic for a military agreement than the British: in fact, Chamberlain had no enthusiasm for it all. Most cabinet ministers were lukewarm, and those like Halifax and Hoare who supported it did so because they feared that otherwise the Soviet Union might turn to Germany. The French were prepared to accept the Soviet interpretation of 'indirect aggression' by Germany; the British were not.[50] The half-hearted nature of the British approach to Moscow was confirmed in Soviet eyes when Britain sent William Strang to Russia to help with the negotiations instead of the cabinet minister the Kremlin had requested, and by the long drawn out voyage by passenger ship to Russia by the Anglo-French military delegations in July – although it has been pointed out that there were reasonable explanations for both these actions.

There was some friction between the British and French over these negotiations, with the French suspecting, with justification, that the British were dragging their feet in their approach to the talks, and the British falsely accusing Phipps and Bonnet, who both hated communism and distrusted the Soviet Union, of withholding from London information about 'a constructive counter-proposal' to the Soviet Union by Daladier.[51] The Foreign Office was taken by surprise when the Soviet foreign minister, Vyacheslav Molotov, and Ribbentrop signed the Soviet-German non-aggression pact on 25 August. While admitting that 'the signature of the German Pact with Russia has changed the whole situation within Europe and the Far East', with Poland now unlikely to hold out for very long against both Germany and Russia, Ivone Kirkpatrick tried to put a brave face on the Soviet *volte face*, in asserting that Italy, Spain and Japan were so disillusioned by Germany's perfidity in turning to Russia that they were likely to remain neutral in the event of war.[52]

With war imminent towards the end of August, the British military attaché in Paris reported that the French had so far mobilised 2,600,000 men in France and North Africa, and, with the air force and navy, had nearly three million men in uniform. After general mobilisation they would have five million men in the armed services. He added that the mobilisation had proceeded more efficiently than it had in September 1938, and that the morale of the French nation was excellent:

> in fact, France to-day presents a spectacle of calm determination which is most impressive and the country is by no means disposed to settle this affair on Hitler's terms. If it cannot have a settlement which will guarantee it against the necessity to mobilise again in another six months or a year, France would prefer to have war now.[53]

Cabinet irresolution and French reluctance to declare war immediately when the German invaded Poland on 1 September 1939 was not an auspicious beginning to the Anglo-French war-time relationship.[54] It proved to be a grave embarrassment to Chamberlain when Bonnet appealed for a delay in declaring war while the French government explored the possibility of Italian mediation. Chamberlain's feeble attempt in the House of Commons on 2 September to explain why an ultimatum had not been sent to Berlin provoked a storm of outrage in Parliament. Simon represented a majority of cabinet ministers when he protested to Chamberlain about the delay. Chamberlain, faced with a major cabinet revolt, was forced to agree to the presentation of the ultimatum to Berlin at 9 a.m., to expire at 11.a.m. on the 3rd. The French ultimatum followed at 12 noon to expire at 5 p.m.[55]

Cadogan blamed Bonnet for the confusion:

> we must regard him as the rallying point of French defeatism and expect that he will continue to exercise his baleful influence on French policy. He may well intrigue, whenever he can, to get France out of the war, or failing that to limit her war effort to the minimum. He may even establish contact with the Germans and Italians. In a word, our recent experience shows that it will be difficult to establish confident and sincere collaboration with the French so long as M. Bonnet is active at the Quai d'Orsay and our well founded suspicions if not M. Bonnet's own activities might easily react on the whole conduct of the war.

He wanted to know what 'discreet measures' could be deployed to get Bonnet out so that 'an honest man' might replace him as foreign minister.[56] All this must have been embarrassing to Phipps, given his close pre-war relations with Bonnet. Whether a result of 'discreet' British measures or not, Daladier transferred Bonnet to the ministry of justice in October, taking over the French foreign ministry himself.

Nor, as Simon complained, was the cordiality of Anglo-French relations assisted when the French '(after their habit) "leaked" the information that our expeditionary force was crossing the Channel', thus increasing the risks of German naval and air interception. The four divisions of the expeditionary force moved to France without any German interference, and by 27 September 160,000 British soldiers and airmen were stationed in France.[57] This force was hardly an impressive reinforcement for the French. It was inadequately trained, deficient in tanks, trench mortar detachments and heavy artillery.[58] Winston Churchill, who had joined the war cabinet on the outbreak of war as first lord of the Admiralty, wondered how long the French would be prepared to accept a division of effort whereby the British concentrated on sea and air operations and 'left them to pay the whole blood tax on land'.[59] Conversely, Inskip, recently ennobled as Lord Caldecote and now lord chancellor, complained that the French were up to their 'usual game' of demanding that Britain 'share the Front Line', ignoring the fact that Britain's air strength was many times greater than that of the French air force.[60] Hore-Belisha supported Churchill's call for a large British army to be sent to France as soon as possible since 'we cannot possibly expect France to stand the strain of a long war if she has to do all the land fighting ... a token force would not be sufficient to persuade the French nation that we were not leaving her to fight our battle.'[61] Simon rejected the war minister's subsequent demand that Britain must raise an army of 50 divisions during the next three years, protesting that more than 20 divisions would result in national bankruptcy. After another 'weary fight', he was overruled when the war cabinet accepted Hore-Belisha's figure.[62]

These were the first of a series of controversies and misunderstandings between the two countries during the ten months of 'phoney war'. Nevertheless, the Foreign Office successfully maintained close and friendly relations with France in this period.[63] The pre-war collaboration between the two countries in economic and trade matters became closer after September. In November 1939, an Anglo-French coordinating committee was set up chaired by the French financial expert, Jean Monnet, to oversee the ten Anglo-French executive committees which had been established to organise Anglo-French resources.[64] Early in January 1940 the Board of Trade concluded that 'by means of these arrangements a degree of co-ordination of the economic war efforts of the two countries, which in the last war was reached only at the end of the third year, has been attained.'[65]

There was, however, no overall Anglo-French ministerial body to oversee the civilian agencies, for which Monnet had pressed, nor was a supreme economic council created.[66] The supreme war council, the first of whose occasional meetings was held at Abbeville on Tuesday 12 September 1939, was not intended to fulfil this task and was mostly concerned with military issues. Its revival, in conscious imitation of its Great War predecessor, had been agreed by the two governments in August, and the Abbeville meeting was suggested to Daladier by Chamberlain as an opportunity to discuss the current situation and future developments and to demonstrate to their publics that the two governments were in active consultation.[67] This first meeting consisted of an exchange of pleasantries, together with expressions of Anglo-French confidence in the military strength of the entente.[68] Chamberlain thought it 'the most satisfactory conference I have ever attended', but it was difficult to see what it had achieved beyond expressions of mutual goodwill.[69] Later meetings in 1939 and 1940 dealt with more contentious military issues, especially over strategy towards Russia, Finland, Sweden and Norway.[70]

During the 'phoney war', the British embassy in Paris monitored French public and political opinion carefully to detect signs either of defeatism or loss of confidence in Britain's steadfastness and determination. Foreign Office nervousness about the stability of French morale reflected its assumptions about the volatile nature of the Gallic temperament, and the knowledge that a clique of French politicians – notably Laval, Flandin and Jean Mistler, the president of the foreign affairs committee in the Chamber – were, according to Phipps, conducting 'an insidious propaganda campaign on the lines that we dragged France into war ... They think this will make them popular if things go badly militarily wrong.'[71]

Phipps had transformed himself from a close collaborator with the defeatist element in France at the time of Munich into an forceful advocate of French unity and strength of purpose. His despatches and telegrams to London played down the influence of the 'peace at the first opportunity' minority and emphasised the high level of morale of the French people.[72] Senior British army officers now serving in France were not so convinced of the truth of this.[73] General Sir John Dill, the commander of I Corps of the British expeditionary force, speculated in September that the will of the French people to continue in the war might eventually weaken:

> The Germans will of course do all in their power to persuade the French that the last thing they want to do is to fight them & that we have let them in for this war for our own selfish purposes. Of course the leaders & the great bulk of the French people will not be taken in by this but there is just a danger that some of the French people may be weakened by it.[74]

Foreign Office fears were only partly allayed by Phipps's assurances since, at the same time, the ambassador was reporting that the views of the French defeatists might, in future, appeal to a wider audience in France if they were able to convince French public opinion that Britain was not pulling its weight within the alliance. From the outset of the war the Foreign Office and the British Ministry of Information wanted to mount an energetic challenge to German radio propaganda to France about the limited contribution the British were making towards the entente war effort.[75] Their efforts to publicise the British military presence in France were frustrated by the War Office and the Royal Air Force, neither of whom wanted any publicity about the arrival of British troops or air contingents in France, since this, they claimed, 'will jeopardize or eliminate the element of surprise inherent in a swift and early entry of the British Army into the field'. This issue was resolved only after Halifax secured the war cabinet's approval on 16 September for the release to the French press of 'maximum, if innocuous ... information' about the presence of Britain's armed forces in France, which, it was hoped, would open French eyes to the positive efforts the British were making to support them.[76] Thus, when General Sir Alan Brooke's II Corps landed at Cherbourg on 29 September, he was ordered to take it straight to the front line on the Franco-Belgian border, although it needed about one month's training before it would be combat-ready. When Brooke protested, General Sir Ronald Adam, the Commander of III Army Corps, told him 'that the early move of the corps was a political gesture for the French'.[77]

British publicity dwelling on the positive aspects of the Anglo-French relationship was regarded as crucial by the Foreign Office as a means of countering German propaganda and of boosting French morale. It encouraged British newspapers to publish favourable reports about France and the French and not to publish articles which denigrated the French, for instance by describing them as 'mean and grasping'.[78] The Foreign Office remained alert to reports of French 'lukewarmness about the prosecution of the war', and did what it could to improve press coverage and other publicity in France about the magnitude of the British war effort.[79]

There were, of course, a number of British observers of France who were sceptical about the steadfastness of the French. In January 1940 Captain Louis Mountbatten wrote to Eden, who had re-entered Chamberlain's government as dominions secretary in September 1939, drawing his attention to an article in *The Week*[80] on 17 January which described falling French industrial production, the prevalence of communism in the French army and the intense anti-British feelings in many parts of France. Since the editor of this newsletter was a communist who, after the German-

Soviet pact, opposed the 'capitalist' war, Eden was probably justified in dismissing its 'alarmist' views. The foreign secretary accepted that the long period of military inaction was 'trying', but told Mountbatten that reports reaching the Dominions Office from France suggested that the 'temper' of the French people was satisfactory:

> Personally I have never taken the view that the French temperament is flighty and ours stoic. I am not sure that it wouldn't be nearer to the truth to say that the French is tenacious and ours sentimental ... It is clearly our duty to do everything we can to encourage the French and keep heart in them.[81]

The British high command was not consulted when, in November, Gamelin decided that, in the event of a German invasion of Belgium, Anglo-French forces would move to the River Dyle, deep inside Belgium, instead of the line of the River Scheldt which had been his initial choice. The British army would have preferred to remain on the Franco-Belgian frontier. Gort, who had become commander-in-chief of the British expeditionary force on the outbreak of war, felt that the relatively tiny British army contribution to the land effort inhibited him from contesting Gamelin's strategy, while General Sir Edmund Ironside, the chief of the imperial general staff since September, while initially opposed, allowed himself to be talked out of his opposition by Gamelin at an Anglo-French military conference at Vincennes on 9 November. The advance to the Dyle strategy was approved by the supreme war council on the 17th.[82] Brooke feared that, as a result of Gamelin's revised plan, 'by trying to save the whole of Belgium, instead of half, not only would we lose the whole of Belgium but probably the war as well' – a prophesy which turned out to be only too accurate in May 1940.

Serving officers also entertained doubts about the likely reliability of the French army when fighting began. While Eden, who had been an infantry officer in the Great War, paid tribute to 'the wonderful quality of the French Army' after visiting the front in November,[83] British officers in the field were not similarly impressed. In October, General F.H.N. Davidson's I Corps of Artillery took over French positions in the Lille–Valenciennes area. What Davidson found there 'shocked' him – the French positions were 'untidy', with ammunition strewn about unprotected from the weather and there was virtually no camouflage. He was told by a French artillery officer at Valenciennes that one division of the French III Corps was 'so infected with communism that it had to be sent to the Maginot Line!'[84] Brooke complained about 'French slovenliness, dirtiness & inefficiency'.[85] He accused the allies of 'facing this war in a half-hearted way', with rear demolitions still unprepared in October, shortages of barbed wire, and the forward area 'crammed with civilians' who should have been evacuated. In his command area near Lille, he discovered that the clothing industries, coal fields and agriculture were short of French labour, and were forced instead to employ Belgians, Poles, Saarlanders and Italians, with the 'consequent opportunities of spying unlimited. Also large communist element to deal with. Belgium full of German spies and attitude of population not very satisfactory.'[86]

When he lunched with General M.B.A. Fagalde, the commander of the XVI French Army Corps, on 23 October, Brooke found him 'a pleasant ruffian and an amusing companion but does not inspire me with unbounded confidence as far as his efficiency is concerned.' At least there was no shortage of food for high-ranking Anglo-French officers – Brooke consumed a large lunch with the prefect of Lille and assorted French dignitaries on 31 October, which comprised champagne, oysters, chicken, paté de fois gras, cheese, fruit, coffee and liqueurs.

In November, he 'could not help wondering whether the French are still a firm enough nation to again take their part in seeing this war through.' He toured French defences on part of the front on 28 November and found them 'to all intents and purposes non-existent'. He visited a Maginot line fort and while he found 'the whole conception ... a stroke of genius', he harboured deep reservations about its impregnability:

> And yet! It gives me but little feeling of security, and I consider that the French would have done better to invest the money in the shape of mobile defences such as more a[nd] better aircraft and more heavy armoured divisions than to sink all this money into the ground.

Later he commented:

> The most dangerous aspect is the psychological one, a sense of false security is engendered, a feeling of sitting behind an impregnable iron fence; and should the defence perchance be broken the French fighting spirit might well be brought down with it.

He was depressed about 'the lack of any real finish in the French Army', and 'its amateur appearance' by comparison with 'the ultra-efficiency' of the German army. 'I only hope they still possess the same fighting qualities which they showed in the last war.'[87]

Ironside doubted it, confiding to his diary in December 1939 that 'there is none of the fire which animated them in 1914.'[88] General Davidson noted that, when he 'ran into' a French anti-aircraft regiment near Cassal in May 1940, a number of German Stukas flew over and began dropping 'their screaming bombs. But not a shot did the French fire as all the personnel quitted their guns and bolted into funk-holes – till the danger had passed.'[89]

Liddell Hart was equally doubtful about French staying power. In early September he wrote:

> it would be wise to reckon with the possibility that the French, a realistic people, may prove unwilling to lend themselves for long to an offensive strategy aimed to recover someone else's territory already lost and lying far behind the fortified barrier which faces them. If the French should decline to continue such an unpromising effort, of which they would have to bear the brunt, the position in which we should be placed would be both dangerous and ridiculous.[90]

By November Liddell Hart had become so depressed by what he believed to be the inability of the entente to defeat Germany once war began in earnest that he became, like Lloyd George, an advocate of a compromise peace.[91]

Nor were relations between French *poilus* and British tommies in the field very comradely. The Saar Sector Detachment of the British Field Security Police (FSP) reported jealousy and discontent amongst the French soldiery in their area about the differentials between the pay of the French and British troops. 'It is amusing how peeved certain Frenchmen are because the well-paid English soldier has most of the luck with the girls.' Further, many British soldiers angered the local citizenry by behaving 'as though we were in a conquered country'. British service personnel 'falsely imagine we are on holiday in France and … we never go near the Maginot Line except for an occasional Cook's tour.'[92]

This FSP's sector lay in the industrialised areas of northern France where the French Communist Party was at its strongest, and where it engaged in intense anti-war propaganda. However, as Donald Cameron Watt has shown, the FSP felt constrained from reporting these communist activities to their superiors, and preferred not to accept the evidence which was presented to them on a daily basis of the declining morale of the French people and the rank and file in the French army. No doubt the need for military solidarity and 'the team spirit', together with the fear of being considered defeatist explained in part this reluctance to report the true facts of the situation.[93]

Only General Spears, who visited France frequently during the 'phoney war', and the Duke of Windsor, who joined the British liaison mission in Paris in October 1939, reported the appalling state of morale in French army units, and were highly critical of the lack of preparedness for war of the French armies, and the inadequacies of the Maginot line.[94] The tendency, however, to ignore apparent French shortcomings was partly explained by a comment Ironside recorded in his diary in January 1940:

> But I say to myself we must have confidence in the French Army. It is the only thing in which we can have confidence. Our own Army is a little one, and we are dependent upon the French. We have not even the same fine Army we had in 1914. All depends on the French Army and we can do nothing about it, except to back it up and not to deny it ... Gort has given me no inkling that he finds anything serious amiss in the French Army. None of his staff have even whispered any doubts ... The issue is in the lap of the gods and we can do nothing to alter things. We must remain loyal to the French.[95]

On the diplomatic front, a new problem arose when the French government called for a 'no separate peace' declaration by the two powers as a means of convincing the French people that Britain was determined to fight to the finish. This issue first surfaced in the semi-official *Le Petit Parisien* on 11 September.[96] The Foreign Office was initially reluctant to pursue this idea,[97] but was eventually converted to it as a means of pre-empting another French demand that the two countries should formulate postwar guarantees against the revival of German aggression.[98] The British did not want this potentially divisive issue, which would inevitably entail French demands for the severance, this time permanently, of the Rhineland from Germany, to be raised so early in the war. They subsequently adopted the 'no separate peace declaration' in the hope that it would reassure the French that 'after victory, the conflicts which had plagued Britain and France between the wars would not recur.'[99] Furthermore, Chamberlain's insistence that the war was being fought against Hitlerism and not the German people alarmed the French, since it suggested that Britain might be willing to make peace with a non-Hitler Germany, which was not far from the truth at that time.[100] Chamberlain told his sister on 5 November that, if the Nazis could be got rid of, the Allies would have no trouble doing a deal with Germany over Poland, Czechoslovakia, the Jews and disarmament:

> Our real trouble is much more likely to be with France. As a rule they are very wooden on these matters and they do not easily learn from their mistakes. If Germans themselves desire to split their country up, well and good. I should be delighted; but for the Allies to do it against the will of the German people would I fear only sow afresh the seeds of

> trouble. But I haven't yet discussed war aims with the French though I hope to do so soon. It may be that Daladier will prove more reasonable than some of his predecessors.[101]

In September, Lord Robert Cecil told Halifax that he hoped the Foreign Office would 'restrain the extravagances of our Allies … and … show the Germans that we were not planning the destitution of Germany – as to which we were both clear that any policy of that kind was madness.'[102] A.J. Sylvester told Lloyd George 'that our troubles will really start with the French when we talk about War Aims and peace conditions. They have made up their minds that this time it is going to be a FRENCH peace and not an English one.'[103]

On 23 October the French government presented an *aide-mémoire* to Halifax requesting a discussion of war aims.[104] Until he retired at the end of October, Phipps sent a stream of telegrams and despatches warning the Foreign Office about the dangers of giving the French any reason to suppose that Germany would be treated leniently after her defeat,[105] and that anxiety about Britain's postwar intentions towards Germany was widespread among Frenchmen 'of every political colour and in all parts of France'. Roger Makins agreed:

> there is here a real divergence between us and the French, which has its roots in the essential difference between the Anglo-Saxon and the Latin mentality and outlook. It is useless to talk to the French about 'the fight against evil' … They do not understand this sort of talk, which they are apt to consider hypocritical. The French are fighting as, fundamentally, we are also fighting, for their own security, and nothing else.[106]

The arguments put forward by senior Foreign Office officials against the imposition of a harsh peace on Germany suggested French fears about Britain's postwar intentions were not entirely groundless. Strang remarked:

> we are fighting to preserve our position in the world against the German challenge; to establish peace and freedom in Europe; and to safeguard Western civilisation … We must … try to convince the German people that war is not a paying proposition, and it is in their interest to re-enter the Western European system.[107]

Sir Ronald Hugh Campbell, who replaced Phipps as ambassador on 1 November, repeated Phipps's warnings about the dangers of Britain appearing to ignore this issue.[108] He pointed out:

> To the French temperament inaction is more trying than action. The period of waiting, without movement on the Front, is a hard trial of

> nerves ... It is a tribute to the intelligence and essential toughness of the Frenchman ... that internal quarrels have been largely laid aside and that there is a general determination to see the war through to the end ... The cement which is binding the country together in the will to victory is the determination not merely to overthrow Hitler, but to put an end once and for all to German aggression. Meanwhile the fear persists that Great Britain will insist upon a peace which will not contain what France considers to be adequate political and military guarantees against any further threat.[109]

The Foreign Office wanted to persuade the French to leave peace aims and territorial questions aside until victory had been achieved, and concentrate in the meantime on the defeat of Germany as the sole entente war aim. Any indication by Britain and France that they would dismember a defeated Germany would, the Foreign Office believed, unite all Germans behind Hitler.

Further French pressure for a 'no separate peace' declaration[110] forced the war cabinet to place it on the agenda of the fourth supreme war council meeting in Paris on Tuesday 19 December.[111] At that meeting Chamberlain agreed to support such a declaration for its psychological effect. Fortunately, Daladier accepted the British contention that detailed discussions of joint war aims should be left for a later stage and that only the no separate peace declaration should be studied at present.[112]

The Foreign Office drafted a declaration at the end of January 1940 that the two governments 'mutually undertake that during the present war they will neither negotiate nor conclude an armistice or a treaty of peace except by mutual agreement'.[113] Then Sir Ronald Campbell suggested to the Foreign Office that the declaration be widened to provide some contractual form to the continuation of economic collaboration and for a military alliance for a specified period after the war, both as a means of lowering German morale and encouraging that of the French. A pledge of postwar collaboration might also reduce French pressure for the imposition of postwar guarantees on Germany. Accordingly, the Foreign Office added a clause to the declaration that 'the two Governments declare their intention to continue the fullest co-operation in their financial, economic and defence policy after the conclusion of peace.'[114] The declaration was approved by the war cabinet on 21 March,[115] and Paul Reynaud, who replaced Daladier as French prime minister on the 21st, signed it on 28 March.[116]

Financial and trade issues also caused dissension between the two countries.[117] To save foreign exchange the British imposed restrictions on imports of luxury goods after the outbreak of the war. The French protested that these measures would hit French silk, textile, wine and liqueur producers.[118] This led to a long controversy when the Treasury refused to lift the restrictions, claiming that the cost of maintaining the British expeditionary force in France was already consuming Britain's reserves of francs, while the French protested that they were destroying the livelihood of French workers whose age made them ineligible for military service.[119] Francis Hirst, the editor of *The Economist*, wrote to Simon in September 1939 that the French 'ought not to tax our coal & we their vegetables, now that our men are fighting and dying side by side.'[120]

The dispute became more serious in November when the French threatened to retaliate by imposing duties on British imports into France.[121] A French economic official told the Board of Trade, 'No French soldier would be able to understand that the United Kingdom Government were not prepared to lend a helping hand to French industry ... This was inviting the break-up of the French economy and would begin to sap the basis of the Alliance.'[122] Eventually, after a long series of negotiations between the two sides, an Anglo-French financial agreement was signed on 12 December whereby, in exchange for a French loan to defray the expenses of the British expeditionary force, the British agreed to lift the restrictions on a wide range of French imports.[123]

A similar controversy erupted over the restrictions on exit visas and on the conversion of sterling into francs, which the British government imposed on British nationals wishing to visit the French Riviera and French winter sports centres outside the war zone. The French wanted to revive its tourist industry, which had collapsed on the outbreak of war, and claimed that the British restrictions were imposing immense hardship on the local people in these areas, who, as a result, were blaming their impoverishment on Britain for dragging France into the war.[124] After a long argument, the Treasury finally relented and agreed to release francs for tourists,[125] but the Home Office Aliens Department and the Passport Control Department were reluctant, for security reasons, to relax their rigorous passport controls. While appreciating the importance of security, Roger Makins thought that 'from every other point of view, intercourse between this country and France is in quite a different category from that with other countries, in view of our special relationship.'[126] Eventually an inter-departmental overseas travel committee drafted a 'Franco-British Agreement on Travel between the Two Countries', designed to protect the security interests of both countries, but when this was ready for signature by France and Britain on 22 May, it was abandoned: because of 'recent "events," private travel on any scale is likely to be at a discount for some considerable time.'[127]

By the end of 1939 the Foreign Office had concluded that only by promoting an Anglo-French union could such mutual suspicions between the two peoples be eradicated. It might also help to solve the problem of postwar security against a revival of German militarism. On 28 February 1940, Orme Sargent, a leading exponent of such a union, believed that 'the cooperation which we are prepared to offer them would constitute a far surer and more lasting guarantee than any occupation of German territory, which is what they will certainly press for – much to our embarrassment.' He called for a publicity campaign to educate the British people to appreciate the advantages of such a union.[128] Halifax, who tentatively supported closer union, argued that 'France might want the Rhine frontier – we must cajole her away from this by saying we shall stand by her in close collaboration after the war was over.'[129] R.A. Butler wanted the creation of a Europe 'within the fortress of civilisation, that is, this side of the Maginot Line'.[130] Reginald Leeper, now head of the Foreign Office Political Intelligence Department (PID), thought that something should be done 'to stir the imagination of two peoples who do not easily understand or appreciate each other', and suggested cultural exchanges and the compulsory teaching of the English and French languages in each other's schools as one means of achieving this.[131]

Halifax persuaded Hankey, who had been appointed minister without portfolio in Chamberlain's war cabinet, to chair a committee of experts from the Foreign Office, the Treasury and the Board of Trade to examine the administrative and procedural aspects of closer Anglo-French union.[132] At their first meeting the committee had before them as a discussion paper a 'Draft Act of Perpetual Association between the United Kingdom and France', drawn up jointly by the PID and a group of academics at Chatham House.[133] Leeper told Sargent:

> we felt that a short and striking document summing up a scheme for Anglo-French co-operation might be the best answer to Hitler's claim that he is establishing a new order in Central and Eastern Europe. Our new order, if it embraces the British and French Empires, would have far wider scope and would provide a real peace aim for the youth of England and France.[134]

The memorandum proposed that the supreme war council should be developed into a peace-time institution to pursue common policies in foreign affairs, defence, economic and financial relations, and that there should be a common Anglo-French nationality. The Chatham House group also called for 'systematic action in the field of education and culture' and the 'sympathetic presentation to young people of the moral and practical principles common to both countries in their unity-in-diversity, as opposed to the traditional treatment of "French and English" as rivals and opposites'.[135]

It was soon clear that Hankey, the Treasury and Board of Trade representatives on the committee were by no means sympathetic towards the idealist sentiments expressed in the draft. From the outset Hankey 'realised that the association would not necessarily be based on feelings of sympathy between the two peoples, but upon their common fear of Germany'. The committee soon emasculated the more far-reaching articles in the Chatham House draft, noting that, since both countries had sovereign parliaments, the supreme council could only act as a coordinating body and as a court of appeal for decisions reached by the respective parliaments.[136] At its next meeting on 21 May, the Board of Trade representative, Sir Arnold Overton, dismissed plans for an Anglo-French customs union as politically, economically and administratively unworkable. Similarly the Treasury ruled out a common currency.[137]

As a result the proposed association was to be merely an extension into the postwar period of the war-time cooperation in military planning and intelligence between the two countries, since the committee thought that war might not end in outright victory for the entente but in a stalemate, which would mean that the postwar situation would be a state of armed truce during which the entente would have to organise and build up its resources in preparation for the next war. Hankey concluded that the most Britain could commit herself to after the war, beyond a military alliance with France, was the development of the closest possible economic and financial cooperation which did not impinge on the sovereignties of either country. Sargent, despite his enthusiasm for closer co-operation between France and Britain, also opposed a federalist solution.[138]

Hankey wrote to Halifax on 11 July that the deliberations of the Committee 'did not, I think, encourage the idea that very much could be done outside the spheres of defence and foreign policy'. The committee did not meet again, since, as Hankey put it, after the events of May 1940, 'France appears to me to have been a debit rather than an asset in the present war.' He doubted the British people would want closer union now, 'and I do not think that I should favour it myself.' Halifax concluded that 'it certainly does not look very likely that there will be any resumption of that co-operation which we have known since 1904.'[139]

The destruction of the Anglo-French-Belgian armies and the subsequent collapse of France have been the subject of numerous studies and I do not intend to deal with this here.[140] With the fall of France, France's detractors in official circles felt free to indulge in the recriminations against that country which had been muted since September 1939. Hankey, never fond of the French connection, told Halifax that he had travelled extensively in France before the war and had discovered then that 'France was pretty rotten', with communism rife everywhere.[141] He wrote to Simon, 'The more I reflect on the events of recent years the more I realise that the French have been our evil genius from the Paris Peace Conference until today, inclusive.'[142] In a letter to Halifax, Hankey declared that, while 'the French are an attractive people', they were 'most unstable', and Britain's association with them had brought it nothing but disaster. The Maginot line had 'permeated the whole [French] nation with false military conceptions', their land preparations had been inadequate, they were hopeless in the air, and their incompetent generals had sacrificed the British army, while the French army 'as a whole has not fought well'.[143] Halifax agreed with Hankey that 'the one firm rock on which everyone was willing to build for the last two years was the French army and the Germans walked through it like they did through the Poles.'[144]

A military intelligence memorandum of 6 July 1940 on the 'Causes of French Collapse' reported at great length on the bitter political and class divisions in France before the war, the advanced age of many French generals, which prevented them from responding flexibly to the changing military fortunes of the entente in May, the adverse influence of German and communist propaganda on French morale, French dependence on the Maginot line, which discouraged training in mobile warfare, and the debilitating effects on morale of the phoney war.[145]

While this catalogue of the faults of the French army and its poor performance in battle did not, of course, lack substance (and the failure of the French command to take any steps to defend the Ardennes gap adequately was a deplorable and ultimately fatal oversight), these critics wilfully overlooked that fact that Britain shared much of the blame for its ally's and its own misfortune. The ill-informed and constant denigration of France and the French by Chamberlain and his supporters, the failure to give any material backing to French security needs by increasing the size and strength of the British army, or by giving France a definite promise of the despatch of a British expeditionary force to France in an emergency, and the condescending treatment meted out to the French government in 1938, further weakened French self-confidence, already undermined by its own foreign policy miscalculations since 1933. More often than not British policy towards the French was characterised by an unthinking complacency, as shown by Hoare's remarks to the committee of imperial defence in December 1938 that 'whatever the French may think, their interests were so bound up with ours that they could not afford to stand aloof from us.' When it finally dawned on the British early in 1939 that this assumption was not to be relied upon, they found that they had left it rather late in the day to reverse long standing foreign and defence policies which had not only neglected their only continental ally, but also the British army, an army which had shown itself more than a match for the German imperial army in 1918, and whose victories British foreign policy-makers had subsequently squandered. In Correlli Barnett's vivid words:

> While the British were resolutely viewing an ex-enemy [Germany] with benevolence and charity, their attitude to their old ally and friend, France, grew colder. Towards her they adopted an exactly opposite kind of irrationality; darkly suspecting her aims and actions; seeing her as an ogre of militarism and power; ignoring or dismissing in a passing phrase the gigantic human and material losses she had suffered during the war, and which left her critically weakened.[146]

After France's collapse, the British reverted to the neo-isolationism which had characterised their policy towards France before 1939, only now their attitude towards the French was one of downright contempt and hostility.[147] Hankey concluded, as did many other British observers at that time, including the king, 'In a way it is almost a relief to be thrown back on the resources of the Empire and of America.'[148] Simon agreed: 'nothing can serve us *now*: nothing but *a British* resolve *never* to yield.'[149] Chamberlain, who had of course long entertained deep suspicions of the French, was relieved that 'we are at any rate free of our obligations to France, who have been nothing but a liability to us.'[150] It was hardly surprising that the Francophobe Henry Channon should welcome France's collapse, writing on 10 July 1940: 'The Third Republic has ceased to exist and I don't care; it was graft-ridden, ugly, incompetent, Communistic and corrupt, and had long outlived its day. ... The old France is dead. The French National Féte day is no more; it is abolished, as is that tiresome motto "Liberté, Egalité, Fraternité."'[151]

The 'honeymoon', if it can be thus described, between Britain and France had been of short duration. Nevertheless, despite the legacy of suspicion which had clouded Anglo-French relations since the Great War, the two countries had made a serious attempt in 1939 and 1940 to bury many of their differences and to collaborate in the face of a powerful enemy. While Britain's ten divisions (by May 1940) on the Western front were totally inadequate as a means either of assisting the French militarily or of moulding the alliance into a genuine collaboration of military equals, economically and politically the short-lived association between the two countries had been relatively successful, at least in the civilian dimension. Those who welcomed the return to 'isolation' from the continent in 1940 and savaged the French for their so-called 'betrayal' were indulging in wishful thinking. It was clear that, with the collapse of the French army, Britain, even after fully mobilising the military resources of its empire, could not hope to defeat Germany on its own, even if it was able successfully to defend its homeland from a German invasion. This was, of course, appreciated by Halifax, ever the realist, who argued in the war cabinet towards the end of May for an Anglo-French approach to Italy to arrange peace negotiations with Germany.[152] Winston Churchill, now prime minister, successfully resisted Halifax's pressure, although it was a close run thing, and, until the Franco-German armistice, tried to encourage the French to continue the struggle. It was a fruitless effort.

7 Conclusion

> I am more passionately convinced than ever that the only hope for civilisation is for France and Great Britain to draw together and stick together and I am quite optimistic as to that view ultimately triumphing in England.
>
> (Philip Noel-Baker)[1]

For a brief period in 1939 and in early 1940 Noel-Baker's optimism seemed to have been fulfilled. After the outbreak of war, officials tried to determine what had gone wrong with Anglo-French relations since 1919. Reginald Leeper, writing in December 1939, believed that:

> we were so anxious to make friends with Germany that we underestimated the importance of remaining friends with France, forgetting the simple fact that our own interests were so closely interlocked with those of France that if we were to be friends of Germany it had to be an Anglo-French friendship with Germany on terms which were as acceptable to France as to ourselves. In other words the maintenance of Anglo-French cooperation was the only foundation for peace in Europe.

Now Leeper wanted to go further and put the war-time close relationship between the two countries on a permanent footing, since both countries sought 'a peaceful Europe made secure against aggression', which, in his opinion, could only be achieved by Anglo-French cooperation after the war. He continued:

> Already at the beginning of the war this cooperation is making rapid strides and it is fairly clear that by the end of the war we shall be acting as a solid unit. That unit may well be the only stable element in Europe, the only element in fact to which America will lend money for the reconstruction of Europe.[2]

Once the war started, former appeasers like Barrington-Ward became converted to the necessity of the Anglo-French connection, and, like Leeper, campaigned for the closest possible links between the two nations.[3] Thus Barrington-Ward suggested the rewriting of school history textbooks in both countries so that future generations would become imbued with 'the real community of ideals and interests which united the two countries' and would learn that the only basis for the future was lasting friendship between them. 'We can now see that the fatal inability of each country to understand the other's point of view in the years after the war led to the political estrangement that is directly responsible for the failure to cope in time with the menace of a renascent Germany.'[4]

During 1939 and 1940 there appeared to be no shortage of people anxious to do everything in their power to improve Anglo-French relations, a refreshing change from the situation before 1939 when only a few hardy souls like Spears and Churchill campaigned in favour of close Anglo-French relations. Hankey spent an hour at the Athenaeum in August 1939 talking to a Roger Pezzani, who, according to Halifax, although 'rather a tiresome fellow', was anxious to improve Anglo-French relations and 'had a remarkable series of contacts with French politicians'. When it came down to practicalities, however, Pezzani had no positive suggestions to make, and Hankey and Halifax did not use his services, no doubt much to their relief.[5]

In March 1939 the theatrical manager and producer, Henry Sherek, wrote to Spears from His Majesty's Theatre offices in the Haymarket hoping to bring a French theatrical company to London to perform a play 'simply because I am so keen on the Entente Cordiale and realise it's [*sic*] importance for the future of civilisation.'[6] Aubrey Jones, a former journalist on the foreign desk of *The Times*, approached Sir Walter Monckton, the deputy director of the Ministry of Information, on 7 May requesting employment as a liaison officer in Paris between the French and British information ministries, because 'France is a country which I know and, I think, understand. Anglo-French cooperation is something which I have at heart.'[7]

The outpouring of pro-French sentiment may have been intended as a means of assuaging guilty consciences about the way Britain had treated the French before 1939 and the underlying fear that the French might pay Britain back in its own coin by reaching a compromise peace with Germany – and there were a number of French politicians who were quite prepared for this solution even before Vichy. As Philip Bell has put it, in connection with the war aims debate, 'Distrust of France … was seldom below the surface … and expressions of unity and undying friendship gave out a slightly hollow ring.'[8]

Those like Geoffrey Dawson and Barrington-Ward, who had been vociferous supporters of Chamberlain's appeasement policy, having been converted to an anti-Hitler line after 1939, became, as has been shown, eager supporters of the entente. Others, convinced of the volatile nature of the French temperament, especially when facing a long war of inaction, indulged in a torrent of pro-French publicity in the belief that this evidence of British steadfastness to the entente would be reciprocated in France. The need to maintain a climate of optimism as far as the French were concerned prompted many officials and senior service officers to discount negative reports about low French military and civilian morale and to blame them on the malign influence of these defeatist French politicians.[9] As Philip Bell has put it, it was essential to ensure that at least 'outward appearances were well maintained'.[10] The British consul-general in Marseilles, Sir Norman King, was probably nearer the mark when he described 'all ... propaganda, explaining what nice and interesting people the English are ... [as] a waste of time. The French are not interested in Great Britain or the British Empire except as allies to help them beat the Germans.'[11]

Indeed, those politicians and officials who were sceptical about the possibility of achieving a permanent Anglo-French association may well have been correct. Paul Reynaud put his finger on one of the impediments to this in November 1939, when he recited a long list of statistics to Simon to demonstrate how much poorer the French Empire was in raw materials, population and wealth than the British Empire, and demanded that Britain would need to do much more to help France if the alliance was to survive. Nor was he, or indeed any other French politician, greatly impressed with Britain's army contribution in 1939, despite British promises of 50 or so divisions within three years.[12]

Between 1936 and 1938, when France appeared at times to be on the brink of political, social and economic chaos, and when it was fashionable to deride France in British establishment circles, even those who struggled to keep the entente alive nursed secret doubts about its survivability. These concerns were reflected in a report by William Strang, who was not a Francophobe, on a 2000 mile motor car tour he made of the French provinces in the summer of 1938, which deserves quoting at length. During this tour he visited Lille, Rouen, Varennes, Lyons, Cannes and Marseilles. His general impressions were that:

> There is a certain old-fashioned inertness in provincial sentiment, and a lack of the restless intelligence and self-conscious culture, with a hint of revolutionary sprit, which are essential elements in the face which France turns to the outside world and which, curiously wedded to deep-seated habits of order and an ancient civilisation, make up a good part of her special contribution to the life of Europe .... France, unlike Germany, does not put all her goods in the shop window. Her people have a degree of education and culture of which their outward appear-

ance will often give little sign, and a reserve of material resources which they might be loath to confess. Under an appearance of makeshift and sometimes of chaos, the country has a system of administration founded more precisely than any other on the principle of reason and order ....

But the question one asks oneself is whether, in the world as it is today, this is enough; whether the confidence of the average Frenchman that France will be united in case of peril does not take it too much for granted that a last-minute closing of ranks is all that is required; whether, in fact, a reliance on improvisation, backed though it no doubt would be by powerful moral and material reserves among the population and by a passionate devotion to the national cause, is an adequate defence, when France may be threatened on three frontiers, when her most powerful potential enemies are developing the technique of 'permanent war,' in which the first overt blow is intended to be the last, and when no immediate help can be expected from Great Britain. The Frenchman's inveterate individualism has its value as a civic virtue and may save him from the dangers of both communism and Fascism; but it can be practised at too heavy a price; and France would perhaps be safer than she is now if Frenchmen were less ready to think of giving their lives in the future, and more ready to put their hands in their pockets here and now in order both to solve the social problem and to mobilize France's economic strength as a foundation for an accelerated rearmament.[13]

The question which sympathetic British observers of France asked was whether the French were capable of pulling themselves together in the way that Strang suggested in the final paragraph. In 1939 the question appeared to have been answered satisfactorily. The French economy had began to revive and its armaments production was increasing, while Daladier was widely respected as a 'strong man' and his relatively lengthy term in office suggested that a degree of political stability had at last been established. The French were feeling more self-confident, while opinion polls after March 1939 produced large majorities who were prepared to stand up to Hitler.[14] This was a great relief to British officials like Vansittart, who had long supported the maintenance of the entente, particularly at a time when Hitler was showing himself to be more dangerously aggressive than ever before. If there is one person who was vindicated in this period, it was Vansittart, who lost his office and his reputation by his outspoken Francophilia and his warnings of the danger of Nazi Germany when all about him were cheering on Chamberlain's fruitless efforts to secure a *rapprochement* with Hitler.

With the fall of France, Winston Churchill sought to replace France as Britain's major ally by the United States. This was not to prove an easy task, although the Foreign Office began planning for a 'special association' with the United States in July 1940. Halifax thought that this could 'replace the idea of Anglo-French Union'.[15] Lord Lothian, now British ambassador to Washington, echoed the thoughts of many when he wrote that 'one interesting aspect of the collapse of France' was that 'it may make it easier to get the British Commonwealth and the United States together if we are disentangled from the European alliances which always scare America to death.' At least this remark demonstrated his consistency of thinking, since he had always opposed entangling alliances with European states.[16] However, after 1946, Britain did enter into alliances with the Fourth Republic, first, through the Treaty of Dunkirk in 1947, then through the Brussels Pact, and finally through the multinational North Atlantic Treaty.[17] Post-Second World War relations with France were never easy. A legacy of mutual suspicions remained, especially as Britain preferred to cultivate its so-called 'special relationship' with the United States.

Appendix

Propaganda leaflet written by Sir Campbell Stuart, the Chairman of the Imperial Communications Advisory Committee, London, to be disseminated to Germany. It was approved by Edouard Daladier and was intended to stress to the German people the unity of Britain and France. 22 December 1939. PREM 1/140.

13

LEAFLET NO.23

EH. 264
No.42/

F R A N C E and G R E A T B R I T A I N

FIGHT

as

ONE AND THE SAME NATION

ON LAND

ON SEA

AND IN THE AIR.

"When in certain French districts the German wireless, pursuing its vain campaign to separate France from Great Britain, was saying that Great Britain wished to wage war with the blood of Frenchmen, the voice was drowned by the uninterrupted rumble of the convoys taking soldiers and cannons of the British Army towards our frontiers".

Edouard Daladier. 10.10.39

"We are proud to know that our men are thus standing to arms beside the soldiers of France, for whose patriotism, determination and magnificent fighting qualities we have so deep an admiration. The understanding between the French and British Higher Command is complete".

Neville Chamberlain. 18.10.39

GREAT BRITAIN and FRANCE

F I G H T

A S

ONE AND THE SAME NATION !

Their Armies fight shoulder to shoulder in the trenches.

Their Navies command the seas side by side.

Their Air Fleets together sail the skies.

<u>FOR ONE AND THE SAME CAUSE</u>

To preserve their own freedom and the freedom of all Europe.

To rid themselves and all Europe of recurrent Nazi threats.

To secure therefore for themselves and all Europe a lasting peace.

<u>FOR ONE AND THE SAME FUTURE</u>

in which, when Nazism is banished, a Germany prepared to live in friendship with other nations will find her rightful place.

And a war will not be the inevitable lot of each succeeding generation.

Frankreich und England kämpfen wie EIN Volk — zu Lande, zur See und in der Luft!

„Die Stimme des deutschen Rundfunks, die England anklagte, den Krieg mit französischem Blut führen zu wollen, und so vergeblich einen Keil zwischen Frankreich und England zu treiben suchte, wurde übertönt von dem unaufhörlichen Dröhnen der englischen Truppen- und Artillerietransporte auf dem Wege nach unseren Grenzen."

Edouard Daladier 10. 10. 39.

„Es erfüllt uns mit Stolz, daß unsere Soldaten Seite an Seite mit den Soldaten Frankreichs stehen, deren Vaterlandsliebe, Entschlossenheit und Kampfgeist wir tief bewundern. Zwischen dem französischen und englischen Oberkommando herrscht absolute Einmütigkeit."

264

Neville Chamberlain 19. 10. 39.

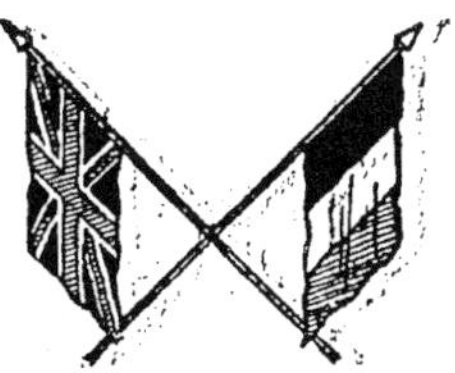

England und Frankreich kämpfen wie EIN Volk!

Ihre Armeen stehen Schulter an Schulter im Schützengraben.

Ihre Kriegsflotten beherrschen gemeinsam die Meere.

Ihre Luftflotten kämpfen Seite an Seite.

Für EINE Sache!

um ihre eigene Freiheit und die Freiheit ganz Europas zu erhalten:

um sich selber und alle Völker Europas von der ständigen Bedrohung durch das Nazi-System zu befreien:

um dauernden Frieden für sich selber und für alle Völker Europas zu erringen.

Für EINE Zukunft—

in der das Nazi-System geschlagen am Boden liegt;

in der Deutschland, zur Freundschaft mit allen Völkern bereit, seinen würdigen Platz findet;

in der Krieg nicht mehr das unabwendbare Schicksal jeder Generation ist.

264

Notes

CHAPTER 1

1. Quoted in John Robert Ferris, *The Evolution of British Strategic Policy, 1919–26* (Basingstoke: Macmillan, 1989), p. 128.
2. P.M.H. Bell, *France and Britain 1900–1940: Entente and Estrangement* (London and New York: Longman, pbk, 1996), p. 6. The following account is based on this excellent study. For French policy in this period, see Anthony Adamthwaite, *Grandeur and Misery: France's Bid for Power in Europe, 1914–1940* (London: Edward Arnold, 1995).
3. Nicholas Rostow, *Anglo-French Relations 1934–1936* (London: Macmillan, 1984), p. 7.
4. Brigadier T.G.G. Heywood, Aldershot Command to G-O-C., Aldershot, 16 June 1938, Davidson Mss, House of Lords Record Office (hereafter HLRO) JCCD DAV/227.
5. For details of Anglo-French disputes over strategy on the Western Front, see William James Philpott, *Anglo-French Relations and Strategy on the Western Front, 1914–1918* (London: Macmillan 1996).
6. Curzon at a meeting of the eastern committee, 2 December 1918, quoted in John Noble Fisher, 'Curzon and British War Imperialism in the Middle East, 1916–1919', unpublished PhD thesis, University of Leeds, 1995, pp. 382–3.
7. Smuts memorandum 'Our Policy at the Peace Conference', 3 December 1918, quoted in *ibid.*, p. 384.
8. Quoted in Michael Dockrill, 'Britain, the United States, and France and the German Settlement, 1918–1920', in B.J.C. McKercher and D.J. Moss (eds.), *Shadow and Substance in British Foreign Policy, 1919–1939: Memorial Essays Honouring C.J. Lowe* (Alberta: the University of Alberta Press, 1984), p. 203.
9. See Correlli Barnett, *The Collapse of British Power* (Gloucester: Alan Sutton, pbk, 1987 reprint), pp. 318ff. There is an immense literature on the Paris Peace Conference. See Alan Sharp, *The Versailles Settlement: Peace-making in Paris, 1919* (Basingstoke: Macmillan, 1991); Michael L. Dockrill and J. Douglas Goold, *Peace without Promise: Britain and the Peace Conferences 1919–1923* (London: Batsford, 1981); Howard Elcock, *Portrait of a Decision: The Council of Four and the Treaty of Versailles* (London: Eyre Methuen, 1972); A. Lentin, *Lloyd George, Woodrow Wilson and the Guilt of Germany: An essay in the pre-history of appeasement* (Leicester University Press, 1984).
10. Dockrill, 'Britain, France and the German Settlement ...', p. 204.
11. Quoted in *ibid.*, p. 204.

12. Quoted in Correlli Barnett, *The Collapse of British Power* (Gloucester: Alan Sutton, pbk, 1987), p. 330.
13. Quoted in John C. Cairns, 'A Nation of Shopkeepers in Search of a Suitable France, 1919–1940', in *The American Historical Review*, no. 3, vol. 79, 1974. This amusing and scholarly article should be consulted for further British opinions of the French in the period.
14. Both quotations are from Ferris, pp. 128 and 129.
15. Cairns, p. 725.
16. For a detailed discussion of this subject, see Carolyn Judith Kitching, 'Britain and the Problem of International Disarmament, 1919–1934', Unpublished PhD thesis, University of Teesside, 1995.
17. Quoted in Keith Robbins, *Munich 1938* (London: Cassell, 1968), p. 108.
18. A.J.P. Taylor, *English History, 1914–1945* (Oxford, Clarendon Press, 1965), p. 215.
19. Quoted in Cairns, p. 729.
20. Quoted in Rostow, p. 47.
21. For details, see Rostow, pp. 83ff.
22. Quoted in *ibid.*, p. 150.
23. *Ibid.*, p. 154.
24. *Ibid.*, pp. 168–171.
25. Quoted in *ibid.*, pp. 224 and 225. Clerk to Eden, tel 142, 31 January 1936, FO 371/19855.
26. Cabinet conclusions, 47(55), 16 October 1935, CAB 63/50.
27. Anthony Adamthwaite, *France and the Coming of the Second World War* (London: Frank Cass, 1977), pp. 17ff.
28. For details, see Philippe Bernard and Henri Dubief, *The Decline of the Third Republic, 1914–1938* (Cambridge: Cambridge University Press, 1987). See also Eugen Weber's fine study, *The Hollow Years: France in the 1930s* (New York: W.W. Norton, 1994), Chapter II.
29. Weber, pp. 245–56. For a meticulously researched and well-written account of French defence policies in these years, see Martin S. Alexander, *The Republic in Danger: General Maurice Gamelin and the Politics of French Defence, 1933–1940* (Cambridge: Cambridge University Press, 1992). See also Robert J. Young, *In Command of France: French Foreign Policy and Military Planning 1933–1939* (Cambridge: Harvard University Press, 1978).
30. See Rostow, p. 231; Mendl to Vansittart, 8 December 1935, CAB 63/50.
31. For details, see Paul Stafford, 'Political Autobiography and the Art of the Plausible: R.A. Butler at the Foreign Office', *Historical Journal*, 28 (4), 1985, pp. 901–22.
32. Martin Gilbert and Richard Gott, *The Appeasers* (London: Weidenfeld and Nicolson, 1963), p. 78.
33. Dawson to H.G. Daniels, 11 May 1937; Dawson to Nigel Law, 4 October 1938; Dawson to Lord Linlithgow, 18 October 1938, Dawson Mss., 79 and 80.
34. Peter Borneau to Clark-Kerr, 14 February 1936, Inverchapel Mss., General Correspondence, 1936.
35. Robert Rhodes James, *Chips: The Diaries of Sir Henry Channon* (London: Weidenfeld, 1993, diary entry, 22 March 1939, p. 188 (hereafter referred to as *Channon Diaries*).

36. Quoted in J.A. Cross, *Sir Samuel Hoare, a Political Biography* (London: Jonathan Cape, 1977), p. 188.
37. Jack Greenway to Clark-Kerr, 23 July 1939, Inverchapel Ms., General Correspondence, 1939.
38. For an excellent biography, see Norman Rose, *Vansittart: Study of a Diplomat* (London: Heinemann, 1978). See also Special Section on 'Robert Vansittart and an Unbrave World, 1930–37', in *Diplomacy and Statecraft,* Vol. 6, March 1995, No. 1, pp. 1–175; and Ian Colvin, *Vansittart in Office* (London: Gollancz, 1965).
39. Quoted in Rose, p. 91.
40. Brian McKercher, 'Old Diplomacy and New: the Foreign Office and Foreign Policy, 1919–1939', in Michael Dockrill and Brian McKercher (eds.), *Diplomacy and World Power: Studies in British Foreign Policy 1980–1950* (Cambridge: Cambridge University Press, 1966). Rose, p. 112.
41. Hankey to Major Casey, 20 April 1936, CAB 63/51.
42. On this, see *The Mist Procession: The Autobiography of Lord Vansittart* (London: Hutchinson, 1958), p. 405.
43. Rose, pp. 81–3.
44. Eden Diary, 16 November 1936, Avon Mss., 20/1/1–32. Also quoted in Dutton, *Eden*, p. 277. See Rose for an assessment of Vansittart's emotional condition, pp. 75–7.
45. Vansittart to Eden, 14 September 1936, Avon Mss, 14/1/631.
46. Claud Russell to Ponsonby 28 February 1938, Ponsonby Mss, c.680.
47. Vansittart to Eden, 9 December [1937] Avon Mss., AP 20/5/32.
48. Dalton Diaries, 7 April 1938, Dalton Mss., I, vol. 19.
49. A.J. Sylvester to Lloyd George, 3 January 1938, HLRO: Lloyd George Mss., G/22/4/2.
50. Cadogan Diary, 24 September 1936, Cadogan Mss, ACAD 1/5.
51. Rose, p. 233. Cadogan minute for secretary of state, 26 February 1939, FO 800/294.
52. Jack Greenway to Clark-Kerr, Tientsin, 23 July 1939, Inverchapel Mss, General Correspondence, 1939.
53. David Dilks (ed.), *The Diaries of Sir Alexander Cadogan, 1938–1945* (London: Cassell, 1971), entry 29 April 1938, pp. 73–74 (hereafter *Cadogan Diaries*).
54. Clive Wigram to Cadogan, 1 April 1935, Cadogan Mss., ACAD 4/1.
55. Rostow, p. 287.
56. *Cadogan Diaries*, 14 March 1938, p. 62.
57. Sargent to Phipps, 11 November 1933, Phipps Mss., PHPP 2/10.
58. Gerothwohl memorandum, 1 September 1938, HLRO, Lloyd George Mss., G/27/3/40.
59. Sargent to Phipps, 29 December 1936, Phipps Mss, PHPP I, 2/10.
60. Sargent minute, 2 January 1936, FO 371/19855.
61. See Donald Cameron Watt, 'Chamberlain's Ambassadors', in Michael Dockrill and Brian McKercher (eds.), *Diplomacy and World Power*, pp. 136–70.
62. Henderson to Halifax, 22 August 1938, FO 800/269.
63. Dalton Diaries, 28 October 1937, Dalton Mss., I, 18.
64. Henderson to Halifax, 23 February 1938, FO 800/270.

65. Henderson to Maxwell Garnett, League of Nations Union, 14 July 1937, FO 800/268.
66. Sir Miles Lampson, Cairo to Henderson, 4 January 1938, FO 800/269. Information about Loraine and Lampson comes from a forthcoming article by Peter Neville, 'The Appointment of Sir Nevile Henderson, 1937. Design or Blunder'. Neville points out that Henderson was not alone among British ambassadors in his eagerness for a settlement with Germany. Furthermore, his appointment to Berlin was fully supported by Vansittart, who had been a friend of long standing, despite Vansittart's subsequent attacks upon him. I am grateful to Dr Neville for letting me see a draft of his article before publication.
67. For Phipps, see John Herman, 'The Paris Embassy of Sir Eric Phipps, 1937–1939', unpublished PhD thesis, the London School of Economics, April 1996. See also Donald Cameron Watt, 'Chamberlain's Ambassadors', pp. 136–70. For an earlier discussion of Henderson, see Felix Gilbert, 'Two British Ambassadors: Perth and Henderson', in Gordon A. Craig and Felix Gilbert, *The Diplomats 1919–1939* 2 vols (New York: Atheneum, 1965), Vol. 2, pp. 537–54.
68. Quoted in Herman, p. 15.
69. *Cadogan Diaries*, 29 April 1938, p. 74.
70. Rostow, p. 130; Rose, p. 114, fn. Collier minute 1 January 1936, FO 371/19855.
71. For further details, see Richard Cockett, *Twilight of Truth: Chamberlain, Appeasement and the Manipulation of the Press* (London: Weidenfeld and Nicolson, 1989), pp. 3–32.
72. R.H. Hadow to Henderson, 11 May 1938, FO 800/269.
73. O'Malley, Mexico City, to Henderson, 10 June 1937, FO 800/268. Rose, pp. 111–12, 204.
74. David Dutton, *Anthony Eden: a Life and Reputation* (London: Edward Arnold, 1997) p. 41.
75. *Ibid.*, pp. 57 and 69.
76. For a more sympathetic portrayal, see David Dutton, *Simon: a Political Biography of Sir John Simon* (London: Aurum Press, 1992), on which I have relied for the following information about Simon.
77. Quoted in Dutton, *Simon*, p. 261.
78. John Harvey (ed.), *The Diplomatic Diaries of Oliver Harvey, 1937–1940* (London: Collins, 1970). Diary entry 15 October 1937, p. 15 (hereafter *Harvey Diaries*).
79. See Cross, *Hoare*, p. 79.
80. *Harvey Diaries*, 15 October 1937, p. 15.
81. For a recent biography, see Andrew Roberts '*The Holy Fox': A Biography of Lord Halifax* (London: Weidenfeld and Nicolson, 1991).
82. *Channon Diaries*, 3 June 1940, pp. 255–6.
83. Kenneth Young (ed.), *The Diaries of Sir Robert Bruce Lockhart, 1915–1938, Vol. 1 1915–1938* (London: Macmillan, 1973), p. 49.
84. Minister of health from 1935 to January 1939 and then secretary of state for air.
85. Lord privy seal, 1937–8 and then president of the board of education.
86. Colonial secretary and dominions secretary between 1935 and 1940.

87. Colonial secretary, 1937–8.
88. President of the board of trade, 1937–9.
89. *Harvey Diaries*, 15 October 1937 and 27 February 1938, pp. 51 and 103.
90. Keith Feiling, *The Life of Neville Chamberlain* (London: Macmillan, 1946). For two recent analyses, see R.A.C. Parker, *Chamberlain and Appeasement: British Policy and the Coming of the Second World War* (Basingstoke: Macmillan, 1993); and J.D. Charmley, *Chamberlain and the Lost Peace* (London: Hodder and Stoughton, 1989).
91. Quoted in Young, *Chamberlain*, p. 323.
92. See Stephen Roskill, *Hankey: Man of Secrets*, 3 vols (London: Collins, 1974).
93. Hankey to Phipps, 2 January 1936, Hankey Mss, HNKY 5/5.
94. David Carlton, *Anthony Eden: a Biography* (London: Allen Lane, 1981), p. 87.
95. Eunan O'Halpin, *Head of the Civil Service: a Study of Warren Fisher* (London: Routledge, 1989), p. 245.
96. For a full account of this debate, see Brian Bond, *British Military Policy between the Two World Wars* (Oxford: Clarendon Press, 1980), Chapter 7.
97. The above discussion is based on *ibid.*
98. *Ibid.*, Chapter 8.
99. N.H. Gibbs, *Grand Strategy: Volume 1, Rearmament Policy* (London: HMSO, 1976) p. 611, footnote.
100. Rothermere to Churchill, 7 October 1937, in Martin Gilbert, *Winston S. Churchill, Vol. V, Companion, Part 3, Documents: The Coming of the War, 1931–39* (London: Heinemann, 1982), pp. 865–6.
101. Spears to Lord Kennet, 21 December 1937, Spears Mss., SPRS 1/9.
102. Max Egremont, *Under Two Flags: The Life of Major General Sir Edward Spears* (London: Weidenfeld and Nicolson, 1997), pp. 135 and 143.
103. Spears to H. Alexander, 21 December 1939, Spears Mss, SPRS 1/9.
104. H.E. Drew, Ambares, Gironde, to R.A. Butler, 2 February 1939, FO 371/22929.
105. *History of The Times, 1920–1948, the 150th Anniversary and Beyond* (London: Times Publishing, 1952), Vol. IV, Part II, Chapters X111–XXIV, pp. 902 and 914.
106. Gilbert and Gott, *The Appeasers*, p. 8; John Turner, 'Introduction: Lord Lothian and His World', in John Turner (ed.), *The Larger Idea: Lord Lothian and the Problem of National Sovereignty* (London: The Historians' Press, 1988), pp. 13–15. For a sympathetic biography, see J.R.M. Butler, *Lord Lothian, 1882–1940* (London, Macmillan, 1960).
107. E.L. Ellis, *T.J.: A Life of Dr Thomas Jones, CH.* (Cardiff: University of Wales Press, 1992), pp. 398–421.
108. Quotations from Gilbert and Gott, *The Appeasers*, pp. 8–9.

CHAPTER 2

1. Minute by Orme Sargent, 18 January 1936, FO 371/19855.
2. Cabinet Conclusions, 3(36) 9 January 1936, CAB 23/83.

3. Rumbold to Dawson, 13 December 1935, Dawson MSS., Box 78, ff. 138–9.
4. Clerk, tel 2S, 3 January 1936, FO 371/19855.
5. Eden minute, 17 May 1936, FO 371/19856.
6. For a detailed account, see J.T. Emmerson, *The Rhineland Crisis, 7 March 1936: a Study in Multilateral Diplomacy* (London: Maurice Temple Smith, 1977).
7. Rostow, p. 233.
8. *Ibid.*, p. 240.
9. Adamthwaite, *France and the Coming ...*, p. 37.
10. Cabinet Conclusions, 15(36), 5 March 1936, CAB 23/83. See also Gibbs, pp. 252–3.
11. B.J. Bond, *Chief of Staff, The Dairies of Sir Henry Pownall*, 2 vols (London: Leo Cooper, 1972), Vol. 1, diary entry, 8 March 1936, p. 104 (hereafter *Pownall Diaries, I*).
12. Chiefs of staff memorandum, 'The Condition of our Forces to meet the Possibility of War with Germany', 16 March 1936; joint planning sub-committee report, 16 March 1936, CAB 53/27.
13. Gerothwohl to Lloyd George, 7 March 1936, HLRO: Lloyd George Mss., LG 9/24/1/84.
14. Lothian to Lloyd George, 8 March 1936, Lothian Mss, GD/17/310.
15. Cecil to Churchill, 22 April 1936, Cecil Add Mss 51073; Nigel Nicolson (ed.), *Harold Nicolson: Diaries and Letters* (London: Collins, 1966), diary entries, 10 and 23 March 1936, pp. 248–9 (hereafter *Nicolson Diaries*).
16. Austen Chamberlain to Hilda Chamberlain, 28 March 1936, in Robert C. Self (ed.), *The Austen Chamberlain Diary and Letters* (Cambridge: Cambridge University Press, 1995), p. 503.
17. Roger Lumley, MP, to Eden, 7 September 1936, Avon Mss., 14/1/600.
18. Emmerson, p. 70.
19. Eden to Clerk, Paris, tel 42, 7 March 1936, no. 37; memorandum by Eden, 'Germany and the Locarno Treaty, 8 March 1936', no. 48, W.N. Medlicott, Douglas Dakin and M.E. Lambert (eds.), *Documents on British Foreign Policy, 1919–1939* [hereafter *DBFP*]. Second Series Vol. XVI, *The Rhineland Crisis and the Ending of Sanctions, March 2–July 30 1936* (London: HMSO 1977) [hereafter *DBFP*, 2, XVI].
20. Lloyd-Thomas to Wigram, 19 March 1936, FO 371/19855.
21. Wigram and Eden minutes, 28 April 1936, FO 371/ 19856.
22. Carlton, p. 77.
23. Adamthwaite, *France and the Coming ...*, p. 40; Emmerson, p. 140.
24. Emmerson, pp. 183–5.
25. Cranborne to Eden, 10 March 1936, Avon Mss., 14/1/57J.
26. Emmerson, pp. 127–30; 'Record of Conversation between representatives of the Locarno Powers at Quai d'Orsay, Tuesday 10 March 1936 at 10.30', DBFP., 2, XVI, no. 63; Eden to Ovey, Brussels, tel 21, 11 March 1936, *DBFP.*, 2, XVI, no. 69.
27. Emmerson, pp. 133–7, 143. Cabinet conclusions, 11 March 1936, CAB 23/83, and 'Special Cabinet Meeting Minutes', 11 March 1936, BDFP, XVI, no. 70, fn. 1; Keith Middlemas and John Barnes, *Baldwin: a Biography* (London: Weidenfeld and Nicolson, 1969), p. 918. See also Gibbs, p. 241.

28. Vansittart, 'Record of conversation with M. Corbin', 13 March 1836, *BDFP*, XVI, no 68.
29. Eden to Clerk, tel 73, 17 March 1936, *DBFP*., 2, XVI, no. 119.
30. Emmerson, p. 128.
31. 'Notes: Vansittart', 14 March 1936, Templewood Mss., VIII, 6.
32. Vansittart to Eden, 7(?) March 1936, Avon Ms., 14/1/628.
33. Eden to Clerk, tel 73, 17 March 1936, DBFP., 2, XVI, no. 119; minute by Cranborne, 'British Commitments in Europe', 17 March 1936; minutes by Sargent and Vansittart, *DBFP*, 2, XVI, no. 122. See also Gaines Post Jr, *Dilemmas of Appeasement: British Deterrence and Defense, 1934–1937* (Ithaca: Cornell University Press, 1993), pp. 197–8.
34. Neville Chamberlain Diary, 12, 14 and 15 March 1936, Chamberlain Mss., NC2/23A.
35. Emmerson, pp. 191–2.
36. Eden to Clerk, tel 73, 17 March 1936, *DBFP*, 2, XVI, no. 119; minute by Cranborne, 'British Commitments in Europe', 17 March 1936, minutes by Sargent and Vansittart, *DBFP*, 2, XVI, no. 122; Cabinet Conclusions, 21(36), 18 March 1936, CAB 23/83.
37. Quoted in Emmerson, p. 190.
38. Chamberlain Diary, entries on 19 and 20 March 1936, Chamberlain Mss, NC2/23A; Cabinet conclusions, 22/36, 19 March 1936, CAB 23/83; Emmerson, p. 177.
39. Neville Chamberlain to Hilda Chamberlain, 21 March 1936, Chamberlain Mss., NC 18/1/952.
40. Simon to Baldwin, 25 March 1936, Avon Mss., 14/1/621.
41. 'Extract from the Minutes of a Meeting of Ministers on 30 March 1936', *DBFP*, 2, XVI, no. 102.
42. Gibbs, pp. 609–11 and footnote, p. 611. See also chiefs of staff memorandum, 'Staff Conversations with the Locarno Powers', 1 April 1936, CAB 53/27.
43. Cabinet conclusions, 25(39), 1 April 1937, CAB 23/83.
44. Vansittart to Eden, 31 March 1936, *DBFP*, 2, XVI, no. 189.
45. Emmerson, p. 208.
46. *Ibid.*, p. 222.
47. Eden, Geneva, to Lord Tweedsmuir, Ottawa, 9 April 1936, Avon Mss., 14/1/626A.
48. Hankey to Major Dick Casey, 20 April 1936, CAB 63/51.
49. 'Memorandum communicated by French delegation in Geneva, 8 April 1936, ' *DBFP*, 2, XVI, enclosure to no. 222; record of Anglo-French conversation in Geneva, 8 April 1936, *DBFP*, 2, XVI, enclosure to no. 223; Sargent minute, 10 April 1936, *DBFP*, 2, XVI, no. 236; Memorandum by Eden on questions to be addressed to the German government, 28 April 1936, *DBFP*, 2, XVI, no. 277.
50. Phipps, tel 175, 14 May 1936, *DBFP*, 2, XVI, no. 234.
51. Anglo-Belgian-French military staff conversations, 15–16 April 1936, WO 106/542. See also Martin Alexander, pp. 193–4.
52. Adamthwaite, *France and the Coming ...*, p. 40; Emmerson, p. 200.
53. Eden to Clerk, tel 102, 28 March 1936, *DBFP*, 2, XVI, no. 102.
54. Quoted in Gibbs, p. 611, footnote.

55. Quoted in Martin Thomas, *Britain, France and Appeasement: Anglo-French Relations in the Popular Front Era* (Oxford: Berg, 1996) p. 3.
56. Quoted in Emmerson, p. 218.
57. Pownall, *Diaries*, I, 30 March 1936, pp. 107–8.
58. Committee of imperial defence, 276th Meeting, 3 April 1936, CAB 2/6.
59. For an excellent analysis of the Popular Front government's foreign policy towards Britain, see Martin Thomas, *Britain, France and Appeasement*.
60. Vansittart minute, 14 May 1936, FO 371/19856.
61. The Earl of Avon, *The Eden Memoirs: Facing the Dictators* (London: Cassell, 1962), p. 381.
62. Eden, Paris, despatch 899, 15 May 1936, FO 371/19879.
63. Phipps to Sargent, 6 June 1936, FO 800/275.
64. Vansittart minute, 9 May 1936, FO 371/19856.
65. Vansittart minute, 17 June 1936, FO 371/19857.
66. Vansittart minute, May 1936, FO 371/19856.
67. Phipps, Berlin, tel 145S, 16 June 1936, Vansittart minute, 17 June 1936, FO 371/19877.
68. Wigram to Phipps, 11 June 1936, Phipps Mss., PHPPS I, 2/25. Eden minute, 22 May 1936, FO 371/19879. For details of Franco-German contacts in this period see Adamthwaite, *France and the Coming ...*, pp. 53ff.
69. Eden, Paris, to Clerk, despatch 898, 15 May 1936, *DBFP*, 2, XVI, no. 329; Phipps tels 183 and 129S, 26 and 27 May 1936, Sargent minute, 28 May 1936, Vansittart minute, 1 June 1936, and Eden minute 3 June 1936, *DBFP*, 2, XVI, nos 339 and 343.
70. 'Joint Planning Staff Appreciation: Strategical Review', 3 July 1936, CAB 53/28.
71. 'Cabinet Discussion of Plans for Agreement with Germany', 6 July 1936, *DBFP*, 2, XVI, Appendix II, pp. 748–57; Cabinet Conclusions, 50(36), 6 July 1936, CAB 23/80.
72. Eden to Baldwin, 6 June 1936, CAB 53/28.
73. Chiefs of staff committee, 178th Meeting, 16 June 1936, CAB 53/6.
74. Cabinet committee on foreign policy, 2nd meeting, 15 July 1936, CAB 27/222.
75. Cabinet Conclusions, 53(36), 16 July 1936, CAB 23/85.
76. Eden Diary, 31 July 1936, Avon Mss., 20/1/1–32.
77. Cabinet committee on foreign policy, 5th Meeting, 25 August 1936, CAB 27/622; Adamthwaite, *France and the Coming ...*, p. 71.
78. Cabinet conclusions, 56(36), 2 September 1936, CAB 23/ 85. See also Thomas, p. 20.
79. Lothian to Lloyd George, 23 May 1936; Lothian to Curtis, 23 July 1936, Lothian Mss., GD 40/17/319.
80. Sir Patrick Duncan, Pretoria, to Lothian, 24 September 1936, Lothian Mss., GD 40/17/328/307.
81. Austen Chamberlain to Hilda Chamberlain, 28 March 1936, *Austen Chamberlain Diary and Letters*, p. 503.
82. Gerothwohl to Lloyd George (telephoned), 15 March 1936; Note by Professor Gerothwohl, 25 March 1936, HLRO Lloyd George Mss., G/26/5/17; Gerothwohl memorandum for Lloyd George, 14 April 1936, HLRO, Lloyd George Mss., G/26/6/5.

83. For a useful analysis, see Glyn Stone, 'The European Great Powers and the Spanish Civil War, 1936–1939', in Robert Boyce and Esmonde M. Robertson, (eds), *Paths to War: New Essays on the Origins of the Second World War* (New York: St. Martin's Press, 1989) pp. 199–232.
84. Carlton, pp. 88–9; Adamthwaite, *France and the Coming* ..., pp. 43–4; Stone, p. 213.
85. Stone, p. 208.
86. Parker, pp. 84–5.
87. See Adamthwaite, *France and the Coming* ..., p. 53; and Parker, p. 72.
88. Vansittart memorandum, 6 October 1936, FO 371/19856.
89. 'Annual Report on France for 1935; Extracts from Economic and Financial Sections, ' 18 January 1936, FO 371/19861.
90. Clerk to Eden, despatch 764, 11 June 1936, FO 371/19857.
91. Vansittart to Clerk, 10 June 1936, FO 371/19857.
92. Lloyd-Thomas to Vansittart, 11 June 1936, FO 371/19857.
93. Clerk to Vansittart, 1 June 1936, FO 371/19857.
94. Clerk, despatch 121, 22 September 1936, enclosing report by the British military attaché, FO 371/19871.
95. Beaumont-Nesbitt to Clerk, no. 73, 11 June 1936; memorandum by the British military attaché, Paris, no. 643, 3 September 1936;, Wigram and Sargent minutes, 26 September and 1 October 1936, FO 371/19871.
96. E. Rowe-Dutton, Paris, 'Note of a Conversation with M. Baudouin', 27 June 1936; Sargent minute, 6 July 1936, FO 371/19859.
97. Bernard and Dubief, p. 322.
98. Lloyd-Thomas to Vansittart, 29 July 1936, FO 371/19859.
99. Phipps, Berlin, tel 190, 12 June 1936; Clerk, tel. 132S, 15 June 1936, Collier and Sargent minutes, 16 and 17 June 1936, FO 371/ 19857; Clerk, despatch 1164, 8 September 1936, FO 371/19856. Herman, p. 11.
100. Group Captain Colyer, air attaché, to Phipps, 9 June 1936; Wigram minute, 12 June 1936; air staff note, 1 July 1936, FO 371/19871.
101. Gladwyn Jebb minute, 8 October 1936, FO 371/19871.
102. Clerk, despatch 1058, 17 August 1936, Eden minute, 20 August 1936, FO 371/19859.
103. Clerk, despatch 1288, 12 October 1936, FO 371/19859.
104. Clerk, tel 5361S, 1 October 1936, Lloyd-Thomas, despatch 1310, 14 October 1936, minutes by Wigram, 24 September 1936, Sargent, 20 October, Cadogan, 20 October, Vansittart, 22 October and Eden, 27 October 1936. FO 371/19879.
105. For details, see Alexander, *The Republic in Danger*, pp. 296–301.
106. Emmerson, pp. 234–5; Bond, *British Military Policy*, pp. 232ff.
107. Bond, *British Military Policy*, p. 233.
108. Clerk, tel 313, 4 December 1936, Wigram minute, 4 December 1936, FO 371/19871.
109. See Sean Greenwood, '"Caligula's Horse Revisited". Sir Thomas Inskip as Minister for the Coordination of Defence, 1936–1939', *Journal of Strategic Studies*, vol. 17, no. 2, 1994.
110. Chamberlain Diary, 25 October 1936, Chamberlain Mss., NC V2/23A.
111. 'The Army': memorandum by Sir Warren Fisher, 23 October 1936, Warren Fisher Mss., Misc 461 2.

112. Gibbs, pp. 445–7; see also 'The Role of the British Army', Duff Cooper memorandum, CP 326(36), 3 December 1936; 'The Role of the British Army', Chamberlain memorandum, CP 34(327), 11 December 1936, FO 371/198222.
113. Neville Chamberlain Diary, December 1936, Chamberlain Mss., NC2/24A. For the Treasury's influence see G.H.C. Peden, *British Rearmament and the Treasury, 1932–1939* (Edinburgh: Scottish Academic Press, 1979).
114. Vansittart minute, 14 December 1936, FO 371/19882.
115. 'The Role of the British Army', Duff Cooper memorandum, CP 337(36), 14 December 1936.
116. Extract from Cabinet Conclusions, 75(36), 16 December 1936, FO 371/19882.
117. Vansittart minute, 18 December 1936; Eden minute, 19 December 1936, FO 371/ 19882.
118. Gibbs, pp. 444–5. See also Gaines Post, Jr, pp. 159–63.
119. Neville Chamberlain Diary, 19 January 1936, Chamberlain Mss., NC2/23A.
120. Pownall, *Diaries* 1, 27 January 1936, p. 99.
121. Gibbs, pp. 441–60.
122. Thomas, p. 14.
123. Hankey's remarks on Vansittart's memorandum, 'The World Situation and Rearmament', 21 December 1936, CAB 63/51.
124. Quoted in Thomas, p. 21.

CHAPTER 3

1. Cranborne to Cecil, 25 January 1937, Cecil Add Mss., 51087.
2. Clerk, despatch 173A, 30 January 1937, FO 371/20697.
3. Clerk, tel 59S, 31 January 1937, Stevenson minute, 2 February 1937, FO 371/20690.
4. Sargent minute, 18 January 1937, Vansittart to Eden, Geneva, 25 January 1937, nos 86 and 116, W.N. Medlicott, Douglas Dakin, assisted by Gillian Bennett (eds.), *Documents on British Foreign Policy, 1919–1939*, second series, vol. XVIII, *European Affairs, January 2–June 30, 1937* (London: HMSO, 1977) [hereafter *DBFP*, 2, XVIII].
5. Andrew J. Crozier, *Appeasement and Germany's Last Bid for Colonies* (Basingstoke: Macmillan, 1988), pp. 175 and 195. Eden to Leith-Ross, 19 January 1937, Leith-Ross to Sargent, 26 January 1937, W.N. Medlicott, Douglas Dakin, assisted by Gillian Bennett (eds.), *DBFP*, 2, XVIII, nos 92 and 118, Martin Thomas, chapter 5.
6. Crozier, pp. 174ff.
7. Quoted in Crozier, p. 196.
8. *Ibid.*, p. 196.
9. Gerothwohl to Lloyd George, 29 January 1937, HLRO, Lloyd George Mss., LG G27/1/2.
10. Phipps, tel 74S, 4 February 1937; Leith-Ross minute for the chancellor of the exchequer, 4 February 1937, Torr minute, 6 February 1937, *DBFP*, 2, XVIII, nos 74 and 148.

11. Crozier, pp. 197–8 and 204–6.
12. Adamthwaite, *France and the Coming …*, p. 56.
13. Lothian to General J.C. Smuts, House of Assembly, Cape Town, 16 March 1937, Lothian Mss., GD 40/17/333.
14. Lord Arnold to Lothian, 4 June 1937, Lothian Mss., GD 40/17/334.
15. Lothian to Smuts, 14 May 1937, Lothian Mss., GD 40/17/343.
16. Memorandum by Hankey, 18 January 1937, CAB 63/52.
17. Vansittart memorandum (probably 3 February 1937) on cabinet paper, CP 41(37), 'The Role of the British Army', 28 January 1937, FO 371/20746.
18. 'Role of the British Army'. Memorandum by Inskip for the cabinet, 2 February 1937; Strang Minute, 11 February 1937, FO 371/ 20746.
19. Cabinet Conclusions, 5(37), 3 February 1937, FO 371/20746.
20. 'Record by Mr Baxter of conversation with Colonel Clark', 29 January 1937, *DBFP*, 2, XVIII, no. 126. For further details about French pressure for a British mechanised force, see Alexander, pp. 25ff.
21. *The Memoirs of Captain Liddell Hart*, 2 vols (London: Cassell, 1965), Vol. Two, p. 3.
22. Gibbs, p. 466.
23. Alexander, p. 255.
24. Vansittart minute for Eden, 12 July 1937, no. 52, W.N. Medlicott, Douglas Dakin and Gillian Bennett (eds.), Documents on British Foreign Policy, 1919–1939, second series, vol. XIX, *European Affairs, July 1 1937–August 4, 1938* (London: HMSO, 1982) [hereafter *DBFP*, 2, XIX].
25. Phipps, tel 382S, 5 July 1937; Clerk, despatch 382S, 18 February 1937, FO 371/20696.
26. 'Talk with Deverell', 18 November 1937, Liddell Hart Mss., 11/1937/94b; Dalton Diary, 'latter half of November 1937', Dalton Mss, I, p. 18.
27. Neville Chamberlain to Hilda Chamberlain, 12 September 1937, Chamberlain Mss., NC 18/1/1620.
28. Hoare to Neville Chamberlain, 17 March 1937, Templewood Mss., IX, 3.
29. Roberts, p. 62.
30. Hoare to Chamberlain, 17 March 1937, Templewood Mss., IX, 3.
31. Henderson to Sargent, 20 July 1937, enclosing memorandum by Henderson on British policy towards Germany, 10 May 1937, *DBFP*, 2, XIX, no. 53.
32. 'Draft Despatch to Sir N. Henderson', 18 October 1938, *DBFP*, 2, XIX, Annex to no. 504; Strang minute, 13 November 1937, *DBFP*, 2, XIX, annex to no. 319.
33. Sargent to Phipps, 29 November 1937, FO 800/274.
34. Sargent to Phipps, 15 October 1937, Phipps Mss, PHPPS II, 2/1.
35. Halifax, 'notes for talk with Hitler', undated but probably November 1937, Hickleton Papers, Reel 1.
36. Eden to Chamberlain, 16 November 1937, Avon Mss., AP 20/5/13.
37. Cabinet conclusions, 48(37), 1 December 1937, CAB 23/90.
38. 'Record of Conversations between British and French Ministers held at No. 10 Downing Street on November 29 and 30, 1937', *DBFP*, 3, XIX, no. 354; see also Adamthwaite, *France and the Coming …*, pp. 67–70.
39. Neville Chamberlain to Hilda Chamberlain, 5 December 1937, Chamberlain Mss., NC 18/1/1030a.
40. Sargent to Phipps, 4 December 1937, Phipps Mss., PHPPS II, 2/1.

41. Sir Alexander Hardinge to Halifax, 30 November 1937, Hickleton Papers, Reel 1.
42. See pp. 00–0. Also Adamthwaite, *France and the Coming ...*, p. 71.
43. Gibbs, chapter VIII, pp. 279–319, 467ff.
44. Chamberlain to Hore-Belisha, 12 October 1937; Notes by Hore-Belisha, 12 October 1937, Chamberlain Mss., 5/9–5/26.
45. For a sympathetic, if critical, account, see Brian Bond, *Liddell Hart: a Study of his Military Thought* (London: Cassell, 1976), in particular chapter 4.
46. Liddell Hart to Burnett-Stuart, 9 November 1939, Liddell Hart Mss 1/323/25; Liddell Hart Notes, 6 November 1936, Liddell Hart Mss., 11/1936/26, *The Times* article, 'The Role of the Army', 11 November 1936, Liddell Hart Mss., 10/1936/92; 'Talk with F.M. Sir C.J. Deverell, 12 November 1936', Liddell Hart Mss., 11/1936/99.
47. 'Note on the Question of the Channel Ports and the Role of the British Expeditionary Force', by Liddell Hart, 24 August 1937, 'sent to H-B, 26 August', Liddell Hart Mss., 11/hb/1937/23; Note by Liddell Hart, 20 October 1937, 'compiled at H.B.'s request (for the PM)', Liddell Hart Mss., 11/HB 1937/62; 'Talk with H-B', Liddell Hart 16 November 1937, Liddell Hart Mss., 11/HB 1937/98B.
48. 'British Defence Policy', memorandum by General Sir John Burnett-Stuart, GOC-in-C., Southern Command, April 1935, Liddell Hart Mss., 1/132/22; Quotation from Bond, *British Military Policy*, p. 216. See also *ibid.*, pp. 93–95 and note 9, p. 116.
49. '"Army Reform." Notes by The Rt Hon. Leo S. Amery'. Undated but attached to reply by Liddell Hart to Amery dated 2 March 1937, Liddell Hart Mss., 1/14/15A and 1/14/16.
50. Adam to Liddell Hart, 17 November 1937, Liddell Hart Mss., 1/4 ADAM.
51. Chiefs of staff's report, 'Comparison of the Strength of Great Britain with that of Certain other Nations as at January 1938', 12 November 1937, CAB 53/34.
52. Bond, *British Military Policy*, p. 253.
53. Inskip to Hankey, 26 and 28 January 1938, Hankey minute, 29 January 1938, CAB 21/554.
54. Inskip minute, 26 April 1938, CAB 21/554.
55. Hankey to prime minister, 19 April 1938, FO 800/311.
56. Bond, *British Military Policy*, p. 257.
57. Memorandum by Eden, 26 November 1937, CAB 4/27.
58. Eden to secretary of the committee of imperial defence, 16 December 1937 and 1 January 1938, *DBFP*, 2, XIX, no. 396, fn. 2. Eden to Duff Cooper, 17 December 1937, Avon Mss., 13/1/60F.
59. Minutes by Strang, 21 December 1937; Ingram 21 December 1937; Sargent, 22 December 1938 and Eden, 23 December 1938, FO 371/20698.
60. Eden to Swinton, 31 December 1937, Avon Mss, 13/1/60G.
61. Swinton to Eden, 24 January 1938, Avon Mss., 13/1/60J.
62. 'Memorandum by the Chiefs of Staff Sub-Committee of the Committee of Imperial Defence on Staff Conversations with France and Belgium', 1 February 1938, *DBFP 2* series, XIX, no. 491. Also quoted in Gibbs, p. 625, but no date is given.
63. Vansittart to Eden, 17 December 1937, Avon Mss., AP 20/5/33.

64. 'Memorandum by the Chiefs of Staff Sub-Committee of the Committee of Imperial Defence on Staff conversations with France and Belgium', 1 February 1938, *DBFP*, 2, XIX, no. 491. Also quoted in Gibbs, pp. 626–7.
65. Thomas, pp. 12–14, 16.
66. Quoted in *ibid.*, pp. 16 and 20.
67. Eden to Chamberlain, 14 September 1937, Avon Mss., AP 20/5/11. Eden believed that Nyon had demonstrated 'that the Western democracies can still play a decisive part in European affairs'. Eden to Churchill, 14 September 1937, Avon Mss., 20/5/16.
68. Neville Chamberlain to Hilda Chamberlain, 1 August 1937, Chamberlain Mss., NC 18/1 /10/4.
69. Alexander, p. 271.
70. Board of Trade memorandum, 23 October 1936; Clerk, tel 287, 26 Sep 1936; FO 371/19861. Thomas, p. 70.
71. Memorandum by Rowe-Dutton on 'Financial Situation in France', 1 December 1936; Barclay minute, 4 December 1936, FO 371/19861.
72. Phipps, tel 408S, 12 July 1937, Sargent and Eden minutes, 15 and 16 July 1937, FO 371/20286.
73. Ashton-Gwatkin minute on Phipps, despatch 767E, 22 June 1937, FO 371/20690.
74. Clerk, tel 12, 24 January 1937; Eden, Geneva, to Chancellor of the Exchequer, tel 11, 25 January 1937, FO 371/20688.
75. Chancellor of the exchequer to Montagu Norman, 23 January 1937, FO 371/20688.
76. Ashton-Gwatkin minute, 5 February 1937, FO 371/20688.
77. Hugh Lloyd-Thomas, Paris, to Sargent, 5 February 1937, FO 371/20689.
78. Message from chancellor of the exchequer to Morganthau, 10 February 1937, FO 371/20689.
79. Sargent minute, 8 February 1937, FO 371/20689.
80. Rowe-Dutton minute, 20 February 1937, FO 371/20688.
81. Gladwyn Jebb minute, 26 February 1937, FO 371/20688.
82. Sargent minute, 1 March 1937, FO 371/20688.
83. Clerk, tel 23, 5 March 1937, FO 371/20688.
84. Eden to Lindsay, Washington, despatch 229, 11 March 1937, FO 371/20688.
85. Rowe-Dutton, Paris, to S.D. Waley, Treasury, 19 March 1937, FO 371/20688.
86. Rowe Dutton memorandum, 6 April 1937, FO 371/20689.
87. Phipps, tel 311, 3 June 1937, FO 371/20689.
88. Phipps, tel 332, 15 June 1937, FO 371/20689.
89. Law had left the diplomatic service in the early 1920s after having been cited as co-respondent in divorce proceedings brought by Sir Milne Cheetham, the counsellor at the Paris embassy, where Law was employed as a junior official, against his wife. The Cheethams were divorced in 1923 and Law married Lady Cheetham in 1929. See Rose, *Vansittart*, p. 56 and footnote.
90. Memorandum by Nigel Law, 11 February 1937; Vansittart minute, FO 371/20689.
91. Phipps to Sargent, 16 June 1937, FO 371/ 20689.

92. Peter Borneau to Clark Kerr, 4 April 1937, Inverchapel Mss., Gen. Corr, 1937.
93. Barclay minute, 23 June 1936, FO 371/20686, Adamthwaite, *France and the Coming ...*, pp. 98–102.
94. Conversation between the prime minister and the French ambassador, 20 September 1937, FO 371/206907.
95. Rowe-Dutton memorandum, 6 October 1937; Strang and Ashton-Gwatkin minutes, 13 and 16 November 1937, FO 371/20691. See also G.C. Peden, 'A Matter of Timing: the Economic Background to British Foreign Policy, 1937–9', *History*, vol. 69, 1984, pp. 15–27.
96. Foreign Office memorandum, 'The French Financial Situation and the desirability of giving assistance to the French Government', 29 September 1937, FO 371/20691.
97. Strang to Waley, 5 October 1937; Waley to Strang, 5 October 1937; Jebb and Strang minutes, 6 and 7 October 1937; Vansittart to Eden, Brussels, tel 13, 12 November 1937; FO 371/20691.
98. Phipps, despatch 692, 4 June 1937, Sargent and Vansittart Minutes, 10 and 11 June 1937, FO 371/20686.
99. Phipps, despatch 1347, 25 November 1937, FO 371/20286.
100. Adamthwaite, *France and the Coming ...*, pp. 65–6.
101. Colonel Roderick Macleod and Dennis Kelly (eds.), *The Ironside Diaries, 1937–1940* (London: Constable, 1962), 29 December 1937 (hereafter *Ironside Diaries*), p. 65.
102. *Ibid.*, pp. 65–6.

CHAPTER 4

1. Churchill to Derby, 12 April 1938, quoted in Gilbert, *Churchill, Companion to Volume V, part 3*, pp. 963–4.
2. *Ironside Diaries*, 25 March 1938.
3. Neville Chamberlain Diary, 19 February 1938, Chamberlain Mss., NC2/24A; 'Cabinet Committee on Foreign Policy meeting at the Prime Minister's room at the House of Commons,' 5 February 1938, *DBFP*, 2, XIX, no. 488.
4. Phipps, tel 50, 18 February 1938, *DBFP*, 2, XIX, no. 554.
5. Henderson, tel 54, 18 February 1938, Sargent, Strang and Cadogan minutes, 19 February 1938, *DBFP*, 2, XIX, no. 555 and fn.3.
6. *Pownall Diaries*, I, 21 February 1938, p. 135.
7. Message from Phipps to Halifax (telephone) undated, February 1938, FO 800/311; Phipps to prime minister, tel 20, February 1938, FO 371/21590.
8. Phipps, tel 117S, 24 February 1938, FO 371/21590.
9. Phipps to Hankey, 23 February 1938, Phipps Mss., PHPP 3/3. Hankey felt 'a strange feeling of relief' when Eden resigned: 'Today I felt there was just the possibility of peace.' Hankey to Phipps, 21 February 1938, Phipps Mss., PHPP I. 3/3.
10. Chamberlain to Phipps, tel, 20 February 1938, FO 371/21590.

11. Roberts, p. 95. For Butler see Anthony Howard, *RAB: The Life of R.A. Butler* (London: Jonathan Cape, 1987), chapter 8.
12. Phipps, tel 63, 25 February 1938, Strang minute, 25 February 1938, FO 371/21590.
13. Parker, p. 140.
14. Phipps, tel 81, 13 March 1938, FO 371/21598. Sargent minute, 17 March 1938, FO 800/274.
15. For further details about this incident, see Herman, pp. 150ff. In January 1936 Laurence Collier wrote that it was not 'proper for us to try to influence French internal politics ... We cannot influence the composition of the next French Government.' Collier minute, 1 January 1936, FO 371/19855.
16. Sargent to Phipps, 17 March 1938, enclosing minutes by Sargent and Cadogan, 17 March 1938, Phipps Mss., PHPP 2/10.
17. Clerk, despatch 274, 18 February 1937, FO 371/20690.
18. Phipps, tel 474, 17 July 1938, FO 371/21612.
19. Phipps to Halifax, 22 March 1938, FO 800/311.
20. Phipps to Halifax, 18 March 1938, Phipps Mss., PHPPS. I, 1/20.
21. Phipps to Halifax, 27 & 28 March 1938, Phipps Mss., PHPPS I, 1/20; Halifax to Phipps, 30 March 1938, Phipps Mss., PHPPS II 1/20. See also Gilbert, Winston S. Churchill, Vol. V *Companion*, part 3, pp. 963–4.
22. *Ibid.*, pp. 963, 989, 991 fn 1.
23. Phipps, tel 77, 12 March 1938, FO 371/21598.
24. Phipps, tel 203S, 27 March 1938, FO 371/21599.
25. Adamthwaite, *France and the Coming* ..., p. 95.
26. Phipps to Halifax, 19 April 1938, Phipps Mss., PHPPS, 1/20.
27. Phipps tel 110, 10 April 1938, FO 371/21599; Phipps to Halifax, 11 April 1938; Halifax to Phipps, 13 April 1938, Phipps to Halifax, 13 April 1938, Phipps Mss, PHPPS 1/20.
28. Phipps, despatch 476, 24 April 1938, FO 371/21599.
29. Phipps to Halifax, 30 March and 13 April 1938, Phipps Mss., PHPPS II, 1/20.
30. Chamberlain to Ida Chamberlain, 16 April 1938, Chamberlain Mss., NC 18/1/1047.
31. *Cadogan Diaries*, 28 April 1938, pp. 71–2.
32. For details see below pp. 95–6.
33. Gibbs, pp. 646–8.
34. Parker, p. 145.
35. 'Record of Anglo-French Conversations held at No. 10 Downing Street on April 28 and 29, 1938', *DBFP*, 2, XIX, no. 164.
36. Chamberlain to Ida Chamberlain, 1 May 1938, Chamberlain Mss., NC 18/1/1049.
37. *Cadogan Diaries*, 29 April 1938, pp. 73–4.
38. *Harvey Diaries*, 28 April 1938, p. 134.
39. Crozier, p. 239.
40. Quoted in *ibid.*, p. 240.
41. Cabinet committee on foreign policy, 26th Meeting, 18 March 1938, CAB 27/623.
42. Neville Chamberlain to Ida Chamberlain, 20 March 1938, Chamberlain Mss., NC 18./1/1042.

43. Cabinet committee on foreign policy, 27th Meeting, 21 March 1938, CAB 27/623.
44. 'Draft Memorandum for French Government on Czechoslovakia circulated to Foreign Policy Committee by Lord Halifax, 21 March 1938'. CAB 27/625; Cabinet Conclusions, 15(38), 22 March 1938; Foreign Office to Phipps, tel 141, 22 May 1938, CAB 23/93.
45. 'Report by the Chiefs of Staff Sub-Committee of the Committee of Imperial Defence on the comparison of the strength of Great Britain with that of certain other nations as at January 1938', 12 November 1937, *DBFP*, 2, XIX, no. 316. Air Chief Marshal Sir Cyril Newall had been appointed chief of the air staff in September : Chatfield and Deverell remained in post.
46. See above, pp. 67–8.
47. Memorandum by Group Captain G.C. Colyer, 14 January 1938, FO 371/21593.
48. Phipps to Sargent, 17 January 1938, minute by Cadogan, 24 January 1938, FO 371/21593.
49. Vansittart minute, 27 January 1938, FO 371/21593.
50. Eden minute, 31 January 1938, FO 371/21593.
51. Eden to Chamberlain, 'Personal and Strictly Confidential', 31 January 1938, FO 371/21593.
52. Note by Hankey on 'Staff Conversations with France and Great Britain', 10 February 1938, CAB 63/53.
53. Gibbs, p. 629.
54. Cabinet Conclusions, 18(38), 6 April 1938, CAB 23/93.
55. Committee of imperial defence, 319th Meeting, 11 April 1938, CAB 2/7.
56. Cabinet conclusions, 19(38), 13 April 1938, CAB 23/93.
57. Halifax to Chamberlain, 14 April 1938, PREM 1/308.
58. Gibbs, pp. 622–36; Cabinet conclusions, 21(38), 27 April 1938, CAB 23/93.
59. *Pownall Diaries*, 25 April 1938, p. 144.
60. Deputy chief of the air staff to the chief of the air staff, 25 April 1938; Chief of the air staff to the secretary of state for air, 25 April 1938, AIR 9/78.
61. Dankwerts minutes, 22 April 1938 and 3 May 1938; minute by Chatfield, 3 May 1938; Dankwerts minute, 6 May 1938; Duff Cooper minute, 9 May 1938, ADM 116/3379.
62. Cabinet conclusions, 26(38), 25 May 1938, CAB 23/38.
63. Captain Holland, Naval Attaché, Paris, to Director of Naval Intelligence, Admiralty, 10 June 1938; Dankwerts minutes, 17 June and 7 July 1938, ADM 116/3379.
64. Group Captain J.G. Slessor, Deputy Director, Plans, minute 17 June 1938; note by air staff, 'The Scope of the Staff conversations', 4 July 1938, AIR 9/78.
65. Minutes by Vansittart, 20 November 1937; and Eden, 22 November 1937, FO 371/20696.
66. IIC Report, 21 February 1938; Minutes by Barclay, 15 March 1938; Strang, 17 March and Vansittart, 28 March, FO 371/21594.
67. Cabinet conclusions, 21(38), 17 April 1938, FO 371/21595.
68. H.V. Cole, Mines Department, to Strang, 2 June 1938; Nicholls minute, 20 June 1938, FO 371/21595.

69. Memorandum by the minister for coordination of defence, 1 July 1938, CP 153(38), FO 371/21595; Cabinet conclusions, 31(38), 6 July 1938, CAB 23/94.
70. Vansittart minute for Halifax, FO 371/21595.
71. Phipps, tel 205S, 26 March 1938, minutes by Sargent, 31 March, Cadogan, 2 April, Vansittart, and Halifax, 8 April 1938, FO 371/21612.
72. Phipps to Halifax, 19 April 1938, FO 800/311.
73. Phipps to Sargent, 7 April 1938, FO 371/21612.
74. For a comprehensive analysis of the Czechoslovak crisis and its background, see Keith Robbins, *Munich 1938* (London: Cassell, 1968).
75. Simon Diary, 22 May 1938, Simon Mss., 7.
76. Phipps to Halifax, 23 June 1938, FO 800/311.
77. Henderson to Halifax, 18 July 1938, FO 800/269.
78. Ronald Campbell, tel 483S, 23 July 1938, FO 371/21608.
79. For details of this visit, see Roberts, p. 103; and Charmley, p. 86.
80. Ronald Campbell to Sargent, 11 and 12 August 1938; minutes by D. Howard, Western Dept, Nicholls, Southern Department, A.N. Maclean, Far Eastern Department; Sargent to Campbell, 20 August 1938, FO 371/21592.
81. Simon Diary and Notes, 22 May 1938 and 31 August 1938, Simon Mss., 7.
82. Cabinet conclusions, 36(38), 30 Aug 1938, CAB 23/94.
83. Phipps, tel 597S, 16 September 1938, Frank Roberts minute, 17 September 1938, FO 371/21596.
84. Wing Commander Goddard, Air Ministry A13, to Mallet, 19 September 1938, FO 371/21596.
85. Daladier to Chamberlain, 12 August 1938; minutes by Phillips, 14 August, and Horace Wilson, 15 August; Chamberlain to Daladier, 17 August 1938, PREM 1/267S.
86. Inskip Diary, Tuesday 13 September 1938, Inskip Mss., I, 1/1; Phipps to Halifax, 14 September 1938, FO 800/311.
87. Cabinet conclusions, 38(38), 14 September 1938, CAB 23/95.
88. Chiozza Money to Lloyd George, 14 September 1938, HLRO Lloyd George Mss., G/14/10/42.
89. Dalton diary, 17 September 1938, Dalton Mss., I, vol 19.
90. Cabinet conclusions, 39 (38) 17 September 1938, CAB 23/95.
91. Phipps, tel 563S, 4 September 1938, CAB 53/41. Gamelin added that, if necessary, France would also advance into Italy.
92. Newall to Ismay, 9 September 1938, CAB 53/41.
93. Gort to Newall, 12 September 1938, CAB 43/41.
94. *Cadogan Diaries*, 13 and 17 September 1938, pp. 99–100.
95. Simon Diary, 29 September 1938, Simon Mss 10.
96. Inskip Diary, 19 September 1938, Inskip Mss., INKP I, 1/1.
97. *Cadogan Diaries*, 18 September 1938, pp. 100–1.
98. 'Record of an Anglo-French Conversation held at No. 10 Downing Street on September 18, 1938', E.L. Woodward, Rohan Butler and Margaret Lambert (eds.), *Documents on British Foreign Policy, 1919–1939*, third series, vol. IIO, 1938 (London: HMSO, 1950) [hereafter *DBFP*, 3, II].
99. Simon Diary, 29 September 1939, Simon Mss, 39.
100. See John Herman, *The Paris Embassy of Sir Eric Phipps*, pp. 173–9.
101. See, for example, Phipps to Halifax, 10 September 1939, CAB 37/(38).

102. See Herman, pp. 201–16.
103. Vansittart to Halifax, 17 September 1938, FO 800/311.
104. For details of this meeting, see Charmley, pp. 114–17.
105. Quotation from Roberts, p. 115.
106. Quotations from *ibid.*, pp. 114 and 116–17.
107. Quotation from *ibid.*, p. 117.
108. Simon Diary, 'Godesberg', 29 September 1938, Simon Mss, 10.
109. 'Record of an Anglo-French Conversation held at No. 10 Downing Street on September 25, 1938, 9.25 a.m.', *DBFP*, 3, II, no. 1093.
110. 'Notes of a Meeting held on 26 September 1938 at 11 a.m. to obtain the views of General Gamelin on the Military Aspects of the Czechoslovak Crisis', CAB 21/595.
111. *Pownall Diaries*, II, 26 September 1938, p. 163.
112. Simon Diary, 'Godesberg', 29 September 1938, Simon Mss., 7.
113. For further details, see Keith Robbins, p. 291.
114. Simon Diary, 'Godesberg', 29 September 1938, Simon Mss., 7.
115. Robbins, pp. 303 and 398.
116. Admiral Roger Backhouse, Admiralty, to Cadogan, 26 September 1938, FO 371/21596.
117. 'Record of an Anglo-French Conversation held at No. 10 Downing Street on September 26, 1938 at 11.20 a.m.', *DBFP*, 3, II, no. 1096.
118. Robbins, p. 316.
119. Charmley, pp. 119ff.
120. Colin R. Coote, *The Times*, to Eden, 20 September 1938, Avon Mss., 13/16/66C.
121. Cecil to Jonathan Griffin, 22 September 1938, Cecil, Add Mss. 57156.

CHAPTER 5

1. Mallet minute, 13 December 1938, FO 371/21612.
2. Chamberlain to Hilda Chamberlain, 11 December 1938, Chamberlain Mss., NC 18/1/1079. See also Wesley Wark, 'German Political Intelligence, Moralism and Grand Strategy in 1939', *Intelligence and National Security*, vol. 5, no. 1, January 1990, pp. 150–70.
3. Roberts, p. 125.
4. Chamberlain to Hilda Chamberlain, 15 October 1938, Chamberlain Mss., NC 18/1/1072.
5. Eden to Spenser Flower, 4 October 1938, Avon Mss., 13/1/66J; Eden to Sir Roger Lumley, 6 November 1938, Avon Mss., 13/1/66Q.
6. Warren Fisher to prime minister, 1 October 1938, Fisher Mss.; Roberts, p. 125.
7. Eunan O'Halpin, *Head of the Civil Service, A Study of Sir Warren Fisher* (London: Routledge, 1989), pp. 266–70.
8. Pownall Diaries, 3 and 17 October 1938, pp. 164 and 165.
9. See Herman, p. 232.
10. Hankey Diary, British embassy, Paris, 2 October 1938, Hankey Mss., HNKY 1/8.

11. 'Notes used in Conversation with Horace Wilson, 4 October 1938', Hankey Mss., HNKY 8/32.
12. Cadogan to Phipps, 7 October 1938, Phipps Mss., PHPP II, 2/1; for further details, see Herman, pp. 255ff.
13. Duff Cooper to Phipps, 7 December 1938, Phipps Mss., PHPP 3/2.
14. Phipps to Halifax, 6 December 1938, minutes by Roberts, 13 December 1938, Sargent, 16 December 1938, and Vansittart, 23 December 1938, FO 371/21600.
15. F.O. memorandum by Nicholls, 28 September 1938, Barclay and Mallet minutes, 7 October 1938, FO 371/21591.
16. Phipps to Neville Chamberlain, 30 September 1938, Phipps Mss., PHPP 3/1.
17. Minutes by Roberts and Mallet, 1 October, Cadogan, 1 October, Halifax, 1 October, and Chamberlain, 2 October 1938, FO 371/21621.
18. Chiefs of staff report, 'Staff Conversations with France', 18 November 1938, CAB 35/42.
19. When Ronald Cross, the parliamentary private secretary to the president of the board of trade, stated that he was not keen to accept an invitation to a British chamber of commerce dinner in Paris in December, the Foreign Office encouraged him to go. Loxley minute, 14 December 1938, Mallet minute, 15 December 1938, FO 371/21619.
20. Phipps, tel 657S, 12 October 1938, minutes by Sargent, 17 October, Cadogan, 17 October, and Vansittart, 18 October 1938, FO 371/21612.
21. Minutes by Sargent, 22 October 1938, Cadogan, 24 October 1938 and Halifax 25 October 1938, FO 371/21600.
22. Oliver Harvey minute, 26 October 1938, FO 371/21613. Halifax minute, 28 October 1938, FO 800/311.
23. Halifax to Phipps, 1 November 1938, no. 285, E.L. Woodward, Rohan Butler and Margaret Lambert (eds.) *Documents on British Foreign Policy, 1919–1939*, third series, vol. III, 1938–1939 (London: HMSO, 1950) [hereafter *DBFP*, 3, III].
24. Phipps to Sargent, 31 December 1938, Makins minute, 10 January 1939, FO 371/22912.
25. L.S. Amery to Eden, 10 October 1938, Avon Mss., 14/1/671.
26. Phipps, despatch 1261, 2 November 1938, FO 371/21613.
27. Halifax to Phipps, 1 November 1938; Phipps to Halifax, 7 November 1938, Phipps Mss., PHPP 1/21.
28. Phipps, despatch 129, 28 January 1938, enclosing Annual Report for 1938, FO 371/22934.
29. Phipps despatch 1386E, 26 November 1938, FO 371/21589.
30. Halifax to Phipps, 25 October 1938, FO 371/21591.
31. Halifax minute, 22 October 1938, FO 371/21600.
32. Chamberlain to Hilda Chamberlain, 6 November 1938, Chamberlain Mss., NC 18/1/1675.
33. Strang minute, 17 November 1938, FO 371/21591.
34. Halifax minute, 18 November 1938, FO 371/21591.
35. Colonel van Cutsem, War Office, to Strang, 17 November 1938, FO 371/21591.
36. *Ibid.*

37. Minutes by Roberts, 10 November, Makins, 19 November, Sargent, 30 November, and Cadogan, 30 November 1938. FO 371/21591.
38. W.H. Bartholomew, HQ Northern Command, York, to Hankey, 22 December 1938, Hankey Mss., HNKY 4/30.
39. Address by Captain B.H. Liddell Hart on 'The Role of the Army after Munich', 20 December 1938, Dalton Mss., 4/1.
40. Diary Notes, Liddell Hart, 30 January 1939, Liddell Hart Mss., 11/1939/6; Bond, *Liddell Hart*, pp. 104–5.
41. Speech by Lothian to the Press Luncheon of the Citizen Service League, 24 April 1939, Lothian Mss., GD 40/17/380.
42. *Pownall Diaries*, I, 7 November 1938, p. 169.
43. *Ibid.*, entries, 17, 24, 31 October, 7, 14, 21, 28 November, 1938, pp. 165–72.
44. Chiefs of staff report: 'Franco-British Co-operation in the Organization of National Defence', 21 November 1938, CAB 53/42.
45. Strang minute, 12 November 1938, F.O. Memorandum by Sargent, 16 November 1938, Cadogan and Halifax minutes, 17 November 1938, FO. 371/21591.
46. Charles Peake minute, 17 November 1938, FO 371/21591.
47. 'Record of Anglo-French Conversations held at the Quai d'Orsay on November 24, 1938', *DBFP*, 3, III, no. 325.
48. Chamberlain to Phipps, 30 November 1938, Phipps Mss., PHPPS I, 3/1; Adamthwaite, *France and the Coming* ..., p. 258.
49. Colonel Fraser, Paris to Phipps, 5 December 1939, Phipps despatch 1437, 7 December 1939, CAB 21/510.
50. 'Memorandum by the Secretary of State for War, 13 December 1938', CAB 53/43.
51. 'Memorandum by the Chief of the Imperial General Staff: Present Policy in the light of Recent Developments', 2 December 1938, CAB 53/43.
52. Gibbs, p. 504; committee of imperial defence, 341st meeting, 15 December 1938, FO 371/22922.
53. Vansittart minute for Halifax, 19 December 1938, FO 371/22922.
54. Vansittart minute, 24 January 1939, FO 371/22922. Underlined by Vansittart.
55. Chiefs of staff, 265th Meeting: 'Preparedness of the Army', 21 December 1938; chiefs of staff, 268th Meeting, 'Preparedness of the Army for War', 18 January 1939, CAB 53/10. See also Bond, *British Military Policy*, pp. 296–8.
56. Phipps, tel 402, 13 December 1938, FO 371/21593.
57. Phipps, tel 828S, 20 December 1938, minutes by Roberts, 20 December, Sargent, 22 December, Cadogan, 23 December, Halifax, 25 December, Vansittart, 28 December, and Halifax, 31 December 1938, FO 371/21593.
58. Adamthwaite, *France and the Coming* ..., p. 259.
59. *Pownall Diaries*, I, 23 January 1939, p. 183.
60. 'Notes on Visit of Colonel W.S. Pilcher and K. de Courcy to Paris', undated but contained in a letter forwarded from Ismay to Jebb, 17 January 1939; minutes by Cadogan, 27 January 1939, Vansittart, 29 January and R.A. Butler, 6 February 1938, FO 371/22922.
61. Hore-Belisha to Halifax, 9 January 1939, FO 371/22915.

62. Strang to Hollis, committee of imperial defence, 19 January 1939; Hollis to Foreign Office, 3 February 1939, enclosing chiefs of staff report 'The Strategic Position of France in a European War', 1 February 1939, FO 371/22915.
63. Minutes by Strang, 10 February, Vansittart, 11 February, and Halifax, 13 February 1939, FO 371/22915.
64. Cabinet foreign policy committee, 35th Meeting, 23 January 1939, CAB 27/624.
65. Cabinet conclusions, 6(39), 8 February 1939, FO 371/22922.
66. Simon to Hore-Belisha, 9 February 1939, Hore-Belisha Mss, HOBE, 5/39.
67. Hankey to Hore-Belisha, 2 January 1939, Hore-Belisha Mss., HOBE 5/46.
68. Beaumont-Nesbitt, War Office, to Strang, 16 January 1939, FO 371/22915.
69. Kirkpatrick minute, 4 February 1939, FO 371/22923.
70. Vansittart to Halifax, 7 February 1939, Halifax minute, 7 February 1939, FO 371/22922.
71. 'Notes of a meeting of ministers held at no. 10, Downing Street on Friday 17 February 1939', CAB 21/511.
72. Halifax note for prime minister, 17 February 1939, FO 371/22922. See also Gibbs, p. 502.
73. Peter Dennis, *Decision by Default: Peacetime Conscription and British Defence, 1919–1939* (London: Routledge and Kegan Paul, 1972), pp. 170–1.
74. Ismay to the chief of the air staff, 2 February 1939, AIR 9/78.
75. Vansittart to Halifax, 10 February 1939; Halifax minute, 10 February 1939, FO 371/22922.
76. *Ibid.*
77. Adamthwaite, *France and the Coming …*, pp. 253–7.
78. Chiefs of staff report, 'Staff Conversations with France and Belgium', 6 February 1939, CAB 53/44.
79. 'Staff Conversations with France and Belgium', chiefs of staff paper, 6 February 1939, FO 371/22922.
80. Strang minute, 25 February 1939, FO 371/22923.
81. Strang minute, 27 February 1939, FO 371/22923.
82. Vansittart minute, 10 February 1939, FO 371/22972.
83. Hollis to Strang, 10 March 1939; Sargent to Ismay, 20 March 1939, FO 371/22923.
84. Chiefs of staff, 'British Strategical Appreciation', 20 March 1939, CAB 56/46. See Gibbs, pp. 657–69.
85. Joint planning staff report: 'Staff Conversations with the French', 22 March 1939, CAB 53/46.
86. Chiefs of staff report: 'Staff Conversations with France', 6 March 1939, CAB 53/45.
87. Chatfield memorandum, 23 March 1939, CAB 53/46.
88. Strang minute, 15 March 1939, FO 371/22923.
89. Minister for coordination of defence memorandum for cabinet, 28 March 1938, Barclay minute, 9 March and Vansittart minute, 10 March 1939, FO 371/22923.

CHAPTER 6

1. Orme Sargent to Charles Peake, 30 March 1940, FO 800/274.
2. Foreign Office note (undated) March 1939, FO 371/22923.
3. Peter Jackson, 'France and the Guarantee of Rumania, April 1939', *Intelligence and National Security*, 10, 95, no. 2, April 1995, pp. 242–72.
4. Sir Horace Wilson to prime minister, 28 March 1939. PREM 1/296.
5. See Dennis, *Decision by Default*, pp. 197–9.
6. Campbell, Paris, tel 159S, 23 March 1939, minutes by Barclay, 24 March, and Kirkpatrick, 30 March 1939, FO 371/22932.
7. Phipps, tel 176, 19 April 1939. FO 371/22932.
8. Phipps, tel 223S, 21 April 1939, FO 371/22932.
9. Quoted in Dennis, pp. 220–1.
10. Bond, *British Military Policy*, pp. 308–10.
11. Horace Wilson memorandum, 29 March 1939; Simon to Chamberlain, 17 April 1939, PREM 1/308.
12. Foreign Office to Phipps, tel 76S, 13 March 1939; Phipps despatch 324, 15 March 1939, FO 371/22923.
13. Anglo-French Staff Conversations, 29 March 1939, first meeting. Present were Captain V.H. Danckwerts, Director of Plans, Admiralty, and Head of United Kingdom Delegation, Captain R.C. O'Conor, Assistant Director of Plans, Admiralty, Brigadier J.N. Kennedy, Deputy Director, Military Operations, War Office, Colonel O.M. Lund of the General Staff, Group Captain J.C. Slessor, Director of Plans, Air Ministry, General A. Lelong, Military Attaché and Head of French delegation, Colonel G. Ayme, Assistant to the Head of the French Delegation and representing the French Colonial Office, Commandant R. Noiret of the Army General Staff, Contre Amiral J. Bourrague, French Navy, Commandant P. Bailly, Air General Staff, and the British and French army naval and air attachés. See AIR 9/78.
14. Chatfield to Prime Minister, 21 April 1939; Steward, 10 Downing Street, to Sellar, CID, 22 April 1939, PREM 1/308; 'Committee of Imperial Defence: Strategical Appreciation Sub-Committee, Staff Conversations with the French, Report by Chiefs of Staff, 13 April 1939'; 'Anglo-French Staff Conversations 1939: Report on Stage I by V.H. Danckwerts, 11 April 1939', FO 371/22924.
15. For the minutes of the 16 meetings of the army staffs, see AIR 9/78.
16. Strang minute, 10 March 1939, FO 371/22923.
17. Gibbs, p. 418.
18. *Ibid.*, p. 421.
19. Quoted in *ibid.*, p. 422.
20. *Ibid.*, pp. 422–3.
21. Backhouse to Ismay, 18 April 1939, ADM 205/3.
22. Gibbs, pp. 425–6.
23. Salerno. M. Reynolds, 'The French Navy and the Appeasement of Italy, 1937–1939', *English Historical Review*, vol. CXII, no. 445, February 1997, pp. 64–104.
24. 'Talks between Anglo-French air force representatives, 10 and 27 February 1939 and 1 May 1939', AIR 40/2032.

25. Sargent minute, 27 February 1939, FO 371/22915, Phipps despatch 327, 16 March 1939, FO 371/22916.
26. 'Extract from conversation with the French Foreign Minister', 22 March 1939, Cadogan minute, 27 March 1939, FO 371/22916.
27. Barratt minute, 21 April 1939, AIR 9/7.
28. 'Summary of Discussions of Meeting in Secretary of State for Air's Room at House of Commons between Kingsley Wood and Guy La Chambre, 25 July 1939', AIR 9/78.
29. Chiefs of staff, 316th Meeting, 30 August 1939, ADM 205/1.
30. Beaumont-Nesbitt to Strang, 9 May 1939, FO 371/22930.
31. *Ibid.*
32. Desmond Morton, Industrial Intelligence Centre to J.W. Nicholls, 6 March 1939, enclosing memorandum of 16 January 1939, FO 371/22916.
33. Board of Trade memorandum, 28 December 1938, Strang minute, 16 January 1939, FO 371/22915.
34. E.M.H. Lloyd, Food (Defence Plans) Dept to Nicholls, 30 May 1939; J.R.C. Helmore, Board of Trade to Nicholls, 14 June 1939, FO 371/22916.
35. Nicholls to Ismay, 5 July 1939, FO 371/22916.
36. Phipps despatch 56E, 13 January 1939, enclosing Rowe-Dutton memorandum of 10 January 1939, Barclay minute, 20 January 1939, FO 371/22905.
37. Phipps to Halifax, despatch 50, 11 January 1939, *BDFP*, 3, II, no. 496 and enclosure, Phipps, tel 235S, 22 April 1939, Phipps despatch, 544E, 28 April 1939, memorandum by N.E. Young, 11 June 1939, FO 371/22906.
38. *Channon Diaries*, 20 and 21 March 1939, p. 187; Halifax to Captain E.A. Fitzroy, 24 January 1939, FO 371/22919.
39. Lord Maugham to Halifax, 25 January 1939, Halifax minute, FO 371/22919.
40. Minutes by Halifax, 1 March 1939, and Vansittart, 6 March 1939, FO 371/22919.
41. Sacha Guitry was a popular French comedian of the period.
42. Seymour Hicks and Cicely Courtneidge were two leading British entertainers of that time.
43. Chamberlain to Ida Chamberlain, 26 March 1939, Chamberlain Mss., NC /1/1091.
44. *Channon Diaries*, 23 March 1939, p. 190. He thought that 'the French must have been very impressed by our bejewelled Aristocracy', *ibid.*
45. 'Record of Anglo-French Conversations held in the Secretary of State's Room at the Foreign Office on March 21 1939; Record of Meeting between Chamberlain, Halifax and Bonnet at the Prime Minister's Room in the House of Commons, 22 March 1939'; Halifax, despatch 708 to Paris, 23 March 1939, FO 800/311.
46. Cabinet conclusions, 21 (39) 19 April 1939, CAB 23/98.
47. Halifax to Phipps, 6 April 1939, Phipps Mss., PHPP I 1/23; Phipps to Halifax, 28 April 1939, Halifax to Phipps, 2 May 1939 Phipps Mss., PHPP II, 1/22; Halifax to Phipps, 7 July 1939, Phipps to Halifax, 7 July 1939, Phipps Mss., PHPP I 1/23; Cabinet conclusions, 28 (39), 17 May 1939, CAB 23/99.
48. Chamberlain to Ida Chamberlain, 10 June 1939, to Hilda Chamberlain, 17 June 1939, Chamberlain Mss., NC/18/1/1102 and 1103; Salerno.

M. Reynolds, 'The French Navy and the Appeasement of Italy, 1937–9', *English Historical Review*, Vol. CXII, no. 445, February 1997, pp. 66–104.
49. For details of these negotiations, see Donald Cameron Watt, *How War Came: The Immediate Origins of the Second World War, 1938–1939* (London: Heinemann, 1989), chapters 13, 20, 24 and 25; Adamthwaite, *France and the Coming ...*, chapter 17.
50. Cabinet foreign policy committee, 57th Meeting, 10 July 1939, CAB 27/624.
51. For details, see Herman, pp. 313–16.
52. Kirkpatrick minute, 27 August 1939, FO 371/22930.
53. Fraser, Paris to Colonel W.E. van Cutsem, War Office, 30 August 1939, WO 106/5413.
54. Adamthwaite, p. 358.
55. For a detailed account of these events, see Watt, *How War Began*, chapters 28, 30 and 31.
56. Cadogan to Phipps, 6 September 1939, Phipps Mss., PHPP II, 2/1.
57. Simon, Diaries and Notes, Tuesday 12 September 1939, Simon Mss, 11; Bond, *British Military Policy*, p. 336.
58. For details, see Bond, *British Military Policy*, pp 328–9.
59. Churchill to Chamberlain, 10 and 18 September 1939, Chamberlain Mss., BC 7/9/47 and 51.
60. Inskip Diary, 26 September 1939, Inskip Mss., INSP I, 1/2.
61. 'The Development of our War Potential', by Hore-Belisha, 16 September 1939, Hore-Belisha Mss., HOBE 5/69.
62. Hore-Belisha to Gort, 26 September 1939, Hore-Belisha Mss., HOBE. 5/74.
63. For the military side, see Eleanor M. Gates, *End of the Affair: The Collapse of the Anglo-French Alliance, 1939–1940* (London: George Allen and Unwin, 1981); and Martin S. Alexander, *The Republic in Danger: General Maurice Gamelin and the Politics of French Defence, 1933–1940* (Cambridge: Cambridge University Press, 1992). For civilian relations, see Michael Dockrill, 'The Foreign Office and France during the Phoney War, September 1939–May 1940', in Michael Dockrill and Brian McKercher (eds.), *Diplomacy and World Power: Studies in British Foreign Policy, 1890–1950* (Cambridge: Cambridge University Press, 1996). Some material in this article has been reproduced in this chapter.
64. W.K. Hancock and M.M. Gowing, *British War Economy* (London: HMSO, 1949), pp. 184–90; J. Hurstfield, *The Control of Raw Materials* (London: HMSO, 1953), pp. 246–7 and 251; Eleanor M. Gates, *End of the Affair*, p. 60.
65. Board of Trade Memorandum, 4 January 1940, FO 371/24293.
66. Hancock and Gowing, p. 186.
67. Foreign Office (from Prime Minister) to Phipps, tel 337, 11 September 1939, FO 371/22926.
68. 'Minutes of the Supreme War Council, 1st Meeting, Abbeville', SWC/39, 12 September 1939', FO 371/24296.
69. Chamberlain to Ida Chamberlain, 17 September 1939, Chamberlain Mss., NC 18/1/1121.
70. For a comprehensive account, see Thomas Munch-Peterson, *The Strategy of Phoney War: Britain, Sweden and the Iron Ore Question, 1939–1940* (Stockholm: Militarhistorika Forlaget, 1981).

71. Phipps, tel 786S, 12 October 1939, FO 371/22910.
72. Phipps, tel 735S, 3 October 1939, Phipps, tel 648S, 10 September 1939, FO 371/22913.
73. Conference paper by D. Cameron Watt, 'The British Image of French Military Morale, 1939–1940. An Intelligence Failure?' A copy of this paper was kindly shown to me by Philip Bell.
74. Dill, HQ. 1 Corps, BEF, to Montgomery-Massingberd, 25 September 1939, Montgomery-Massingberd Mss., MM 160.
75. Phipps tel 651S, 11 September 1939, FO 371/22913; Phipps to Halifax, despatch 1249, 14 September 1939, FO 371/2292. For further information about French dissatisfaction with Britain's war effort and her war aims, see 'Memorandum on the French attitude towards Great Britain and the British effort', by Somerset Maugham, communicated by Lord Maugham to Halifax, 24 October 1939, and 'Further Memorandum on the French attitude towards Great Britain', by Somerset Maugham, 5 November 1939, communicated by Campbell, desp 1531, 14 November 1939, FO 371/22927.
76. Halifax minute, 17 September 1939, FO 371/22926.
77. Alan Brooke Diary, 29 September 1939, 5/1.
78. For the attitude of British public opinion towards France, see P.M.H. Bell, 'L'Évolution de l'opinion publique anglaise à propos de la guerre et de l'alliance avec la France (septembre 1939–mai 1940)', in *Comité d'Histoire de la 2e Guerre Mondiale: Français et Britanniques dans la drole de Guerre: Actes du Colloque franco-britannique tenu à Paris de 8 au 12 decembre 1975* (Paris: Éditions de Centre National de la Recherche Scientifique, 1979), pp. 51ff; Campbell tel 850S, 14 November 1939, FO 371/22927.
79. E.H. Carr, Ministry of Information, to Foreign Office, 27 December 1939, FO 371/22915.
80. An anti-establishment newsletter edited by the communist journalist, 'Claud Cockburn'. Cockett, *Twilight of Truth*, p. 71.
81. Mountbatten, *HMS Kelly*, to Eden, 26 January 1940, Eden to Mountbatten, 8 February 1940, Avon Mss., AP 20/8/284 B, C & D.
82. Brian Bond, *Britain, France and Belgium, 1939–1940* (London: Brassey's (UK), 2nd edition 1990), pp. 27–30.
83. Eden to Douglas Fairbanks Jr., 24 November 1939, Avon Mss., AP 20/7/81.
84. Notes by Major General F.H.N. Davidson, October 1939, Davidson Mss., File D.
85. Alan Brooke Diary, 30 September 1939, Alanbrooke Mss., 5/1.
86. Alan Brooke Diary, 9 and 13 October 1939, Alanbrooke Mss., 5/1.
87. Alan Brooke Diary, entries 23, 31 October, 5, 28 November, 20 December 1939, 29 January, 6 February 1940, Alanbrooke Mss., 5/1.
88. *Ironside Diaries*, December 1939.
89. 'Notes', 1939–40, by Major General F.H.N. Davidson, undated, Davidson Mss, file C.
90. 'Can We "Crush Hitlerism"?', 9 September 1939, Liddell Hart Mss., 11/1939/101.
91. 'The Prospect in This War', 7 November 1939, Liddell Hart Mss., 11/193/128.

92. Reports to British army intelligence section 1b by Saar Sector Detachment FSP., 17 and 24 February 1940, WO 197/48. David Reynolds has drawn attention to the similarities between the uneasy relations between the British troops in France and French civilians in 1939 and 1940 and those between American troops stationed in Britain after 1942 and British civilians. David Reynolds, *Rich Relations: The American Occupation of Britain, 1942–1945* (London: Harper-Collins, 1995), p. 63.
93. Watt, 'The British Image of French Military Morale', pp. 7–10.
94. Watt, 'The British Image of French Military Morale', pp. 11–13; Major-General Sir Edward Spears, *Assignment to Catastrophe, Volume I, Prelude to Dunkirk, July 1939–May 1940* (London: William Heinemann, 1954), pp. 86–7.
95. *Ironside Diaries*, 10 January 1940, p. 204.
96. Phipps, tel 649S, 11 September 1939, FO 371/22913.
97. Cadogan minute, 18 September 1939; Halifax minute, 16 October 1939, FO 371/22926.
98. For the wider political ramifications of the war aims issue in Britain, see P. Ludlow, 'Le débat sur les buts de paix en Grande Bretagne durant l'hiver 1939–1940', in *Français et Britanniques dans la drole de Guerre: Actes du Colloque franco-britanniques tenu à Paris du 8 au 12 decembre 1975* (Paris: Éditions du Centre National de la Recherche Scientifique, 1979), pp. 93ff.
99. P.M.H. Bell, *A Certain Eventuality: Britain and the Fall of France* (London: Saxon House, 1974), p. 6.
100. See reports from British consuls in France on French suspicions of Britain's war aims: Phipps, tel 285S, 21 September 1939; Phipps desp 1447, 23 October 1939; FO 371/2294 See also Peter Hoffmann, 'The Question of Western Allied Co-operation with the German anti-Nazi Conspiracy', *The Historical Journal*, vol. 34, no. 2, 1991.
101. Chamberlain to Ida Chamberlain, 5 November 1939, Chamberlain Mss., NC 18/1/1129.
102. 'Note of Interview with Halifax', 26 September 1939, Cecil Add Mss., 51084.
103. Sylvester to Lloyd George, 14 November 1939, HLRO Lloyd George Mss., G/9/24/1/84.
104. Halifax to R.I. Campbell, Paris, desp 2603, 23 October 1939, FO 371/22946; see also Hoffmann's article.
105. For example, Phipps, tel 810S, 23 October 1939, FO 371/22913.
106. *Ibid.* Makins minute, 28 October 1939, FO 371/22946
107. *Ibid.* Strang memorandum, 31 October 1939, FO 371/22946.
108. Campbell, despatch 1518, 9 November 1939, FO 371/22946.
109. Sir R. Campbell, tel 878S, 25 November 1939, FO 371/22947.
110. Cadogan thought that 'It might be better to keep it [the no separate peace declaration] as a manifestation after some disaster. Or it might be better after some success.' Cadogan minute, 9 December 1939, FO 371/22939.
111. Gates, p. 63; Lawford minute to Halifax, 16 November 1939, Halifax minute, 18 November 1939, FO 371/2298; Cadogan minute, 9 December 1939; 'Central Department Brief for Supreme War Council meeting on 19 December 1939', 16 December 1939, FO 371/22928.

112. Sir Edward Bridges to Cadogan, 21 December 1939, enclosing draft minutes of the Supreme War Council meeting, FO 371/24297; minutes of the 4th Meeting of the Supreme War Council, 19 December 1939, FO 371/22928.
113. Kirkpatrick minute, 31 January 1940, FO 371/24297.
114. Campbell to Cadogan, 29 February 1940, Malkin minute, 28 February 1940, FO 371/24297.
115. Halifax to Campbell, desp 658, 21 March 1940, FO 371/24298.
116. 'Supreme War Council Conclusions, 6th Meeting, Tuesday 28 March, 10 Downing Street'; Campbell, telephone, to FO, 29 March 1940, FO 371/24299. For the full text of the declaration, see Gates, p. 65.
117. See also Robert Frankenstein, 'Le Financement français de la Guerre et les Accords avec les Britanniques (1939–1940)', pp. 461ff; and L.S. Pressnell, 'Les Finances de Guerre Britanniques et la Coopération Franco-Britannique, 1939 et 1940', *Français et Britanniques dans la drole de Guerre: Actes du Colloque franco-britannique tenu à Paris du 8 au 12 decembre 1975* (Paris: Édition du Centre National de la Recherche Scientifique, 1979), pp. 489ff.
118. Phipps, tel 639S, 7 September 1939, FO 371/22929.
119. Stacy, Board of Trade, to Kirkpatrick, 13 and 19 October 1939, FO 371/22929.
120. Francis W. Hirst to Simon, 28 September 1939, Simon papers 5.
121. Strang to Cadogan, 31 October 1939, Stacy to Barclay, 23 November 1939, FO 371/22929.
122. Board of Trade minute, 7 November 1939, FO 371/22929.
123. For details, see 'Record of Discussion between Sir John Simon and M. Paul Reynaud at the Ministry of Finance, Paris, 11.00 a.m. Monday 4 December 1939'; Neville Chamberlain to Edouard Daladier, 7 December 1939; Halifax to Lord Lothian, Washington, tel 893, 12 December 1939, FO 371/22930; Hurstfield, p. 250; Hancock and Gowing, p. 190.
124. Hopkinson, Anglo-French Liaison Section, War Cabinet Offices to Kirkpatrick, 30 December 1939; Hugh Dodds, consul-general, Nice to British embassy, Paris, desp 82, 22 December 1939, FO 371/24307.
125. Treasury to Foreign Office, 19 January 1940, FO 371/24307.
126. Makins minute, 24 January 1940, FO 371/24296.
127. Minutes of eight meetings of the Overseas Travel Committee, Feb.–April 1940; J.G. Ward to F.A. Newsam, Home Office, 22 May 1940, FO 371/24307.
128. Sargent minute, to Cadogan, 28 February 1940, FO 371/24298.
129. 'Lord Ponsonby: Interview with Halifax, 1 March 1940', Ponsonby Mss, C682; Halifax to Chamberlain, 13 February 1940, Chamberlain Mss., NC 7/11/33/74.
130. Butler to Halifax, 13 March 1940, FO 371/24288; Halifax to Chamberlain, 29 February 1940; Prime Minister to Halifax, 1 March 1940, FO 371/24298.
131. Leeper minute, 9 April 1940, FO 371/24298.
132. Hankey to Halifax, 9 April 1940, FO 371/24299; 'Inter-Departmental Committee on Post-War Anglo-French Collaboration: Composition and Terms of Reference', Note by the Secretary, H.L. d'A. Hopkinson, 20 April 1940, FO 371/24200.

133. Note by H.L. d'A Hopkinson, 26 April 1940, FO 371/24299.
134. Leeper to Sargent, 26 March 1940, FO 371/24299.
135. 'Memorandum by Sir A. Zimmern on a Proposed Act of Perpetual Union between the United Kingdom and France' (undated but late April 1940), FO 371/24298.
136. 'Inter-Departmental Committee: Post-War Anglo-French Collaboration: Minutes of the 1st Meeting held in Lord Hankey's Room, Treasury, on Tuesday 30 April 1940 at 3.00 p. m.', FO 371/24299.
137. Memorandum by Sir Arnold Overton, Board of Trade, 'Implications of the Proposed "Act of Association" between the United Kingdom and France, with particular reference to a Customs Union', 9 May 1940, FO 371/24300.
138. 'Inter-Departmental Committee: Post-War Anglo-French Collaboration', Second Meeting, Minutes, Tuesday 21 May 1940, FO 371/24300. The idea of a federal Europe was supported at the time by British intellectuals from all sides of the political spectrum. See P.M.H. Bell, 'L'evolution de l'opinion publique anglaise ...' in *Français et Britannique dans la drole de guerre.*
139. Hankey to Halifax, 11 July 1940; Halifax to Hankey, 15 July 1940, Hankey Mss., HNKY 5/4.
140. For a relatively recent account see Gates and bibliography. Also Bond, *Britain, France and Belgium*, and bibliography.
141. Hankey to Halifax, 11 July 1940, Hankey Mss., HNKY, 5/4.
142. Hankey to Simon, 17 June 1940, Simon Mss., Box 86.
143. Hankey to Halifax, 22 June 1940, Hankey Mss., HNKY 4/32.
144. Quoted in Roberts, p. 211.
145. This memorandum is quoted in full in Watt, 'The British Image of French Military Morale', pp. 1–3.
146. Correlli Barnett, p. 325.
147. Stephen Roskill, *Hankey: Man of Secrets, Vol. III, 1931–1963* (London, Collins, 1974), p. 478. See also Gates, p. 381.
148. Hankey to Hoare, Madrid, 19 July 1940, quoted in Roskill, p. 480.
149. Simon to Chamberlain, 17 June 1940, Hankey Mss., HNKY 4/31.
150. Quoted in Young, *Chamberlain* p. 449.
151. *Channon Diaries*, 10 July 1940, p. 261.
152. Martin Gilbert, *Finest Hour: Winston S. Churchill, 1939–1941* (London: William Heinemann, 1983), pp. 404, 411, 413, 421.

CHAPTER 7

1. 'Great Britain & Europe', by Philip Noel-Baker, undated but probably December 1935 or January 1936. Noel-Baker Mss., NBKR.
2. R.W.A. Leeper Memorandum, 'War Aims', 30 November 1939; Leeper to Strang, 1 December 1939, FO 371/22947.
3. Cockett, *Twilight of Truth*, pp. 144ff.
4. Barrington-Ward Memorandum, 'Anglo-French Educational Co-operation', 9 April 1940, FO 371/24299.
5. Halifax to Hankey, 9 August 1939; Hankey to Halifax, 17 August 1939, Hankey Mss, HNKY 5/4.

6. Henry Sherek to Spears, 15 and 27 March 1940, Sherek to Captain F.W. Elles, 21 March 1940, Spears Mss., SPRS 1/9.
7. Aubrey Jones to Walter Monckton, 7 May 1940, Monckton Mss., I.
8. P.M.H. Bell, 'L'Évolution de l'opinion publique anglaise …'.
9. *Ibid.*
10. *Ibid.*
11. *Ibid.*; Campbell, despatch 1476, enclosing memorandum by King, 31 October 1939, FO 371/22914.
12. 'Note of Meeting between M. Paul Reynaud and Sir John Simon at the Treasury', 20 November 1939, FO 371/23298.
13. Minute by William Strang, 30 July 1938: 'Impressions of tour of France by car June 15 and July 3', FO 371/21621.
14. Robert J. Young 'A.J.P. Taylor and the Problem with France', in Gordon Martel (ed.), *The Origins of the Second World War Reconsidered: The A.J.P. Taylor Debate after Twenty Five Years* (London: Allen and Unwin, 1986), pp. 110–14.
15. See David Reynolds, '1940: Fulcrum of the Twentieth Century', *International History*, vol. 66, no. 1, January 1990. See also Halifax to Hankey, 15 July 1940, Hankey Mss., HNKY 5/4.
16. Lothian to Abe Bailey, South Africa, 1 July 1940, Lothian Mss., GD 40/17/398.
17. For the history of Anglo-French relations after 1940, see P.M.H. Bell, *France and Britain, 1940–1994: The Long Separation* (London: Longman, 1997).

Select Bibliography

UNPUBLISHED BRITISH GOVERNMENT RECORDS

Foreign Office Political Files; FO 371
Private correspondence: FO 800
Cabinet, Chiefs of Staff and Committee of Imperial Defence papers: CAB 2, CAB 4, CAB 16, CAB 21, CAB 23, CAB 27, CAB 35, CAB 53, CAB 44, CAB 50, CAB 53, CAB 56, CAB 63
Prime Ministers' Papers PREM 1
Admiralty papers: ADM 1, ADM 116, ADM 205
Air Ministry papers: AIR 9, AIR 10, AIR 40
Treasury papers: T 160, T 172, T 177, T 273
War Office papers: WO 32, WO 33, WO 106, WO 197, WO 282

UNPUBLISHED PRIVATE PAPERS

Field Marshal Lord Alanbrooke, Liddell Hart Centre for Military Archives, King's College, London
Earl of Avon, Birmingham University Library
Sir Alexander Cadogan, Churchill College, Cambridge
Lord Caldecote, Churchill College, Cambridge
Lord Robert Cecil, British Library
Neville Chamberlain, Birmingham University Library
Hugh Dalton, British Library of Economic and Political Science
J.C.C. Davidson, House of Lords Record Office
General Major General Francis Davidson, Liddell Hart Centre for Military Archives
Geoffrey Dawson, Bodleian Library, Oxford
General Sir John Dill, Liddell Hart Centre for Military Archives
Sir Warren Fisher, British Library of Economic and Political Science
Sir Maurice Hankey, Churchill College, Cambridge
Hickleton Papers (Earl of Halifax), Borthwick Institute of Historical Research, University of York
Leslie Hore-Belisha, Churchill College, Cambridge
Lord Inverchapel, Bodleian Library, Oxford
David Lloyd George, House of Lords Record Office
Lord Lothian, Scottish Record Office
Lord Monckton, Bodleian Library, Oxford
Field Marshal Sir Archibald Montgomery-Massingberd, Liddell Hart Centre for Military Archives
Francis Noel-Baker, Churchill College, Cambridge
Sir Henry Page-Croft, Churchill College, Cambridge

Sir Eric Phipps, Churchill College, Cambridge
Lord Ponsonby, Bodleian Library, Oxford
Lord Simon, Bodleian Library, Oxford
Major-General Sir Edward Spears, Churchill College, Cambridge
Lord Templewood, Cambridge University Library
Sir Robert Vansittart, Churchill College, Cambridge

PUBLISHED DOCUMENTS

Medlicott, W.N., Dakin, Douglas and Lambert, M.E. (eds.), *Documents on British Foreign Policy, 1919–1939*, second series, Vol. XVI, *The Rhineland Crisis and the Ending of Sanctions, March 2–July 30 1936* (London: HMSO, 1977).

Medlicott, W.N., Dakin, Douglas, assisted by Bennett, Gillian (eds.), *Documents on British Foreign Policy, 1919–1939*, second series, vol. XVIII, *European Affairs, January 2–June 30, 1937* (London, HMSO, 1977).

Medlicott, W.N., Dakin, Douglas and Bennett, Gillian, *Documents on British Foreign Policy, 1919–1939*, second series, vol. XIX, *European Affairs, July 1, 1937–August 4, 1938* (London: HMSO, 1982).

Woodward, E.L. and Butler, Rohan (eds.), *Documents on British Foreign Policy 1919–1939*, third series, vol. I, March–July 1938 (London: HMSO, 1949).

Woodward, E.L., Butler, Rowan and Lambert, M.E. (eds.), *Documents on British Foreign Policy, 1919–1939,* third series, vol. II, July 1937–September 1938 (London: HMSO, 1949).

Woodward, E.L., Butler, Rowan and Lambert, Margaret (eds.), *Documents on British Foreign Policy, 1919–1939*, third series, vol. III (London: HMSO, 1950).

BOOKS

Adamthwaite, Anthony, *France and the Coming of the Second World War* (London: Frank Cass, 1977).

Adamthwaite, Anthony, *Grandeur and Misery: France's Bid for Power in Europe, 1914–1940* (London: Edward Arnold, 1995).

Alexander, Martin S., *The Republic in Danger: General Maurice Gamelin and the Politics of French Defence, 1933–1940* (Cambridge: Cambridge University Press, 1992).

Avon, the Earl of, *The Eden Memoirs: Facing the Dictators* (London: Cassell, 1962).

Barnett, Correlli, *The Collapse of British Power* (Gloucester: Alan Sutton, pbk, 1987 reprint).

Bell, P.M.H., *A Certain Eventuality: Britain and the Fall of France* (London: Saxon House, 1974).

Bell, P.M.H., *France and Britain 1900–1940: Entente and Estrangement* (London and New York: Longman, pbk, 1996).

Bell, P.M.H., *France and Britain, 1940–1994, the Long Separation* (London: Longman, 1997).

Bernard, Philippe and Dubief, Henri, *The Decline of the Third Republic, 1914–1938* (Cambridge: Cambridge University Press, 1987).
Bond, Brian, *British Military Policy between the Two World Wars* (Oxford: Clarendon Press, 1980).
Bond, B.J., *Chief of Staff, The Dairies of Sir Henry Pownall*, 2 vols (London: Leo Cooper, 1972).
Bond, Brian, *Britain, France and Belgium, 1939–1940* (London: Brassey's (UK), 2nd edition 1990).
Bond, Brian, *Liddell Hart: a Study of his Military Thought* (London: Cassell, 1976).
Butler, J.R.M., *Lord Lothian, 1882–1940* (London: Macmillan, 1960).
Carlton, David, *Anthony Eden: a Biography* (London: Allen Lane, 1981).
Charmley, J.D., *Chamberlain and the Lost Peace* (London: Hodder and Stoughton, 1989).
Cockett, Richard, *Twilight of Truth: Chamberlain, Appeasement and the Manipulation of the Press* (London: Weidenfeld and Nicolson, 1989).
Colvin, Ian, *Vansittart in Office* (London: Gollancz, 1965).
Craig, Gordon A. and Felix Gilbert, Felix (eds.), *The Diplomats 1919–1939*, 2 vols (New York: Atheneum, 1965).
Cross, J.A., *Sir Samuel Hoare, a Political Biography* (London: Jonathan Cape, 1977).
Crozier, Andrew J., *Appeasement and Germany's Last Bid for Colonies* (Basingstoke: Macmillan, 1988).
Dennis, Peter, *Decision by Default: Peacetime Conscription and British Defence, 1919–1939* (London: Routledge and Kegan Paul, 1972).
Dilks, David (ed.), *The Diaries of Sir Alexander Cadogan, 1938–1945* (London: Cassell, 1971).
Dockrill, Michael L. and Goold, J. Douglas, *Peace without Promise: Britain and the Peace Conferences 1919–1923* (London: Batsford, 1981).
Dutton, David, *Anthony Eden: a Life and Reputation* (London: Edward Arnold, 1997).
Dutton, David, *Simon: a Political Biography of Sir John Simon* (London; Aurum Press, 1992).
Egremont, Max, *Under Two Flags: the Life of Major General Sir Edward Spears* (London: Weidenfeld and Nicolson, 1997).
Elcock, Howard, *Portrait of a Decision: the Council of Four and the Treaty of Versailles* (London: Eyre Methuen, 1972).
Ellis, E.L., *T.J.: A Life of Dr Thomas Jones, CH.* (Cardiff: University of Wales Press, 1992).
Emmerson, J.T., *The Rhineland Crisis, 7 March 1936: a Study in Multilateral Diplomacy* (London: Maurice Temple Smith, 1977).
Feiling, Keith, *The Life of Neville Chamberlain* (London: Macmillan, 1946).
Ferris, John Robert, *The Evolution of British Strategic Policy 1919–26* (Basingstoke: Macmillan, 1989).
Gates, Eleanor M., *End of the Affair: the Collapse of the Anglo-French Alliance, 1939–1940* (London: George Allen and Unwin, 1981).
Gibbs, N.H., *Grand Strategy: Volume 1, Rearmament Policy* (London: HMSO, 1976).
Gilbert, Martin, *Winston S. Churchill, Vol. V, Companion, Part 3, Documents: The Coming of the War, 1931–39* (London: Heinemann, 1982).

Gilbert, Martin, *Finest Hour: Winston S. Churchill, 1939–1941* (London: William Heinemann, 1983).

Gilbert, Martin and Gott, Richard, *The Appeasers* (London: Weidenfeld and Nicolson, 1963).

Hancock, W.K. and M.M. Gowing, *British War Economy* (London: HMSO, 1949).

Hart, B. Liddell, *The Memoirs of Captain Liddell Hart*, 2 vols (London: Cassell, 1965).

Harvey, J. (ed.), *The Diplomatic Diaries of Oliver Harvey, 1937* (London: Collins, 1970).

History of the Times, 1920–1948, the 150th Anniversary and Beyond (London: Times Publishing, 1952), Vol. IV, Part II.

Howard, Anthony, *RAB: The Life of R.A. Butler* (London: Jonathan Cape, 1987).

Hurstfield, J., *The Control of Raw Materials* (London: HMSO, 1953).

James, Robert Rhodes, *Chips: the Diaries of Sir Henry Channon* (London: Weidenfeld, 1993).

Lentin, A., *Lloyd George, Woodrow Wilson and the Guilt of Germany: An essay in the pre-history of Appeasement* (Leicester: Leicester University Press, 1984).

McKercher, B.J.C. and Moss, D., *Shadow and Substance in British Foreign Policy, 1919–1939: Memorial Essays Honouring C.J. Lowe* (Alberta: The University of Alberta Press, 1984).

Macleod, Colonel Roderick and Kelly, Dennis (eds.), *The Ironside Diaries, 1937–1940* (London: Constable, 1962).

Middlemas, Keith and Barnes, John, *Baldwin: a Biography* (London: Weidenfeld and Nicolson, 1969).

Munch-Peterson, Thomas, *The Strategy of Phoney War: Britain, Sweden and the Iron Ore Question, 1939–1940* (Stockholm: Militarhistorika Forlaget, 1981).

Nicolson, Nigel (ed.), *Harold Nicolson: Diaries and Letters* (London: Collins, 1966).

O'Halpin, Eunan, *Head of the Civil Service: a Study of Warren Fisher* (London: Routledge, 1989).

Parker, R.A.C., *Chamberlain and Appeasement: British Policy and the Coming of the Second World War* (Basingstoke: Macmillan, 1993).

Peden, G.H.C., *British Rearmament and the Treasury, 1932–1939* (Edinburgh: Scottish Academic Press, 1979).

Philpott, William James, *Anglo-French Relations and Strategy on the Western Front, 1914–1918* (London: Macmillan, 1996).

Post, Gaines, Jr., *Dilemmas of Appeasement: British Deterrence and Defense, 1934–1937* (Ithaca: Cornell University Press, 1993).

Reynolds, David, *Rich Relations: the American Occupation of Britain, 1942–1945* (London: Harper-Collins, 1995).

Robbins, Keith, *Munich 1938* (London: Cassell, 1968).

Roberts, Andrew, *'The Holy Fox': A Biography of Lord Halifax* (London: Weidenfeld and Nicolson, 1991).

Rose, Norman, *Vansittart: Study of a Diplomat* (London: Heinemann, 1978).

Roskill, Stephen, *Hankey: Man of Secrets*, 3 vols (London: Collins, 1974).

Rostow, Nicholas, *Anglo-French Relations 1934–1936* (Basingstoke: Macmillan, 1984).

Self, Robert S. (ed.), *The Austen Chamberlain Diary and Letters* (Cambridge: Cambridge University Press, 1995).

Sharp, Alan, *The Versailles Peace Settlement, 1919* (Basingstoke: Macmillan, 1991).
Taylor, A.J.P., *English History, 1914–1945* (Oxford: Clarendon Press, 1965).
Thomas, Martin, *Britain, France and Appeasement: Anglo-French Relations in the Popular Front Era* (Oxford: Berg, 1996).
Vansittart, Robert, *The Mist Procession: the Autobiography of Lord Vansittart* (London: Hutchinson, 1958).
Watt, Donald Cameron, *How War Came: the Immediate Origins of the Second World War, 1938–1939* (London: Heinemann, 1989).
Weber, Eugen, *The Hollow Years: France in the 1930s* (New York: W.W. Norton, 1994).
Young, Kenneth (ed.), *The Diaries of Sir Robert Bruce Lockhart, 1915–1938, Vol. 1 1915–1938* (London: Macmillan, 1973), p. 49.
Young, Robert J., *In Command of France: French Foreign Policy and Military Planning, 1933–1939* (Cambridge: Harvard University Press, 1978).

ARTICLES

Bell, P.M.H., 'L'Evolution de l'opinion publique anglaise à propos de la guerre et de l'alliance avec la France (septembre 1939–mai 1940)', *Comité d'Histoire de la 2e Guerre Mondiale: Français et Britanniques dans la drole de Guerre: Actes du Colloque franco-britannique tenu à Paris de 8 au 12 decembre 1975* (Paris: Editions de Centre National de la Recherche Scientifique, 1979).
Cairns, John C., 'A Nation of Shopkeepers in Search of a Suitable France, 1919–1940', *The American Historical Review*, no. 3, vol. 79 (1974).
Dockrill, Michael, 'The Foreign Office and France during the Phoney War, September 1939–May 1940', in Michael Dockrill and Brian McKercher (eds.), *Diplomacy and World Power: Studies in British Foreign Policy, 1890–1950* (Cambridge: Cambridge University Press, 1996).
Dockrill, Michael, 'Britain, the United States, and France and the German Settlement, 1918–1920', in Dockrill, Michael and McKercher, Brian (eds.), *Diplomacy and World Power* (Cambridge: Cambridge University Press, 1966).
Frankenstein, Robert, 'Le Financement français de la Guerre et les Accords avec les Britanniques (1939–1940)', *Français et Britanniques dans la drole de Guerre: Actes du Colloque franco-britannique tenu à Paris du 8 au 12 decembre 1975* (Paris: Edition du Centre National de la Recherche Scientifique, 1979), pp. 461ff.
Gilbert, Felix, 'Two British Ambassadors: Perth and Henderson', in Craig, Gordon A. and Gilbert, Felix (eds.), *The Diplomats 1919–1939*, 2 vols (New York: Atheneum, 1965), vol. 2, pp. 537–54.
Greenwood, Sean, '"Caligula's Horse Revisited." Sir Thomas Inskip as Minister for the Coordination of Defence, 1936–1939', *Journal of Strategic Studies*, vol. 17, 2, 1994.
Hoffmann, Peter, 'The Question of Western Allied Co-operation with the German anti-Nazi Conspiracy', *The Historical Journal*, vol. 34, no. 2, 1991.
Jackson, Peter, 'France and the Guarantee of Rumania, April 1939', *Intelligence and National Security*, 10, 95, no. 2, April 1995, pp. 242–72.

Ludlow, P., 'Le débat sur les buts de paix en Grande Bretagne durant l'hiver 1939–1940', in *Français et Britanniques dans la drole de Guerre: Actes de Colloque franco-britanniques tenu à Paris du 8 au 12 decembre 1975* (Paris: Editions du Centre National de la Recherche Scientifique, 1979).

McKercher, Brian, 'Old Diplomacy and New: the Foreign Office and Foreign Policy, 1919–1939', in Dockrill, Michael and McKercher, Brian (eds.), *Diplomacy and World Power.*

Peden, G.C., 'A Matter of Timing: The Economic Background to British Foreign Policy, 1937–9', *History*, vol. 69, 1984, pp. 15–27.

Pressnell, L.S., 'Les Finances de Guerre Britanniques et la Coopération Franco-Britannique, 1939 et 1940', *Français et Britanniques dans la drole de Guerre: Actes du Colloque franco-britannique tenu à Paris du 8 au 12 Decembre 1975* (Paris: Edition du Centre National de la Recherche Scientifique, 1979), pp. 489ff.

Reynolds, David, '1940: Fulcrum of the Twentieth Century', *International History*, vol. 66, no. 1, January 1990.

Reynolds, Salerno M., 'The French Navy and the Appeasement of Italy, 1937–1939', *English Historical Review*, vol. CXII, no. 445, February 1997, pp. 64–104.

Special Section on 'Robert Vansittart and an Unbrave World, 1930–37', in *Diplomacy and Statecraft*, vol. 6, no. 1 (March 1995).

Stafford, Paul, 'Political Autobiography and the Art of the Plausible: R.A. Butler at the Foreign Office', *Historical Journal*, 28 (4) (1985).

Stone, Glyn, 'The European Great Powers and the Spanish Civil War, 1936–1939', in Boyce, Robert and Robertson, Esmonde M. (eds.), *Paths to War: New Essays on the Origins of the Second World War* (New York: St. Martin's Press, 1989).

Turner, John, 'Introduction: Lord Lothian and His World', in Turner, John (ed.), *The Larger Idea: Lord Lothian and the Problem of National Sovereignty* (London: The Historians' Press, 1984).

Wark, Wesley, 'German Political Intelligence, Moralism and Grand Strategy in 1939', *Intelligence and National Security*, vol. 5, no. 1, January 1990, pp. 150–70.

Watt, Donald Cameron, 'Chamberlain's Ambassadors', in Dockrill, Michael and Mckercher, Brian (eds.), *Diplomacy and World Power.*

Watt, D. Cameron, 'The British Image of French Military Morale, 1939–1940. An Intelligence Failure' (conference paper).

Young, Robert J., 'A.J.P. Taylor and the Problem with France' in Gordon Martel (ed.), *The Origins of the Second World War Reconsidered: The A.J.P. Taylor Debate after Twenty Five Years* (London: Allen and Unwin, 1986).

UNPUBLISHED THESES

Fisher, John Noble, 'Curzon and British War Imperialism in the Middle East, 1916–1919', University of Leeds PhD (1995).

Herman, John, 'The Paris Embassy of Sir Eric Phipps, 1937–1939,' London School of Economics PhD (April 1996).

Kitching, Carolyn Judith, 'Britain and the Problem of International Disarmament, 1919–1934', University of Teesside PhD (1995).

Index